D0810683

MANAGING THROUGH PEOPLE

Dale Carnegie
&
Associates

SIMON AND SCHUSTER
New York

COPYRIGHT © 1975 BY DALE CARNEGIE & ASSOCIATES, INC.
ALL RIGHTS RESERVED
INCLUDING THE RIGHT OF REPRODUCTION
IN WHOLE OR IN PART IN ANY FORM
PUBLISHED BY SIMON AND SCHUSTER
ROCKEFELLER CENTER, 630 FIFTH AVENUE
NEW YORK, NEW YORK 10020

DESIGNED BY EVE METZ
MANUFACTURED IN THE UNITED STATES OF AMERICA

1 2 3 4 5 6 7 8 9 10

LIBRARY OF CONGRESS CATALOGING IN PUBLICATION DATA

DALE CARNEGIE & ASSOCIATES.
MANAGING THROUGH PEOPLE.

INCLUDES BIBLIOGRAPHICAL REFERENCES AND INDEX.
1. MANAGEMENT. I. TITLE.
HD31.D19   1975   658.4   75-17993
ISBN 0-671-22106-X

Contents

Introduction

The success or failure of any business can be directly attributed to the competence of its management. Moreover, it is not just the expertise of the senior managers that determines the result but the expertise of all the levels of management from first line supervisors all the way to the chairman of the board.

Indeed, one of the major responsibilities of top management is to make sure that subordinate managers are properly trained to understand and apply the techniques of good management to their jobs.

The ranks of middle management are staffed by persons coming from a variety of backgrounds. Some come from the ranks of factory workers, some are clerks or office employees, some are "cadets" recruited from schools or colleges for management training, and some are professionals in specific areas such as accounting or engineering who have advanced to management positions. Whether these persons are promoted from the ranks or employed as part of the management staff, they require some training in the methods and techniques of management.

Many companies conduct both formal management training programs for new managers and management development programs for persons being trained for any future openings that may occur. Other organizations use colleges, trade associations and public seminars in management either to substitute for or to supplement their own programs.

Dale Carnegie & Associates, Inc., is a business organization with much the same problems as other businesses. We, too, have the need to train our own managers and to prepare personnel to move up into management positions—not only in our parent company, but in the many sponsors of Dale Carnegie courses throughout the world. Our organization has the dual problem of operating as a multi-national parent body with the complexities of a large corporation and as a number of independent local sponsors with the special problems of small businesses.

In 1962 we put together the first of our internal management development programs. Drawing on the many years of business experience of some of our own people—both at the home office and among the sponsors—and on extensive research in the literature of business administration, we identified the major responsibilities of the manager and developed approaches to train our people in how to deal with these responsibilities effectively.

Managerial personnel in our headquarters and at the sponsors' offices were given the opportunity of taking this program. The results were extremely satisfactory. Men and women who had been good salespersons but less than effective as sales managers began to show considerable improvement in managerial performance. Managers in other areas of administration became more proficient.

Some of our sponsors were so enthusiastic about the management seminar that they suggested we offer it to the public as a new Dale Carnegie program. After all, our business was providing courses to the public to improve personal effectiveness; the Management Seminar was a natural extension of our curriculum. It worked well for our own people. We believed it would work equally well for others.

The first public Dale Carnegie Management Seminars were offered in 1967. Since then, similar seminars have been attended by over 20,000 persons in the United States. In addition, seminars have been given in Japan, Brazil, Spain, Germany, Australia, New Zealand, Argentina, Iceland, Ireland, England and other countries throughout the world.

An analysis of participation in these seminars indicates that the attendees come from all ranks of management and from all types of industry. Large companies often send middle-management personnel; smaller firms are usually represented by top management. Individual entrepreneurs come themselves and often bring along (or subsequently send) their entire managerial teams. Many companies have asked us to conduct in-house management seminars for their staffs.

Salespeople being groomed for sales management find themselves sharing ideas with experienced sales managers as well as general managers, factory foremen, office managers, executive assistants, engineers and personnel administrators. All these people learn that their managerial duties are similar, even where their functional responsibilities differ. They learn to set objectives, to plan short-term, intermediate-term and long-term activities, to organize their departments and to direct, coordinate and control their people.

In everything they do the human aspect of management is emphasized. It is the basic philosophy of the seminar that *managing means managing through people.*

The Dale Carnegie Management Seminar is a pragmatic approach to solving management problems. We recognize that many of the innovations in modern management thinking have come from the studies and depth analyses made at the principal graduate schools of business administration, and that many of our concepts of human behavior come from the work of behavioral psychologists and sociologists. But we also know that a good number of the people in business who must work on a day-to-day basis with the problems of running a business have never been exposed to these studies. Even when the top managers of a firm come from prestigious business schools, they do not always find it easy to convey the teachings of these schools to the operating managers.

The purpose of the Dale Carnegie seminar and of this book is to present the latest developments in management thinking in a form that can be readily understood and accepted by supervisors, middle managers and the many senior managers who cannot take time for graduate study.

This book explains in non-technical language the techniques and concepts of good management and offers practical illustrations of how these principles can be applied in the day-to-day activities of a line or staff manager. It emphasizes the human aspects of management. As it is people who make a business succeed—or fail—it is the manager's chief responsibility to motivate his or her people so that they will assure success. There are no magic formulas in this book. The authors believe firmly that each human being has an infinite potential for creativity and for working toward the achievement of managerial goals. The thrust of this book is to guide managers in ways to reach this potential, to stimulate creativity and to foster in their people the desire to succeed and to achieve self-fulfillment through their work.

Although this book was written as a text for the Dale Carnegie Management Seminars, it stands by itself as an integrated text on management principles.

Those who enroll in the seminar will find it an adjunct to the case studies, discussions and participative learning techniques used.

All readers of this book will gain insight into the methods and techniques that have worked successfully for other organizations, here presented in a form that is easily read, easily understood and readily applicable to their own situations.

Dale Carnegie & Associates, Inc.

PART I

The Perspective of Management

Things do not happen in this world—
they are brought about.

John M. Hay

1

THE PERSPECTIVE
OF MANAGEMENT

The success of every organized activity—be it a business, a hospital, a school, an association or a government agency—depends upon the managerial skills of its leaders. These skills are not necessarily inborn. They can be acquired by studying the literature of the field, by participating in seminars and discussions of managerial problems, and by careful observation of successful managers.

Major corporations budget significant sums for the purpose of training and developing managers. Men and women interested in careers in management take courses and seminars in the techniques and processes of effective management.

What is it that makes one manager a success and another a failure? What does the successful manager have or do that the unsuccessful one lacks or fails to do? To answer this question we must analyze the managerial function.

Management has been defined as the ability to obtain desired results through effective utilization of the resources available to the organization. The basic resources with which the manager works are the 5 M's:

M oney
M aterial
M achinery

M ethods
M anpower

Money: In management, the term *money* includes both capital expenditures and working funds. The manager must utilize the money budgeted to his department in the most effective manner. He must understand how money spent today will pay off in the future, and what he can expect as a return on the money he uses. Money is the lubricant of the business world. It is the common denominator which relates to all phases of business. Money management is as essential to business management as the circulation of the blood is to the human body.

Material: In a manufacturing business, the *material* consists of both raw materials and finished products. In a wholesale or retail business, it includes all inventory. Even in a service business, there is a variety of supplies that management controls—although there material is of less importance than in a product-oriented activity.

Machinery: Proper selection and utilization of *machinery,* including computers and office machines, as well as the equipment used in plants, stores or any other place of business, is a major component of the manager's job.

Methods: A systematic approach to organizing and implementing the other resources can make the difference between success and failure. The expertise of many managers consists in their command of techniques and methods. Most major companies have developed effective methods of dealing with their problems, and these methods too make up a major resource of the business.

Manpower: Andrew Carnegie has been credited with saying that if all of the first four M's (money, material, machinery and methods) were taken away from him, and he was left with only his people—his manpower—he could start over again and in a relatively short period of time rebuild his industrial empire. None of the other M's mean anything without the manpower to implement them. Effective utilization of the people in an organization can overcome defects in the other resources. Poor utilization of manpower will negate the effectiveness of the organization even if it is strong in all of the other resources.

Management depends on manpower—not just to be the hands that manipulate the machines, but also to be the brains that determine how the organization should function and to ensure that it does so function.

Peter Drucker, one of the best known management thinkers of our time says that real management is the management of people. People are the key to success, and managing people effectively is the factor that separates the haves from the have-nots.

Let's look now at this key word again:

MANAGEMENT

The syllable that we should accent is

MAN AGEMENT

It is the *man* we concentrate on in developing all other resources—*man* used generically as meaning all human resources, male and female. *MANPOWER* is the catalyst that makes all of the other resources succeed—or fail.

It is the thesis of this book that good management utilizes all resources to the best of its ability, but that by concentrating on the fifth M, we shall be able to achieve our objectives most effectively.

History of the Management Concept

In the early part of this century the first steps in a systematic approach to management were taken by Frederick W. Taylor, an engineer who worked in the steel industry. Taylor's main concern was increasing productivity. Up to this time most management decisions had been made on the basis of the specific knowledge of the immediate supervisor and his experience in handling related problems in the past. The manager thus relied on his own limited knowledge and on the tradition of previous managers in his company. "This is the way we always did it" was the usual rationale.

Taylor changed all that. He studied the various jobs and determined the most effective way to accomplish each. His plan included setting up specific methods of performing each step of the task, scheduling exact time-periods to complete each task and establishing smooth-flowing systems for handling materials.

Taylor's concept of "scientific management" caught on rapidly and was adopted by companies in many industries, as well as by many organizations involved in routine work. It saved these companies countless dollars in wasted time and materials. It saved workers unnecessary effort, too, for Taylor and his colleagues developed methods that reduced the amount of energy needed to meet production goals.

Many of Taylor's ideas were improved upon and made more sophisticated by his successors in the new field of "industrial engineering." The most famous of his successors were the husband-and-wife team of Frank and Lillian Gilbreth. The Gilbreths introduced the concept of time-and-motion study. In this procedure each job is broken down into specific tasks which are studied by careful observation of the exact time each motion takes and then simplified so that the worker can accomplish the task with a minimum of effort and time. Gilbreth's quest for "the one best way" became the watchword of scientific management.

Although this systematic approach to solving production problems achieved its goal of higher productivity, it was not without problems of its own. Many workers resented the almost inhuman manner in which the so-called efficiency experts treated them and their work. Labor unions claimed that industrial engineering was an excuse for a "speed-up" and sabotaged the programs by themselves setting maximum productivity standards much below those that the "one best way" analysis determined was achievable. Managers began to depend on "scientific" techniques to solve all of their problems for them, forgetting that the most important element was the man behind the machine. There was obviously a place for this analytical method, but something was missing.

The missing link was supplied as a result of an experiment made at the Hawthorne plant of the Western Electric Company by Elton Mayo and Fritz Roethlisberger in the late 1920's and early 30's. Engaged by Western Electric to determine how *physical* changes in the environment would affect the production of assembly workers, Mayo and his team selected at random a group of women and had them placed in a separate room for study. The temperature of the room was raised and lowered; the lighting was adjusted at various levels, etc. To the surprise of the observers, no matter what they did productivity continued to rise. The physical factors proved to have little bearing on the work. After much analysis of this situation over several years, Mayo and Roethlisberger determined that the workers were responding, not to components of the work environment, but to the entire work situation. The increase in productivity was due to such intangibles as liking the people with whom they worked, enjoying the feeling of being treated as "special" people, of being considered as each one an individual, rather than all together as "hands" working on an assembly line.

Management was thus made more aware of the human element. People are not machines. Management cannot be purely mechanistic. The human element must be considered. Our key word MANAGEMENT now becomes

HUMAN AGEMENT

Concern over this human element has continued to grow to the present day. Over the past several years management specialists have been studying the behavioral sciences. They have adapted from the fields of psychology, sociology, anthropology and related disciplines many concepts which have not only resulted in an increase in productivity, but also have made the world of work a more pleasant environment. This advance has enabled more and more people to achieve a large degree of satisfaction from their work.

PLORDICOCO

What techniques do successful managers use to attain their goals? How can they properly utilize the 5 M's in such a way as to maximize their chances of success in their endeavors?

The basic components of successful management are summarized in the acronym PLORDICOCO. This acronym utilizes the first two letters of each of these components:

PL—PLANNING
OR—ORGANIZING
DI—DIRECTING
CO—COORDINATING
CO—CONTROLLING

Planning: Before any endeavor can be really launched, a plan of action must be developed. The plan usually starts with a statement of the goal or goals that it is designed to accomplish. It then carries forward in some detail the steps that should be taken to reach this goal.

In the field of management the goals of a company or an organization must be always kept clearly in mind in the development and implementation of plans. In business the goal usually includes profits. The importance of profits as a goal will be discussed in depth in the next chapter. Other goals also exist, and these must be brought into perspective if the plan is to succeed.

Planning is both long-range and short-range. Companies often plan for many years into the future. This is particularly important in situations where long-term commitments of funds, facilities and managerial personnel must be made. Long-range plans often derive from the shorter- and intermediate-range goals of day-to-day operations. Plans must be made for handling repetitive problems so that they need not be thought out each time they arise. Other plans have a single-use purpose—they cover a situation which may only occur once.

Planning includes the development of a variety of possible solutions to problems so that the manager will have alternatives from which to choose and not be limited to a single possible solution. To develop alternatives, one must encourage the creativity of the planners. Most people have creative capability. Good management aids people in bringing this creativity into the open. The more creative the plans are, the more likely it is there will be several viable alternatives to choose from.

Another key part of the planning process is decision-making. Managers reach the higher levels of their organizations only if they can make good decisions. It is primarily for this reason that managers are given power and the rewards that go with power. In today's modern corporation, decisions are often made by joint activity of several persons. The manager must know how to help his people contribute to the decision-making process, and how to enlist the assistance of his staff in carrying out the decision when it has been made. Part II of this book will discuss the entire subject of planning in detail.

Organizing: Once plans have been formulated, the company must be organized in such a manner as to enable it to put the plans into effect. As companies grow more complex because of size, volume of work, geographic dispersion and diversification of products and services, the need for a well-built structure becomes more and more important.

Company structure is usually hierarchial. It is set up in such a way that each manager will have control over a group of subordinate managers who report to him; he in turn will report to a superior, and so on up the chain of command to the chief executive officer.

To understand the implications of this structure, we must explore the job content of each job in the organization and its relationship to the other jobs.

To take advantage of the expertise of specialists in their organizations, most companies divide their structure into line- and staff-positions. The line managers have direct responsibility for the people and functions under their jurisdiction; the staff people concern themselves with individual areas of specialty, wherever in the line-organization that specialty is involved. Integrating these groups is one of the major problems in modern management.

In addition to this formal organization, most companies find built into the organization an informal structure—a people-to-people relationship which sometimes works with and sometimes against the formal structure. Good managers must know how to identify and work with (or against) the informal groups, and must understand the effect of these groups on company policies and politics.

Probably the key to utilizing the organizational structure for the best interests of management is *delegation*. Much of the work and a good part of the authority a manager has can be delegated to his subordinates. The manager, of course, is still accountable for the success of his department, but if he knows how to delegate and does so effectively, he will have a much greater chance of getting his unit to meet its goals.

In Part III of this book we will examine the organization of the company, both formal and informal, and consider its role in the management function.

Directing: The structure of an organization is just a skeleton until it is fleshed out with the human beings who will actually perform the work. Good direction of the personnel of a company starts with the proper selection of men and women able to carry out the duties and responsibilities of the various jobs.

Management of people depends on those people. To obtain the "right person for the right job" requires a careful analysis of the job to determine what factors are needed to succeed in that specific job. Then follow the recruitment, selection, and training of these right people. After all that there must be a constant and consistent program of directing the work and motivating the people chosen to perform at peak capacity.

One of the major aspects of direction is good communication. A leader—and a manager is primarily a leader—should be able to communicate ideas, directions, attitudes and objectives to his subordinates and know they have been received and accepted by them. He must also be alert to their thinking, feelings, hopes and gripes.

The manager who is in direct contact with his subordinates is the key to the success of the business. His leadership style will be reflected in the climate of his department. There is a direct relationship between good leadership and high productivity—no matter what type of work is being performed.

Much has been learned from the behavioral sciences about leadership and motivation. The manager who recognizes the principles involved and applies them in his work will be a better manager. Managing through people requires understanding people. The psychologists have given us much help in learning to work with others. In Part IV we will explore some of the ideas they have suggested and see how the manager can utilize these in his day-to-day activities.

We will also look at problems of discipline and other employee problems. Managers can do much to keep such problems from developing, but so long as people are people, there will always be some human frailties which we cannot overcome, and these will cause management problems. When such problems develop, the manager will know just how to determine what causes them and be able to reach a satisfactory solution in line with the company's objectives.

Coordinating: In a multi-unit activity, the importance of coordinating what is happening throughout the organization is self-evident. How this work can be done without devoting all of one's time to it is one of the headaches business executives face.

Part of the coordinating process can be built into the organization structure. Some will grow out of the way in which the leaders of the company act and the way they react to their subordinates and peers.

Coordination is sometimes implemented by committees consisting of representatives of the areas concerned; sometimes it is a function of a special staff section. In other cases coordination is informal, but because everyone concerned knows the objectives and is working towards them, the coordination is nonetheless effective.

Controlling: This final component of our acronym—the last CO in PLORDICOCO—can be defined as making sure that what has been planned has actually been accomplished.

Managers are accountable for seeing that objectives are met, and it is through control that they do so. The chief tool of the controlling process is the establishment of standards of performance. These standards—set in terms of dollars, units of production, or other quantitative units—can be used as a yardstick against which actual performance can be measured.

There are innumerable techniques for using performance standards. They include budgets, sales reports, production charts and accounting records. These may be brief hand-written reports, or complex detailed computer print-outs. The purpose of all is the same. Here are the standards; here is the actual performance; what deviations exist between them? With the comparisons before him, the manager can devote his efforts to the problem areas, spending no more time than necessary on aspects of the work that are going well.

It is more difficult to control the intangible aspects of the work. Such matters as public image, employee morale, customer acceptance and development of personnel are difficult to measure and therefore to control. Management has nevertheless found certain means of measuring these, and has also developed ways of dealing with problems in these areas. In Part V we will analyze methods of coordinating and controlling both tangibles and intangibles, and applying these methods to the manager's job.

Manage for Results

In the long run the only thing that really counts is the result of your efforts. If a manager thinks of his job as simply following the rules and "not making waves," he is not really a manager. The true manager has his eye on the end-product. He knows the objectives of his department and his company. His own objectives are aligned with these objectives.

In every aspect of his work, from planning to organizing to directing to coordinating to the final controlling, the true manager has the objectives in mind. Unlike the bureaucrat, whose great joy is to follow the rules precisely whether or not his goal is achieved, the manager gives his all to reaching that goal.

As management is managing through people, the manager imbues his people with this results-oriented attitude. He and his staff never lose sight of the objective.

In the chapters that follow we will show how these objectives may be met by using the techniques of good management and applying them to the daily activities of the manager's job.

PART II

Planning

*If a man does not know to what port he is
steering, no wind is favorable to him.*

Seneca

2

SETTING OBJECTIVES

The first step in the process of planning is to determine the goal toward which we aim. Without a clear understanding of our objectives, we cannot formulate our plans.

Objectives must be spelled out. They must be fully understood by all who have to meet them. The managers—whether in the top echelon or in any other level of the managerial hierarchy— must not only be aware of the company's objectives but must also accept them and be fully committed to them, if the objectives are to be achieved.

All organizations have objectives. They may be long-range or short-range. The long-range objectives include company aims and goals for several years into the future. They may cover such areas as share of the market desired, introduction of new products or services and financial condition as well as intangibles such as development of a second or third generation of management or improvement of community relations.

Shorter-term objectives include steps toward reaching the long-term objectives plus specialized goals that may be desirable, such as completing a project on schedule or solving a specific problem facing the organization.

In a multi-unit organization, each of the units will have its own goals, but all should be congruent with the objectives of the parent organization.

In setting objectives, one major goal should always be kept in mind: the continuity of the business. Except in the case of "quick-buck" promotional businesses such as a company created specifically to take advantage of a fad—to make a quick profit and then close up—most businesses are in business to stay. They are willing to sacrifice certain short-run gains for long-run advantages. They not only aim to stay in business, but gear their entire effort toward continuity and the growth and security this encompasses.

These ideas can be summarized in the management triad.

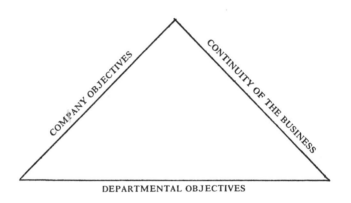

DEPARTMENTAL OBJECTIVES

Each department head must keep all three aspects in mind in setting his objectives. Unless all three sides of the triad are considered, the success of the enterprise cannot be assured.

Benefits of Establishing Objectives

1. Establishing objectives helps motivate the individuals who are performing the task. If a person knows *why* he is required to do something, he is more likely to learn to do it well, and so accomplish the purpose, than if he is just told to do it. People take pride in doing a good job. Unless they know the objectives of the job they are doing, they cannot really know whether they are doing satisfactory work or not.

2. Establishing objectives provides consistency in planning. When several persons are engaged in making the plans for an or-

ganization, a thorough understanding of the goals will make it easier to develop plans that are in line with the overall objectives. Each person involved in the planning process keeps his eye on the major objectives and fits his aspect of the planning into the whole picture.

3. Establishing objectives makes decentralization easier. Many large firms and non-business organizations have decentralized operations for more efficient handling. These decentralized units tend to become fairly autonomous, and unless there is a clear understanding of objectives, they may tend to go off on separate paths—paths often in conflict with the long-range objectives of the parent company.

4. Establishing objectives provides a sound basis for coordination and control. On the basis of these objectives performance standards can be developed, and these in turn become guideposts against which actual performance can be measured.

Objectives, once set, should not be changed lightly. Except in case of major emergencies, the goals of an organization should remain constant. However, as the company grows and as times change, objectives may have to be reevaluated and, if necessary, adjusted to meet the new conditions.

For example, an acquisition of a large subsidiary may require a firm to change its objectives to include the objectives of the new addition. A change in public acceptance of a product may force a company to reevaluate the goals it has had for years and set up new objectives. The American Tobacco Company had long had as its major objectives the manufacturing and marketing of tobacco products. When the cigarette industry was hit by criticism by the government and health organizations, the company changed its objectives to include not just tobacco products but other consumer packaged-goods as well, and in time it changed its name to American Products Company to fit in with its new objectives.

A change of departmental objectives should be made only with due deliberation. No department head should alter his department's goals without serious thought and analysis of any proposed change in the light of overall corporate goals.

Profit as an Objective

In any discussion of company objectives, the first goal usually mentioned is profit. There is no question that in a capitalist economy, profit is a major objective of business. Without profit a business cannot survive for long. However, it is too simplistic to believe that profit is the only goal—or even the most important goal—of management.

One of the reasons for overemphasis on profits has been the tendency on the part of business people to try to measure everything in terms of the lowest common denominator. If profit were indeed the main measurement of success and the chief goal of each intermediate manager as well as of the general management of a company, much long-term growth would suffer to make way for short-term profits.

To survive in the highly competitive markets of today's economy, a company must plan and prepare for expansion and look to the future. Money must be diverted from current profits for research and development, for capital expansion, for personnel development and for other projects that will not pay off until years later.

On the other hand, current earnings are needed to attract additional capital, to make the company a good credit risk now, to encourage current stockholders and employees to stay with the company. Profit—in its proper context—is only one of the many objectives a company should set.

Other Corporate Objectives

In addition to short-range profits, the company wants to assure *long-range profitability.* This may be expressed in terms of return on investment or earnings per share. A company may list as its objective: "To achieve an increasing level of earnings per share at a minimum of 10% each year."

Share of the market: Many companies measure their growth by their percentage of the market for the goods or services they produce. Their objective may read: "To increase our share of the market from its present 12% to 25% over the next five years."

Financial soundness: Another objective might be to improve one's liquidity or to get out of debt. This objective might be stated: "To retire outstanding bonds within six years." A privately held company may have as an objective: "To go public within the next __ years." Such an objective requires the company to take a number of steps both financially and legally in preparation.

Technological Improvement: Companies may have as an objective the introduction of new methods or other technological changes.

Personnel development: A sound objective for most organizations is preparing personnel within the company to take on added responsibility and assure a continuity of management capability for future growth.

Social responsibility: In the past several years many companies have added objectives related to their social responsibility to their statements of goals. Social goals may include better community relations, concern for the environment, integration of minority personnel into the company, and assisting local charitable and civic organizations.

Departmental Objectives

The major goals cited above are a sampling of the many objectives a company might have as an overall policy. Within the company each department has to set its own goals.

Departmental goals are more specific than company goals. They relate to the specialized nature of the department, but they fit also into the company's comprehensive goals.

An example of a Departmental Objective statement:

OBJECTIVES OF PERSONNEL DEPARTMENT

1. To assure that all positions in the company are filled with personnel who are highly qualified to do the job.
2. To maintain a high morale among all employees.
3. To maintain a compensation program which will pay all employees "a fair day's pay for a fair day's work."

4. To provide a benefits program which will give every employee as comprehensive coverage as any company in this area.
5. To provide facilities for encouraging employees to express their ideas, grievances, and problems directly to the management of the company, without resorting to outside organizations.
6. To give every employee a chance to grow with the company by providing promotional opportunity and training programs.
7. To assist all other departments in their dealings with their personnel.
8. To counsel general management on their legal and moral obligations concerning all aspects of human relations within the company.

Sometimes this type of objective list is called a statement of policy. This policy statement for the personnel department will be used to supply broad guidelines for specific plans which the department will use to implement the policies.

In some instances there may appear to be a conflict between different objectives that a company or department may have. For example one company may include in its list of objectives:

. . . to make the best possible product at the lowest possible cost.

. . . to maintain a clean and non-polluted environment in our plant areas.

But keeping the environment free from pollution may involve considerable added cost in producing the product. The management of the company will have to decide what compromises or trade-offs must be made to abide by each of the objectives and so resolve the conflict.

Breaking down goals into bite-sized smaller objectives makes it easier to understand and achieve the goals. A short-run objective in meeting the broader objective of less pollution might be installing a dust-catching mechanism in the plant as an interim step toward rebuilding an entire facility. Another example: The long-range goal is a totally integrated management-development program. The first of a series of short-range goals might be the use of local college facilities to train managers; a second short-range goal to follow this might be instituting an in-plant foreman-training program. If management works toward each of the short-range goals, the long-range goal will eventually be reached.

A company never has just one objective. Although one aspect of the objectives set may dominate the company's thinking, the others will constantly call for attention and cannot be ignored. The dominant objective of a drug manufacturer might be to make a profit by selling his products, yet other objectives must be constantly kept in mind, such as research and development of new drugs, training of research chemists and pharmacologists, creation of new markets, and coordination with hospitals and government agencies on health maintenance programs.

When several people within an organization are competing to have their personal (or departmental) objectives given priority, it is the function of the general management to keep the objectives in balance. A full appreciation of the organization's overall objectives, a keen sense of values, a sensitivity to the needs of the participating personnel and, above all, complete integrity are needed to succeed in this function.

Setting Objectives

Modern management encourages full participation by all concerned in the setting of all objectives, from short-range departmental objectives all the way to long-range corporate goals.

To make sure that the company considers all of the ramifications of the objectives chosen, it is to the advantage of all to utilize the knowledge and perspectives of everyone who will be involved in meeting the objectives.

Objectives can be set in two ways—from above: major policy is handed down to the subordinate divisions; or from below: each division suggests policy which is integrated at the top.

In the former case a company may have some definite overall

concept which must be kept in mind in determining all of the other objectives. An airline, for example, could have as its overall objective the fulfillment of its charter to provide air transportation over its allotted routes. All its other objectives would have to fit into that. With this in mind, subordinate divisions could develop their objectives and present them to management to be incorporated into the major goal—so long as the divisional goals are not in conflict with the overall goal.

If each of the participants in the objective-development process is given an opportunity to help set the goals, the company will have a broader set of objectives, and more important, each of the participants will be committed to the goals, because each feels part of them.

The success of a participatory goal-setting process depends upon the attitude of the top management. If the big boss has an authoritarian approach, there is little likelihood that subordinate managers will contribute significantly. Often all that happens is a rubber-stamp approval of the objectives dictated from above with little real enthusiasm for them. That may result in only half-hearted support in carrying out the objectives set.

On the other hand, if top management by its attitudes and acceptance of suggestions and ideas from the participants encourages participation, a climate of cooperation will be engendered and real participation will occur.

Objectives that come from a participative atmosphere of this sort tend to be more realistic, yet more imaginative because the people who have to work with the objectives have helped create them. They know what the real problems are, and because several different people are involved, may present many different ideas for solutions.

Long-range objectives are usually more abstract than short-range ones. The shorter-range goals should be as specific as possible, and should include definite measurable performance standards. For instance, a long-range goal may be stated as: "To overcome the lead our major competitor has in marketing pocket calculators." The specific short-term objectives might in this case read:

1. For the production department: To reduce cost of producing the pocket calculator by 15 percent over the next two years.
2. For the sales department: To increase sales volume 7 percent each year for the next three years.
3. For the engineering department: To redesign calculator to make it 30 percent lighter in weight and develop new materials that will enable us to reduce cost of raw materials by 10 percent.

Once objectives are set, executives should follow up on them and be encouraged to refer to them constantly as a check on their own effectiveness in carrying out their jobs.

Here are some guidelines executives might follow in setting and carrying out company objectives:

ARE OBJECTIVES FOR EACH EXECUTIVE:
Forward-looking and courageous?
Do they look to the future with imagination and courage?
Are they high enough to require executives to reach out and stretch themselves?
Sound and comprehensive?
Are they based on objective and sound analysis rather than rule of thumb or hunch?
Is there a balanced emphasis on long and short range?
Do they cover all important phases of the business (such as profitability, technical and market leadership, growth and development of human as well as material resources)?
Clear and specific?
Are they in writing?
Are goals specific and measurable enough for each executive to know how he is doing?
Known and Understood?
If each executive were asked to write his understanding of the division's objectives, would you expect to find a high degree of uniformity?
Is each executive expected to set his own goals?

Do executives refer to these goals as guides to daily decisions? *

Relating Objectives to Specific Targets

Most organizations have a specific product or service that they provide. Their objectives relate directly to this product or service and their statements of these objectives are not just abstract statements. A statement of objectives will not usually say: "To successfully develop a market" but will specify which market: "To develop the market for pet foods in the eastern states."

A company must select its objectives with specific purposes in mind. Every organization needs a central purpose from which all of its objectives emanate. As a company grows, it may find itself diverging from this central purpose. If such a change is made purposefully and with careful forethought, it may be successful, but haphazard digression from the central purpose usually wastes the resources of a company. This does not mean that a company must remain always limited to its first—often narrow—purpose, but rather that the changes in the direction a company takes must be made with much planning to ensure that the new directions fit in with the original goals.

Some of the factors a company should examine in establishing its long-range objectives and in considering changes in them are:

1. *What do we do best?* Is it manufacturing? Do we have capability to manufacture high-quaity, low-cost products? Can our facility be utilized in manufacturing products other than what was originally contemplated? (For example, during the early days of World War II, many companies that had manufacturing facilities for consumer goods were able to change their objectives to manufacturing war materiel with the same facilities.)

Is it marketing? A company with a superior marketing staff could easily expand its objectives into areas which would utilize

* W. H. Newman, C. E. Sumner, and E. K. Warren, *The Process of Management*. Englewood, N.J.: Prentice-Hall, 1972, p. 405.

its marketing know-how. Recently the Colgate Palmolive Corporation changed its objectives to include marketing consumer packaged-goods products which were manufactured by other companies, but marketed in the same channels as the toilet goods Colgate has been successful in selling over the years.

Is it in finance? Banks have changed their objectives in recent years to include a number of financial services not previously rendered.

2. *What needs can we satisfy?* If there is a demand for a service or product that is not being met satisfactorily, we may be able to provide it. Many new enterprises have been created because somebody perceived a need. Some years ago two attorneys, Elmer Winter and Aaron Schonfeld, were having difficulty in obtaining temporary secretarial help when they needed it. As a result of the perception of this need, they founded a temporary office service company, Manpower, Inc., which has developed over the years into an international business.

Companies have invested millions of dollars in research and development to fill product needs. Du Pont spent many years and considerable money in developing a synthetic fiber that could replace silk. The payoff was nylon.

3. *What can we do to maximize the resources we have?* Management seeks a synergistic utilization of resources. (By *synergism* we mean a cooperative action in which the combined effect of two or more acts is greater than sum of the effects we would expect from each of the acts taken independently. In other words, the effect of the whole is indeed greater than the sum of the effects of the parts.) A large finance company added an income tax counselling service in each of its offices. The customers of the small-loan division were logical clients for the new service; the persons coming in for income-tax counsel were logical customers for small loans to pay their tax, or to borrow money in advance of receiving their refunds. The synergism of this combination paid off far more than the sum of the two services, each offered by itself.

4. *Are the resources available?* Setting objectives is not an exercise in wishful thinking or daydreaming. For these goals to

have a fair chance of succeeding, you must have the resources to put them into effect.

Unless the finances are available, or can be made available, unless you are assured of a supply of whatever materials are needed, unless there is the manpower available to produce the goods or provide the service, the goals you seek are doomed to failure.

All objectives must be realistic. They should be based on an analysis of the availability of the resources needed. On the other hand, it is not essential that all of the resources be available before you start work. As long as there is a reasonable assurance that resources will be there when needed, the risks involved in meeting the goals will be minimized.

By careful consideration of these questions in setting or revising goals, a company will develop more meaningful objectives, with a better chance of their being achieved. The following is an example of a well written statement of policies and objectives:

A STATEMENT OF POLICIES AND OBJECTIVES OF H. J. HEINZ COMPANY

During the more than 80 years of the Company's existence, certain basic principles and policies have been developed to guide management in the performance of its responsibilties. With the continued growth of the business and the enlarged responsibilities of all levels of management, it is important that every member of our supervisory personnel have a uniform understanding of the present policies and objectives of the House. I hope that you will become thoroughly familiar with both the words and the spirit of these statements.

January 1, 1953   H. J. HEINZ II

There are certain basic policies which define the scope of H. J. Heinz Company operations. The policies of the House are:

1. To manufacture and market processed foods.
2. To limit the marketing of products which are not produced by the Company to not more than 25% of the Company's total sales volume.

3. To distribute in retail stores only those products manufactured by the House.

4. Not to engage in the manufacture of products for sale under private label.

5. To make exceptions to expressed policies only on specific direction of the Board of Directors.

Under these policies the following objectives will be the basis for executive decisions:

PROFITS

Our net earnings after taxes must be sufficient to finance our normal healthy growth and pay reasonable dividends to our shareholders.

In order to achieve this profit objective the following are the expected standards of performance—

1. While the gross profit margin will vary between varieties, we should maintain a sufficient margin on each variety to cover its share of allocated cost.

2. The introduction of new products is necessary to maintain the vitality of the business. We will introduce a new product only if we can anticipate that the profit from it will exceed the average rate of profit of existing varieties.

3. All capital investments will be carefully controlled in order to reach the profit objective. On capital expenditures other than unavoidable expenditures for the replacement of facilities, preference will be given to those projects which have the shortest pay-off period.

QUALITY

The reputation we have enjoyed since 1869 is based upon a public recognition of "Heinz Quality." Yet quality is a relative term which acquires significance only when the kind of quality is defined and the standard of quality established.

Our objective is to make products of maximum recognizable value and desirability to the consumer within a price structure she can be induced to pay.

The pursuance of our quality objective requires—

1. Clear determination of Heinz standard of quality for each finished product.

2. Careful and continuous qualitative evaluation of ingredients, packages and processes.

3. Maximum uniformity of finished products.

FACILITIES

We will maintain grounds, buildings and equipment in safe, orderly and sanitary operating condition at all times.

Factory, office, warehouse and transportation equipment is to be maintained in efficient operating condition.

Good housekeeping standards shall be observed.

We will take advantage of technological developments when economically feasible.

RESEARCH

Research is studious inquiry, exhaustive investigation and directed experimentation, having for its aim the revision of accepted conclusions in the light of newly discovered facts.

A research viewpoint should be constantly applied to all phases of the Company's activity. We believe that there should be continuous challenging of existing practices and constant effort for their improvement.

GROWTH

Our objective is to build a sound business at a moderate rate of growth consistent with our financial resources.

1. Our annual sales growth should be at a rate which equals or exceeds the annual rate of increase of total sales of the processed food industry.

2. We should maintain or increase our share of the total market on each Heinz variety.

3. We will periodically review the contribution which each variety makes to the progress of the House.

4. We should aggressively develop new products.

5. Growth must be profitable.

6. It is not our policy to expand our business through acquisition of other companies.*

* Since this policy was published, H. J. Heinz has modified this position.

7. Growth by acquisition or expansion of facilities in foreign countries or in the United States will be determined by current opportunity to invest corporate resources of capital and personnel where they will yield the maximum return, enhance our reputation and contribute the most to our healthy growth.

DISTRIBUTION

We will distribute by whatever means produces economically the type and adequacy of service that is generally acceptable to our customers.

ORGANIZATION

A sound organization structure in which each position is clearly defined is essential to the attainment of our objectives.

Our organization must be manned by persons of character and ability. We will continually encourage each individual to develop himself to his capacity.

We will promote primarily from within.

We will maintain personnel policies embodying continuous concern for the adequacy of compensation, including insurance, retirement and other employee benefits, and working environment.

Inspiring leadership and effective teamwork are essential.

We believe these policies will attract, develop and hold persons capable of continuing the growth of this business.

REPUTATION

We will guard jealously and strive to enhance our reputation for—

1. Being financially sound and responsible.
2. Considerate and equitable treatment of stockholders, customers, suppliers and employees.
3. Quality products.
4. Able and progressive management.
5. Being a good place to work.*

* Reprinted with permission of H. J. Heinz Co.

3

CATEGORIES
OF PLANS

The objectives set by an organization outline its broad-scope purposes. To translate these into action is the function of planning.

A plan is a specific course of action that is designed to meet a goal. It breaks the objectives into workable pieces and sets up a strategy to achieve the desired results.

In setting up a plan, the following factors should be considered:

1. There should be a clear understanding of what *results* are expected to be attained.
2. These results should be reasonable and achievable. To set a goal which is impossible to reach discourages participants from making a real effort to reach it.
3. A detailed series of *actions* should be indicated leading to a successful achievement of the goals.
4. A specific person should be assigned the responsibility of putting the plan into effect and seeing that it succeeds.
5. The necessary resources should be committed.
6. A timetable should be set for each phase of the plan.
7. Performance standards should be built in to measure the degree of success in attaining the objective.

Standing Plans

Most activities should be planned. In some instances an activity of a company is routine and repetitive. For such functions planning is particularly important. If no standard method were available to cover these matters, a new method would have to be devised each time the situation arose. Plans made to cover recurring problems are called *standing plans.*

There are a variety of types of standing plan. Some are rigid rules which leave little room for managerial discretion; others are just guidelines to help the manager reach a decision consistent with company policy.

An example of a rigid standing plan is the manufacturing instructions for a particular machining operation. The plan calls for very specific tooling requirements ("the point shall be 3mm"), for special assembly instructions ("part A will be riveted 6cm from the top of Part B") and so on.

Company policies and procedures are a form of standing plan. They set standards which must be followed by everybody each time a particular situation arises. Once they have been promulgated, they become directives, and all persons working with them can refer to them at any time so that consistency in performing the tasks is maintained and the established policy is followed.

An example is a company policy on personnel concerning sick leave:

SICK LEAVE POLICY

No employee will be paid for any time lost no matter what the reason may be during the first three months of employment.

For the period from the first day of the fourth month until the end of the first year of employment, sick leave will be granted at the rate of one day for each month worked from the start of employment with the company.

Commencing with the second year of employment employees will be given a maximum of 15 days sick leave each year.

Sick days not taken in any year will be credited to the following year.

This is a rigid policy. No provision is made for deviations from it. But in some companies the manager may have the authority to make exceptions to a company policy. An example is this policy from a bank credit department:

PERSONAL LOAN POLICY

Each applicant for a personal loan will fill out a weighted personal loan application form.

Next to each item is a credit-factor score. Persons whose credit-factor score total is less than 70 are usually poor credit risks and may not qualify for loans.

Managers will keep the credit-factor score in mind when making decisions on granting the loan.

In this instance the "policy" is really a guideline. The credit officer of the bank can still grant a loan if he feels it wise to do so, even if the score is below the critical score of 70.

In setting a policy, the company must determine how much flexibility it wants to give in each instance to the persons carrying out the policy.

It is better to be rigid in cases where deviation would cause reduction of quality, lack of consistency or deviation from a code of ethics, or where deviation from policy would affect the operations of other departments of the company. It is better to be more flexible in cases where individual judgment is needed to make fair or appropriate decisions, or where individual consideration may be required because of specific circumstances.

A very common type of standing plan is the *standard operating procedure,* sometimes called the *SOP.* Some companies call this by other names such as *standard practices,* or irreverently, *The Bible.*

The SOP is a detailed description of a sequence of steps which must be taken to accomplish a specific function. It is formal in that it is set forth either on a "methods card" or more commonly in a company procedures manual.

The following SOP for putting a new employee to work will illustrate the comprehensiveness of standing plans:

PROCESSING A NEW EMPLOYEE

1. All new employees will report to the Personnel Office. A member of the personnel staff will complete the following forms for each employee. [Examples of the forms are usually attached to SOP but are omitted in this example.] One copy of each completed form will be attached to employee's personnel file. Other copies will be distributed as indicated.
   a. New hire form. One copy to Payroll Dept. One copy attached to requisition form and sent to Executive Vice President.
   b. Personnel record form. One copy only. Check: Social Security number; noncitizen visa; minor's working papers; union membership card.
   c. Federal, state and city tax forms. Copy of each to Payroll Dept.
2. Assign payroll number.
3. Assign locker; give employee locker key (50¢ deposit).
4. Orientation program (checklist will be initialed by employee as completed).
   a. History and purpose of company (given by personnel department representative).
   b. Benefits explained and forms completed (by Benefits Mgr.).
      (1) Life insurance (proof of age provided and beneficiary indicated).
      (2) Health and accident insurance.
      (3) Disability insurance.
      (4) Pension plan.
   c. Rules explained concerning hours, punch-in/out, call-in when absent, etc. (by personnel department representative).
   d. Booklet describing above presented to employee.
5. Employee escorted to department head by representative of personnel department.

In developing standard operating procedures, it is important to keep them simple. SOPs tend to become overcomplicated because managers want to cover every possible contingency. This is never possible. The manager will have to make decisions on many factors, no matter how detailed the SOP. In preparing a procedure, specify all of the *usual* aspects of the job and leave the occasional special problems for individual decision.

To ensure that the SOP is effective:

1. It should clearly state the action expected of each person involved.
2. Specific methods of performing a task should be indicated where applicable.
3. The procedure should be instituted only after it has been shown by a test to be "the one best way."
4. Controls are built into SOP so that management can verify that it is being followed.

The Exception Principle

If an organization has prepared standing plans for its regular routine operations, the managers responsible for those operations will not have to concern themselves about the day-to-day performance in those areas.

By having established *control points* at strategic places in the SOP, the manager can determine by a quick inspection whether the plan is going as scheduled. Only when a deviation from the SOP develops, will the manager have to step in and take action.

Control points should be placed at such intervals in the procedure as to enable management to note whether the earlier steps have been accomplished correctly and to take corrective action if needed before other key steps are taken.

For example in the SOP for Processing an Employee (p. 43) a good control point would be after Step 1. If all of the information needed for Step 1 is provided, the employee can immediately proceed to Step 2 without the necessity of any managerial decision. However, if some of the data is missing (such as the Social Security number), the Personnel Manager will have to be consulted to determine whether to proceed with Step 2 or to hold up the procedure until the missing material is provided.

This is the *exception principle*. Management need not concern itself with things that go according to procedure. Only when an exception occurs will a decision by a manager be required.

Another manner in which the exception principle is used is to require all subordinates to follow the standing plans and to make decisions that are covered within the plan. But when something arises which does not seem to be covered, they turn the matter over to a superior, who then decides whether an exception should be made. If the same "exception" occurs frequently the precedent established by the managerial decision may be incorporated into the SOP, so that it no longer is an "exception."

The exception principle is an important part of the modern management concept. A company cannot grow nor can a manager develop if every detail has to be checked and every minor decision made by a member of the management team. By establishing standing plans and requiring that managers concern themselves only with exceptions, the company frees its managers to use their time and energies to plan, create and help the organization move on to bigger and better things.

Advantages of the Standing Plan: To summarize, the Standing Plan is an important tool of good management because:

1. It enables managers to manage more efficiently. Once a plan is established, once participants in the procedure are properly trained and controls set, the manager need concern himself only with exceptions.

2. It allows for consistency and easier coordination of the work.

3. It makes the training of new employees much easier. In his SOP the manager has a structured outline of the work that the new employee must learn. That makes it easier to set training schedules and to test whether the employee has learned the work.

4. It facilitates delegation. Once the procedure is established, the manager can delegate aspects of it, or even assign entire procedures, to subordinates, relieving the superior of the need to be on top of everything all the time.

5. If the plans are well worked out, the procedure will be based on "the one best way," and this should also be the most economical way of doing the job.

6. An SOP helps managers develop themselves and their sub-

ordinate managers by encouraging their participation in the creation of the plans, and frees them from supervising details covered by a plan once it is implemented.

7. A good plan has controls built into it. This enables management to discover and correct deviations before they become unmanageable.

Problems of Using Standing Plans:

1. Lack of flexibility. There is a tendency to consider any plan—once it is put into writing—as immutable. When companies even jestingly refer to their standing plans as "The Bible," we recognize that they tend to confer a reverential attitude on it.

Plans should not be so rigid that they cannot be changed. On the other hand they should not be so loose that a change can be made without serious thought.

Persons working with plans should be encouraged to suggest changes which might improve the procedure. A formal system for considering these suggestions should be established. In this way plans can be kept up to date and can take advantage of new thinking and new developments in the field.

2. Plans tend to become obsolete. In a dynamic environment, new inventions, new concepts and new methods are constantly being introduced. Our procedures may not be flexible enough to incorporate such innovations. Even depending upon suggestions from the staff using the plan may not be adequate to provide sufficient flexibility. A standing plan for reviewing standing plans should exist in every company. Every three or four years at the most, each standing plan in use should be reevaluated to make sure that it is still "the one best way." A committee or a staff department should have the responsibility of reviewing the plan to determine if it should be kept as it is, revised or completely abrogated.

Too many companies have too many plans that have no real relationship to current problems. They are often on the books and ignored—which defeats their real purpose—or are followed rigidly, but fail to accomplish their mission in the most effective manner. Try these plans for their lives. They must be able to meet today's needs; if they do not, they should not survive.

It is not necessary to defer evaluating the parts of a plan until it is possible to evaluate the entire plan. Many companies have a practice of reviewing all printed forms (which are usually covered in the SOPs) each time they are to be reordered. Any changes that would improve them are recommended at that time and incorporated into the SOP. This makes the SOP more flexible, and also saves considerable money in printing charges for forms which would have to be scrapped if the changes were made at other times.

3. Planning is expensive. The time it takes the management people and their specialized staffs to work out a well-planned SOP is costly. It is also expensive to develop forms, systems, etc. and to train the people to use the plans.

4. Planning takes time. And what must be taken into consideration is not just the cost of the time, but also the fact that it is time that might be devoted to direct production.

5. Use of standing plans stifles initiative. If subordinates always have to follow an SOP, they will not learn to think for themselves and will become automatons. Unless managers give the subordinates an opportunity to develop their own thinking, this can be a real problem. Having subordinates participate in making the plans and in reevaluating and revising them gives them that opportunity. Independent thinking can also be encouraged by having sub-managers make the "exception" decisions, rather than passing all of these up to higher management.

Recognizing both the advantages and limitations of standing plans, managers can make use of them in ways which fit into their operations, taking whatever steps are necessary to make the plans profitable for future as well as current organizational development.

Single-Use Plans

A single-use plan is one which is developed for a specific nonrecurring situation. Similar situations may be faced at another time, but as there will most likely be significant differences each time, a new single-use plan can be generated at that time.

Examples of situations calling for a single-use plan are:

moving to a new location, introducing a new product or service, opening a branch store or running a political campaign.

It is essential to plan for these major events to make sure they will be accomplished as desired. Failure to make a detailed single-use plan will result in chaos, wasted time and money, and the likelihood of failure.

As in other types of planning, to assure best results the plan should indicate the steps that should be taken, and the time at which it should be started and completed; it should assign an executive to be responsible for each phase of the plan.

For a program of this type to succeed, it must be broken down into bite-sized pieces, so that each component can be easily handled. It is often frightening to be faced with a very large program—the difficulties then appear almost insurmountable. However, if the program is divided into logical steps, each step is seen as an attainable element. Division of the task also enables the manager to assign the work and accountability for each component to a specific individual or team.

Once the program is broken into parts, the proper sequence of steps can be determined. Certain phases of any program must be completed, or at least well under way, before a subsequent step can be taken.

Each step requires certain resources. These must be prepared and assembled. Resources include the people who will be assigned to the work and the managers who will direct it. If a company does not have the right people available and cannot obtain them, the project is doomed to fail. Often a company will assume that one of its current executives can handle a project without sacrifice of his other responsibilities. This may prove to be short-sighted, and may result in neglect of both the executive's normal work and the new project.

One of the indispensable parts of any single-use plan is a timetable for each of the component steps. This should include the time the step should begin, how long the work should take and the deadline by which it must be completed. A written time schedule usually will be a part of the plan. In some plans it may be very specific: "Step 2 will start on May 2nd and be completed no later than July 24th"; in others it may be more flexible: "Step 2 will start in the first half of May and be completed before the end of July." The length of time allotted to each step depends on a reasonable expectation as to the duration of that aspect of the plan and the need of the organization for completion of it.

Following through a typical program for the introduction of a new product will make the entire concept of the single-use plan clear.

Plan for introducing new product into the market: Before the actual commencement of this plan, certain decisions had been made by the company. The Research and Development Department had come up with a workable formula for a new toiletry, and the market-research people had made a preliminary survey and recommended it be introduced. The executive committee had budgeted adequate funds to finance the project. A product manager had been assigned to develop this plan and be responsible for its implementation.

The Objectives: To introduce the new product on a national basis and to reach sales of 300,000 units per month by the end of 12 months.

Sub-objectives: To gain consumer acceptance via advertising and a wide sample distribution.

To open channels of distribution in food, drug, chain store, department store and jobber outlets throughout the United States.

To manufacture adequate supplies of the product to meet anticipated demand.

To have the product in all outlets in sufficient quantities to meet sales objectives concurrent with advertising and sampling campaigns.

To accomplish these objectives the Product Manager set up three separate but interrelated programs: Marketing, Manufacturing and Distribution. He assigned an executive to take charge of each program. Naturally, the programs had to be coordinated for both work done and time limits imposed.

So that you can better understand how such a plan works, we will discuss each phase separately. The plan and schedule chart on pages 52–53 will help you see how the three divisions of the plan were interwoven and coordinated.

Marketing Plan (Overall responsibility assigned to Divisional Marketing Manager)
1. The Market Research section (Responsible person: Market Research Manager) had made preliminary studies of this market. The new program starts Jan. 2 and will cover:
    a. Statistical analysis of market areas to determine potential by geography and type of outlet; to be completed no later than Feb. 15.
    b. Motivational market study to be assigned to——(a consultant) to determine what our product's potential customers seek in selecting this type of toiletry. (To be ready by Feb. 28)
    c. Pricing analysis of competitor's lines. (To be ready by Feb. 28)
2. Marketing strategy committee, consisting of Product Manager, Divisional Marketing Manager, Market Research Manager and Sales Manager will commence strategy sessions as soon as all market studies are completed. (No later than Mar. 1)
    Based on the results of these studies:
    a. Packaging department will submit recommendation for packages. Committee will decide which design to accept no later than Mar. 31.
    b. Advertising Manager will commence work with ad agency on advertising campaign. Work to be completed by Apr. 15.
    c. Sales Manager will start plans for sales strategy, including projections of needs for additional salesmen. Plans to be completed by Mar. 31.
3. Product Manager will select three test areas for market testing and be prepared to start test marketing on May 1. Testing will run simultaneously in all three areas for 2 months.
4. Advertising Manager will have completed first set of ads for print and radio-TV. Will test ads in test areas in conjunction with test marketing. Complete ad selection by Apr. 30. Run tests in May and June. Start evaluation June 30.
5. Sales Manager will start recruiting new salesmen and, as they are hired, will start basic sales training. All new hiring completed by Apr. 30. Training of new and regular staff on the new product will start May 1 and be completed by May 22.

6. Actual sales begin to all outlets in East and Central regions on June 1.
7. Final decisions on market strategy by Marketing Committee after evaluating test market results by July 15. Sales begin in Mountain and Pacific regions July 15.
8. National consumer advertising begins on TV and in national media on Aug 1. Continue through end of program.
9. A major aspect of this marketing program is sending a sample of the new toiletry to millions of consumers, using the "Occupant" postal address system. Marketing research has determined that samples should be sent to middle-income and high-income areas nationally. This assignment has been contracted to a direct-mail company. Responsibility has been assigned to the Assistant Advertising Manager in charge of Sales Promotion. He has initiated contact and has been working with the contractor since January. The mailing of samples commences in August and continues through end of September. By Oct. 15 every consumer on the list should have received a sample. This is tied in with the advertising campaign so that the impact of the ad and receipt of the sample will make the product stand out in the consumer's mind.
10. Complete marketing program is studied and evaluated during month of October. Results presented to top management in November with suggestions for standing plans for continued operations.

Manufacturing Plan (Responsible person: Assistant Manufacturing Manager)
1. Final research and development to be completed by Feb. 15.
2. Production Planning (assigned to Product Control Manager) begins by Feb. 1.
3. Necessary materials for production to be ordered by Mar. 31.
4. Packaging to be ordered by Apr. 15.
5. Production begins on May 1 of sample sizes. A special unit for production of the samples has been established and will produce only sample size until Aug. 1.
6. Production of regular sizes begins on May 15.
7. Production continues after ironing out problems which may have developed in original manufacturing. Rate set at 100,000 units in June, 200,000 in July, 250,000 in August, 300,000 units each in September and October.

8. Complete evaluation of production picture in October. Recommend standing palns for continuing operations.

Distribution Plan (Responsible person: Distribution Manager)
1. Distribution analysis made in January, February and March by territories, types of outlets, quantities to be shipped, etc. Close coordination with Sales Promotion Manager concerning sample distribution.
2. Distribute product to test markets by May 10.
3. Regular distribution begins to East and Central regions June 5.
4. Regular distribution begins to Mountain and Pacific Regions July 5.
5. Distribute as required for balance of program.
6. Evaluate distribution picture in October and November and recommend standing plan for continuing operations.

You will note that each of the major areas of activity was assigned to an executive who was to be responsible for attaining the goals in that area. The Product Manager had complete overall control and coordination of the program. Note also that a time limit was set for each phase.

A well-drawn single-use plan is essential for any major undertaking such as the introduction of a new product, and the time spent in developing a good one pays off in the much greater degree of success the project is likely to achieve.

PLAN AND SCHEDULE FOR INTRODUCING NEW TOILETRY TO MARKET

MONTH	MARKETING	MANUFAC-TURING	DISTRIBUTION
Jan.	Start mkt. research Stat. analysis Motivational analysis	Start R & D	Start distribution analysis
Feb.	Complete mkt. studies	Complete R & D Start production planning	Distr. anal. cont'd.
Mar.	Design package Start ad plans Plan sales strategy	Order materials	Complete distr. anal.

MONTH	MARKETING	MANUFAC-TURING	DISTRIBUTION
Apr.	Recruit salesmen	Order packages Complete Production Plan Produce samples	Prepare for test marketing
May	Test Marketing Train salesmen Run ads in test market areas	Production starts Samples cont'd. Regular sizes begin	Distr. to test markets
June	Test marketing Run ads in test market areas Sales begin in East and Central regions	Produce 100,000 units	Distribute to East and Central regions
July	Evaluate test market results Sales begin in Mtn. and Pacific regions	Produce 200,000 units	Distribute to Mtn. and Pacific regions
Aug.	Consumer ads run Sales continue Samples mailed to East and Central regions	Produce 250,000 units	Distribute nationally on sales orders
Sept.	Consumer ads cont'd. Mailings cont'd.	Produce 300,000 units	Continue distr.
Oct.	Evaluate complete marketing picture	Produce 300,000 units Evaluate production picture	Continue distr. Evaluate distr. picture
Nov.	Develop standing plans for continuing operations	Develop standing plans for continuing operations	Develop standing plans for continuing operations

Long-Range Plans

Standing plans and single-use plans have their places in handling specific situations. In addition to these types of plan, most companies engage in long-range planning to guide them in implementing their objectives over a period of several years.

In smaller companies, and also in some large organizations, long-range planning is informal. It is developed by a few top executives among themselves, and much of it is done verbally without any formalized system. Often long-range planning is a reaction to events rather than a projection of well-thought out ideas. For example, a competitor opens a branch store in a suburban shopping center. The management of the company panics and immediately plans to open a branch of its own in a nearby shopping center. No analysis is made, no needs-study— no real thought has been given as to actual potential.

To avoid this type of "planning," more and more companies have turned to formal planning systems, which involve the careful thought and analysis essential in real planning. A formal planning system usually requires that plans be written out in specific detail by each of the participants in the planning, and that these plans be coordinated and reviewed before final acceptance by a high company officer or committee.

A formal long-range plan usually covers a period of from three to ten years; five years is the term most commonly used. Unless the plan involves commitment to purchase equipment or build facilities that take many years to complete, it is better to limit the plan to five years. Otherwise the changes in our society, economy or technology may make the latter years of the plan unrealistic. Any matters for which we plan more than five years ahead are so uncertain that the planning may not be really useful.

Many companies have a series of "short-range plans" tied together to make a long-range plan. "Short-range" usually refers to periods of from one to two years. Even though many circumstances cannot be planned with any degree of accuracy beyond a short range, it is essential that wtihin that range these plans be complete and comprehensive. On the basis of the short-range plans long-range plans can be projected.

The terms long- and short-range plans, as used in this context, refer to plans that encompass the entire organization, not the standing and single-use plans which concern specific aspects of the company's activities. To ensure that these over-all plans are given proper consideration, they should be developed by persons with authority in the company, persons fully supported by top management. Planning which is delegated to a low rank-ing member of a department, given cursory attention by the department executive and only lip service by top management is rarely successful.

Both short- and long-range plans should always be reduced to writing. Copies must be distributed to all persons who will work on the plan, all who are responsible for its effectuation. The plan must be used. It should not be a show-piece brought out to impress visiting dignitaries but not taken seriously by the managers themselves.

Steps in long-range planning:

1. Evaluate the overall situation. This includes the world economy and the national economy, local and community pres-sures, the state of the industry you are in, and as fair an estimate as you can make of the future in this situation.

For example: Your company manufactures a plastic product which has as its basic raw material petro-chemicals. In order to do long-range planning, you must estimate the probability of obtaining petro-chemicals over the next several years, the likeli-hood that either the local community or national government will change its regulations on pollutants which your manufac-turing process emits, and both the changes that are occurring in the plastics industry and those that you can foresee on the basis of your studies of this field.

2. Examine your organization's objectives and translate them into specific terms. In the previous chapter we discussed objec-tives. In order to make these objectives into plans, we now have to take into account such matters as rate of growth (if we plan to grow); specific methods of accomplishing this growth (acquisi-tions, increasing sales, opening branches, etc.); timetables for this growth; funding of the plan; availability of resources; and risks involved.

3. Determine what results are expected at each phase of the

plan. Assess your "as is" situation: that is, know just where you are right now in each of the areas affected by the plan (facilities, manpower, management, capability, etc.) and compare it to the "should be" situation—the situation you are attempting to reach through the plan.

4. Utilize the planning steps which will be discussed in the following chapters. This will enable the planners to systematically take into consideration a variety of essential information, and to apply creative thinking to making a well-rounded plan.

5. Put the plan to work. *Use it.* Management should not merely give verbal support to the plan, but should make "working by the plan" an integral part of the company's operations.

6. Review and reevaluate. At least every six months, the plan should be reviewed to see how it is holding up and what changes should be made.

At the end of each year, a plan for another year should be developed and added to the long-range plan. Thus, at the end of 1976, an addition to the five year plan for 1976 to 1980, the plan for 1981, should be devised.

Cautions in long-range planning: Too often, companies assume that if they have a long-range plan they have solved their growth problems. This assumption can be very misleading. Here are some cautions the manager must consider:

1. Have the plans been adequately prepared? If the plan was slipshod to begin with, it will not be effective. You cannot have managers make long-range plans in their spare time. It is a major part of their jobs and must be so considered. It takes time and a great deal of thought.

2. Have the managers who will be required to carry out the plan participated in making the plan? Companies often have special staff personnel do the planning and present the result to the operating people for implementation. This rarely works. Specialists may be used to assist, to suggest ideas and to contribute their expertise where required, but the actual final plan should be made by the people who have to use it.

3. Do the plans call for commitment of funds or other re-

sources before they are actually needed? The existence of a plan encourages executives to pursue it. However, if circumstances change, the plan may have to be adjusted; resources should not be committed until they are needed.

4. Are concerned personnel reluctant to change a plan once it is made? Much work and emotional involvement goes into a plan. The persons who have prepared it often "fall in love" with their work. In long-range planning, however, the dynamics of our society are such that we cannot become rigid about what we have planned. Management must be willing to review and to revise when that is appropriate.

5. Do you expect immediate results? Some managers are disappointed when a five year plan doesn't start paying off the first year. Give a plan time to accomplish what it is supposed to accomplish.

Measuring Results

As long-range plans tend to become abstract, it is essential that a system be developed to measure just how much progress is being made each six months or each year of the plan.

Establishing a concrete criterion for each aspect of the plan in the form of *results expected* is the best way of accomplishing this.

Where the results are quantifiable, measuring is relatively easy. You expect an increase in sales or productivity; you determine the amount of increase for each year and measure the actual increase against it.

Where phases of completion of the plan are measurable, the same type of comparison can be made. For example, a building is scheduled for completion over a three-year period. You know how much should be completed each year.

It is more difficult when the long-range plan includes intangibles. The objective is to improve public image. Results are measurable only by attitude surveys or analysis of press and media comments, etc. Nevertheless, even here certain criteria should be developed against which measurement can take place.

4

FIRST STEPS
IN PLANNING

Planning must always be tied in with objectives. Unless one knows the objectives, the planning will be haphazard. The persons in the company who do the planning should be thoroughly familiar with the overall corporate goals as well as the goals of the department or unit for which the plans are being made.

Who Should Plan?

Planning should be a function of all managers. In some cases, one type of manager may be more deeply concerned with planning than others—for example, a production control manager would spend more time planning production than the foreman of the department—yet all persons who will work with the plan should be encouraged to take part in the work.

There are a variety of approaches to the problems of who does the planning, and how much of this work is to be done by specialists, how much by direct-managers. Some companies require that the department manager do all of his own planning. This is effective because this individual is directly involved with the work and knows the problems and the ramifications of the decisions made. However, that method is not always practical because some managers are so busy with the day-to-day activities of their departments that they tend to do a superficial job in planning. Their real efforts are devoted to operations, and planning is done only when time allows.

It is much more common to have the manager work in conjunction with specialists or associates. Variations on this method may include having subordinates work up plans for approval by the manager or, in a completely participative situation, having the subordinates do all the planning with the manager as an equal participant.

Most companies find that the operating executives cannot do the planning by themselves, but should participate in developing any plans that affect their work. They are close to the operating problems and therefore can visualize the situation more effectively than staff people alone. On the other hand, the planner should have adequate time and objectivity to see beyond the present situation into the broader picture.

Some companies have planning specialists who act independently to develop various types of plans for the company. Some concentrate on long-range planning; these are often older operating executives who are moved into planning at the end of their careers with the company. After many years in day-to-day operations, they can utilize their experience and mature judgment in a planning function.

As a general rule, plans pertaining to long-run activities are made by specialists and by top management of the company. Plans concerning short-run and current problems are handled at lower levels.

What Are the Problems?

Once the objectives are clearly defined and the responsibility for planning assigned, the planners must diagnose the problems that the plan is to cover. To do this, certain steps should be followed:

Clarify the problem. Make sure that each of the planners understands the problem in the same way. If the objective of an overall plan is to increase sales, and one participant diagnoses the situation as a problem in better sales techniques, while another sees it as a problem in pricing, no solution can be reached. One way to make sure that the problem is correctly evaluated by everybody is to have each state it concisely in writing.

Look at the situation objectively. Ask the questions every investigator is trained to ask: What? Why? When? Where? Who? How?

What must be done to correct an inefficiency, to prepare for contingencies, to change a method, etc.?

Why must it be done? If it is not done, what will happen? Is the action essential to solve present problems or to prepare for the future? How will this action affect our objectives?

When should it be done? Is there an immediate urgency? What timetable should this plan have tied to it?

Where will it take place? Are facilities available for the plan and its implementation?

Who will be assigned to develop the plan? Will it be assigned to a special group or to the operating people?

How will it be done? In what manner will the plan be made and later implemented?

Too often businessmen are superficial in diagnosing their problems. They assume they know what the problem is when it is actually much deeper than it appears. Just as a medical diagnostician seeks beyond the symptoms to find the real cause of an illness, so the manager must not confuse symptoms with causes. The manager must dig deep to find the root cause of a problem. The symptom might only mask what really has caused the gap between what is happening and what was supposed to happen.

A major cafeteria chain in New York City, once noted for its quality food at low prices, found itself losing money. Its management immediately assumed the cause was that the rising cost of food made it impossible to make a profit without either cutting quality or raising prices. First, they raised prices, and business fell off significantly. Then they reversed themselves and reduced prices but lowered quality. Business fell off still more. A deeper look at the problem would have uncovered the fact that neither of the obvious answers was the root cause of their losses. A depth-analysis of their operation in relationship to the fast food segment of the restaurant business would have shown that the fall-off was due to a changing pattern of eating habits. The hamburger-fries-soda outlets had taken the business away from the meat-vegetable-dessert restaurants. The real cause was not the price, but the type of food served.

The root cause usually lies several layers below the symptoms. The manager responsible for the diagnosis must question each result until the root cause is uncovered. In the example of the cafeteria chain, when higher prices reduced the gross business to a point where the additional income per unit did not make up for the total loss, the obvious answer was to reduce prices and make up the loss by lower quality. Before making this decision, the company should have delved into what effect lower prices would have on volume. A careful study of industry figures would have shown that price was less important than type of product sold. A review of their own product mix would show which items were selling and which were not. Analysis of the changes in type of customer would have shown that the younger people, who were making up a larger and larger percentage of the potential market, were not coming into their cafeterias. If time and effort were available, the manager might want to go still further and determine why the market had changed, but at some point the search for the "cause of the cause" must cease. That point is the one where the diagnosis is clear enough for action to be taken—the point where the action taken will be useful to the management. In this example the determination of how the market had changed enabled the company to plan to meet the change. It was not necessary to go beyond this.

Get the Facts

Digging up facts is essential for a proper diagnosis, but it becomes even more critical once the problem is identified. In order to find a solution for the situation and to make the plans needed to help meet the objectives, it is essential to have as much information as possible.

The manager must use whatever tools are at his disposal to get as much data pertaining to the problem as can be developed. Some of these tools are:

Previous experience: A logical start is to examine how similar problems had been handled earlier. If the problem is the introduction of a new product, one should check on how the company had introduced previous products. If it concerns the institution of a new system for processing paper, how was the current system developed? If the company has not had a similar problem in the past, the experience of executives with other companies that have faced this sort of problem should be utilized. This does not mean that the method of the past should be followed blindly. Rather it should be used as a guide to the sort of facts that are needed to prepare for the current planning activity. There is no reason to reinvent the wheel each time a problem arises. Neither is there any guarantee that old solutions will always work.

Observation: The manager or planner can obtain many of the pertinent facts by observing the situation at first hand. He can determine the "as is" situation, putting together all the data on hand that describes what is currently being done.

Observation should be supplemented by *discussions with people currently working on the matter.* This includes both supervisory and operating personnel. These men and women can not only provide facts that are not obvious on surface observation, but can fill in the intangibles that are so important to the real meaning of any situation. Attitudes of the employees, gripes and grievances about current practices, state of morale, etc., all bear on the success of an activity. The planner must give careful attention to such matters in order to have the real facts. Often discussions with rank-and-file workers bring out important aspects of the problem that have not been previously noted.

Research. Many companies have research facilities which can be used to obtain data that is not available through observation or questioning persons on the job. Such facilities range from research on technical matters to compiling statistics on sales trends, economic forecasts, etc.

Technical research includes work done in the laboratory, investigation of new methods and procedures, and determining what technical problems may arise when planning for business areas in which the company has limited experience. If the company does not have technical research facilities, the planner should arrange for outside specialists to make the technical studies.

Market research is the study of the potential market for a product or service. The data is derived from a variety of sources. Some market research can be done right in the company's own files. Checking sales records can help project potential sales in various territories. Checking industry sales records can help determine the total sales of your type of product or services and what share of the market your company has.

Market research consultants can be used to survey the market to determine consumer preferences, whether or not a demand for a particular product or service, what the buyer's ability to purchase the product is likely to be, etc. Marketing planning requires all this and more, and planning in other aspects of the business is often dependent on projected sales figures.

Another type of fact-finding that market research can provide is motivational studies. This is a psychological analysis of why consumers make the choices they make. The researcher interviews a sampling of consumers in depth and determines what inner motivations influence the buyer's decision. For example, motivational studies showed that many women were reluctant to purchase cake-mixes to which nothing but water had to be added. The psychologists reported that there was a guilt feeling on the part of purchasers because they were not adding "healthy" ingredients like butter, eggs and milk. Even though the cost was higher, when the food producers removed the powdered dairy products from the formula and instructed the user to add butter, eggs and milk, sales soared. Uncovering this hidden fact solved the problem.

Other fact-gathering methods include use of government figures on population trends, changes in make-up of areas, and the development of new industries which may be markets for your product. This information is available from various government agencies and in trade journals in fields of interest to your firm.

Assembling the Facts

Once the facts have been gathered, they must be put into order so they can be properly interpreted. In many instances the data accumulated are so voluminous that it is difficult to sift through the material and make sense of it.

When the facts are primarily of a quantitative nature, the computer can be utilized to help in this task. Many firms have Management Information Systems (MIS) units that are primarily concerned with analyzing data and keeping management aware of the information they need to help them plan and make decisions.

A system that carries fact-assembling one step further is Operations Research. This is valuable in several aspects of planning. It helps in diagnosing complex problems, in evaluating the facts and in forecasting the effect of the data on the total picture. Later Operations Research can be used to test the decisions made.

Operations Research (OR) is performed by reducing the problems to a complex mathematical equation called a "model." Each of the facts can then be analyzed as it relates to other facts and to the whole problem. By using a computer the most complex models can be worked out. OR allows for consideration of many variables; the solution of the equation provides the planner with a prediction of what will happen as a result of each possible variable separately, or of several together.

For example, an automobile manufacturer wanted to plan how many units of each type of replacement part should be provided in each regional warehouse for each month of the ensuing year. By using previous experience, market forecasts for sales of new cars, history of replacement needs for parts of older models, weather conditions in various parts of the country (which affect wear and tear of certain parts), road conditions and speed limits in various areas, etc., the OR people developed a model. When the model was fed into the computer, the automobile firm knew what the need would be for each part in each region. With this information they were able to plan to meet these needs at a savings of millions of dollars. If they had not had all these facts, and had not been able to relate them to each other, they would have either failed to meet customer demands for certain parts or would have overstocked parts, a costly investment in inventory.

One of the dangers of relying exclusively on quantitative matters (an easy trap to fall into when OR or computer data is available) is that it is often intangibles that are the key to understanding and solving a problem. As part of the fact-gathering and fact-assembling process, the planner should take into consideration such matters as employee morale, public opinion of the company, community relations, possible government actions that will affect the plan, acceptance of the plan by the persons concerned and so on.

In addition to the manager's personal "feel" of the situation, there are some specific methods for determining these intangible factors. Surveys can be made by outside consultants who specialize in employee-attitude studies or in public and community relations analysis. These surveys can be structured to provide the specific data needed to assist in making the plans. If a company is planning to open a plant in a new community, it would be helpful to know the attitude of the people in that community toward the type of business the company is in, toward any pollution problem the plant may cause and other such matters. If a survey determines that there may be a problem in these areas, the facts have to be considered in the planning.

The manager responsible for the planning should be confident that he has the whole story before he begins the formulation of the plan itself. Once he is sure, the next steps can be undertaken.

Developing Alternatives

There is rarely only one way to handle a problem. The planners must attempt to develop a variety of alternatives before choosing the "one best way." Most executives depend on past experience in solving problems. If the past experience has been successful, it may very well provide the answer to the current problem. On the other hand, before the decision is made, other possible solutions should be explored.

In gathering the facts about a situation, one often comes across information concerning the solution of similar problems by other organizations. The experience of others can often provide alternatives worth considering. One of the side benefits of attending management seminars or trade association meetings is the exchange of such information that often occurs informally over cocktails or dinner.

Seeking alternatives more directly and systematically should be part of the planning process. Often managers holding related positions in companies in the same or similar industries talk things over with each other and give each other information on mutual problems. It is good business to make such contacts and use them when needed.

Reading trade papers, attending trade association meetings and just talking shop with people in management, all help develop a storehouse of ideas which can be applied to business problems. Such organizations as the American Management Association, the Society for the Advancement of Management and the Conference Board put out reports and publish articles which can be valuable to managers in broadening their knowledge of how other companies have solved similar problems. Regular reading of papers like *The Wall Street Journal* and magazines like *Business Week, Fortune* or the *Harvard Business Review* should be part of the regimen of business managers. There is nothing shameful about copying someone else's successful methods if they apply to your situation. By reading, listening and exchanging ideas, the manager will broaden his scope and increase the number of possible alternatives he can consider.

Encouraging Individual Creativity

In developing alternatives the manager should use the creative talents of his people. Everybody has creativity. Psychologists have shown that this great faculty is within all of us but is often suppressed or inhibited. As effective management is managing through people, it is the responsibility of the manager to unleash the creative ability in each of his people.

Many people do not really believe that they are creative. All of their lives they have been made to believe that creativity was a special gift of artists, writers, advertising specialists and similar "geniuses." Often their original suggestions and ideas have in the past been ridiculed or rejected out of hand by parents, teachers and supervisors.

Why do people fear being creative? Chiefly it is because they are afraid their ideas will be criticized, that they will be made to appear foolish or stupid if their ideas are not accepted. The manager has to overcome this fear by encouraging his people to initiate or recommend improvements, to contribute ideas and to participate in planning. However, to really encourage creativity, the manager should be careful never to ridicule an idea, no matter how unrealistic it may be. He should evaluate—not condemn—a poor idea. By showing that originality is welcome, he can gradually lift the fear of being put down.

If the manager understands the creative process, he will be able to improve his own creative powers and assist others to develop theirs. Psychologists break the creative process into five steps:

1. Saturation: Before the mind can start working on an idea, it must be "saturated" with knowledge about the problem. This includes obtaining the facts, as discussed earlier in this chapter, as well as acquiring a broader knowledge of the area involved.

2. Analysis: All the facts and data are sorted out in the mind. They are arranged in some form of system, rearranged and re-rearranged until a pattern begins to take shape. The mind is constantly selecting aspects of the facts and comparing them with other facts that have been fed to it, and with the vast memory (never lost) of every experience it has had. It is like the computer which compares new input with material already programmed into it. The mind is far more complex and has much vaster resources than any man-made computer.

3. Incubation: Once the computer between our ears completes its arrangement and analysis of the facts, we may come up with some answers. Often, however the mind is now so cluttered with facts and concepts that we find ourselves completely confused. Time is needed for the mind to get it all together. Most people have experienced this type of situation, and know that if they turn to other pursuits, the mind will relax, and ideas will begin to incubate in the subconscious. Many ideas incubate while we sleep or are relaxing. It is good to allow this to happen. When you or your staff feel frustrated in solving some problem, keep in mind that the frustration is only a step in the creative process and should not be a cause of worry but is rather a sign that it is time to put the problem aside for a while and let it incubate.

4. Illumination: The comic strip cartoonist shows his character getting a new idea by drawing a flashing bulb in the balloon above his head. Frequently the mind works just that way. After one has been saturated with the data, has analyzed the facts and deliberated on the relationships among them, after one has incubated the material for a period of time, a solution suddenly becomes evident. CAUTION: Do not expect illumination unless all the previous steps have been taken. To sit back and wait for inspiration to solve one's problems will rarely work. Edison's formula that genius is ninety-nine percent perspiration and only one percent inspiration should not be forgotten.

5. Adaptation: Once the idea has germinated, it has to be tested and adapted to the specific situation. Adjustments have to be made to accommodate the requirements of different aspects of the work, the different viewpoints of participants and all the other factors that develop when an idea is fully understood. The manager must always keep in mind that although the new idea appears to be viable when it is presented, it still must be tested and checked to make sure it will really work. A common danger is to fall in love with one's own ideas and become defensive of them when changes are suggested, instead of adapting to suggestions.

Developing Creative Thinking

Certain attitudes encourage the production of ideas, while other attitudes inhibit creativity. The human mind works in two ways. There is a judicial or analytical mind which analyzes, compares and chooses; and there is a creative mind which visualizes, foresees and generates ideas.

If the judicial mind dominates, the individual sometimes becomes negative. His concern is to determine why an idea won't work rather than to create new ideas. Our judicial mind has been nurtured from childhood on, while our creative mind has usually been inhibited. We are taught to ask: "What's wrong with this?" rather than to say: "Let's try that." To stimulate our people to become creative, we have to inculcate a positive attitude. We have to be enthusiastic and optimistic. When looking at a new idea, we should consider all the ways it can be made to work, rather than just judge it unworkable.

Another problem in developing creativity is that most people are timid about presenting new ideas. Unless they are encouraged to develop self-confidence, they will never fully function creatively. You can help your staff become more self-confident by showing confidence in them. Some persons need special help in this important area. Programs such as the Dale Carnegie Course Effective Speaking and Human Relations have assisted many people in developing self-confidence.

A manager can help people overcome their blocks to creativity. One of the chief barriers to creative thinking is the tendency of most people to conform to the customs and practices of their environment. They fear being different in their thinking, just as they fear being different in the way they dress, talk and act. Usually, it takes an iconoclast to come up with radical new ideas that may really make a significant contribution to solving problems. Almost every major invention has emanated from someone (or some group) who has had the courage to defy the customs or conventions of his time.

A manager can encourage innovative thinking by listening carefully to all ideas presented by his subordinates, no matter how illogical they may appear. Instead of jumping to the conclusion, "That won't work," go over the idea carefully with the initiator and see if there is any merit in it or any part of it that is useful. In your evaluation, give the person who presented the idea encouragement by praising his orginality and pointing out the defects in a positive way, rather than by discouraging negation of the whole idea. For example, instead of saying: "That will cost too much," it is more effective to ask: "Joe, have you costed this out?" Joe will then recognize the cost problem for himself, and maybe come up with a better answer. Always keep in mind that a person who "dares to be different" may often present offbeat ideas that are impractical, but if not stifled by constant disparagement by his superiors and peers may eventually develop innovative and viable ideas.

Another major barrier to creativity is the inclination of many people to cling stubbornly to a concept once they have made up their minds about it. They close their eyes and ears to new evidence if it is opposed to their own ideas. Dale Carnegie wrote: "Keep your mind open to change all the time. Welcome it. Court it. It is only by examining and reexamining your opinions and ideas that you can progress." This is a principle that managers must follow themselves and encourage their subordinates to follow if creativity is to be developed in an organization. Never let the excuse "We've always done it this way" prevent consideration of new ideas.

More complicated is the block to creativity caused by the different ways in which different people perceive a situation, or even in the way the same person perceives the same situation at different times. Psychologists have written in depth about such problems of perception. People tend to ignore what disturbs them or tends to disrupt their basic ideas. Only when pushed off center by outside influences, or at the other extreme, by the realization that they are in a perceptual rut, do people even attempt to change their perceptual outlook.

In the example of the cafeteria chain discussed earlier (p. 60) the perception of management was based on a previous experience of dealing with problems on a cost basis. It required a completely new perspective for management to perceive the problem in its proper light—as a problem of changing demand. Had the management team not changed their perspective, the problem would never have been diagnosed, let alone solved.

Some people misunderstand the true meaning of creativity. They believe that to be creative one must produce completely new ideas, inspired by some inner force over which one has no control. This is untrue. Most creative ideas are based on combining, changing, rearranging or finding new uses for already existing elements.

Alex Osborne provides this check list in his book *Applied Imagination* as a summary of some of the kinds of questions one might ask oneself about any concept:

Put to other uses? New ways to use as is? Other uses if modified?
Adapt? What else is like this? What other idea does this suggest? Does past offer parallel? What could I copy? Whom could I emulate?
Modify? New twist? Change meaning, color, motion, sound, odor, form, shape? Other changes?
Minify? What to subtract? Smaller? Condensed? Miniature? Lower? Shorter? Lighter? Omit? Streamline? Split up? Understate?
Substitute? Who else instead? What else instead? Other ingredient? Other material? Other process? Other power? Other place? Other approach? Other tone of voice?
Rearrange? Interchange components? Other pattern? Other layout? Other sequences? Transpose cause and effect? Change pace? Change schedule?
Reverse? Transpose positive and negative? How about opposites? Turn it backward? Turn it upside down? Reverse roles? Change shoes? Turn tables? Turn other cheek?

Combine? How about a blend, an alloy, an assortment, an ensemble? Combine units? Combine purposes? Combine appeals? Combine ideas? *

If managers encourage all of their people to increase their creativity potential by establishing a climate of reception to new ideas, by urging them to read books and attend seminars that will stimulate their creative buds and by exposing them to the creative processes of other members of the organization, the process will pay off with innovative, productive ideas that will help the organization grow. But even more important, it will help the people who contribute this new thinking to grow too and make them more dynamic and self-fulfilled human beings.

Encouraging Group Creativity

Most people visualize the creative person as one working by himself and generating ideas or inventions like Einstein or Edison. Actually many creative concepts come from groups of people working together. The interaction and cross-fertilization of ideas stimulates ideation.

The old adage "two heads are better than one" and its amplification that many heads are better than a few has been shown over and over again to be true. Committees and conference groups have been used for years in business and government to mull over problems, and by group effort to come up with answers.

In recent years there has been developed a new use of group thinking specifically geared to encourage creative ideas. Originally used in advertising agencies to come up with new advertising programs, it soon was adapted for use by a variety of organizations to stimulate group creativity.

Alex Osborne is credited with originating this concept when he headed the prestigious advertising agency, Batten, Barton, Durstine and Osborne; he christened it *Brainstorming*.

* Osborne, Alex F., *Applied Imagination.* New York: Charles Scribner's Sons, 1953, p. 284.

The difference between the usual kind of conference and brainstorming is that in the usual conference evaluation and criticism of ideas dominate the meeting, rather than the actual production of ideas themselves. The chairman often controls the meeting and because he is usually the boss, stifles any opposition to his ideas. New ideas that are presented are immediately analyzed and judged, and this inhibits the development of more ideas.

In brainstorming, the objective is to spawn as many ideas as possible *regardless of their value*. Even poor ideas, crazy ideas, irrelevant ideas, may spark off an idea in the mind of another participant which may be worthwhile.

Osborne says, "The power of association is a two-way current. When a panel member spouts an idea, he almost automatically stirs his own imagination toward another idea. At the same time, his ideas stimulate the associative powers of all the others." *

In a typical brainstorming session, a group, usually five to ten people, tackle a single subject which has been announced in advance of the meeting. The chairman usually does nothing but present the problem and then take his place as an equal member of the group. One of the members acts as secretary to jot down all the ideas that are suggested. (In some cases a secretary joins the group just for this purpose, or a tape recorder is used.) One person starts by throwing out an idea. It is *NOT* criticized or analyzed—no comment is made at all. Another participant may suggest an idea based on what the first member has offered, or he may suggest a completely different idea. There are no restrictions on the ideas. Some of the wildest may have within them the cue for a good idea on someone else's part. Out of such meetings more alternatives are usually developed than would come from the same people each working independently.

The four basic rules of brainstorming are:

1. There will be no criticism of ideas. Judgmental comment is ruled out. All analysis is to be done after the session, not during it.

* *Ibid.*, p. 299.

2. "Free-wheeling" is encouraged. The wilder the idea, the better.

3. The more ideas, the better. The greater the number of ideas presented, the more likely it is that some of them will be usable.

4. Improve and combine the ideas of participants. Members of the group should be encouraged to turn the ideas of others into better ideas.

Brainstorming is not applicable to all kinds of problems. In some instances, individual attention to a problem can be more effective. Brainstorming is most useful when the subject is specific rather than general. The problem should be clearly stated. The participants should be thoroughly immersed in the data needed. Brainstorming sessions are no place to discuss new data. All members of the group should recognize what brainstorming is, and be ready and willing to verbalize ideas, no matter how foolish they may appear. Unfortunately, many businessmen have been trained to hold their tongues until they have thought out all of the ramifications of what they intend to say, and so are much too inhibited to be effective in brainstorming. Once this barrier is overcome—usually only after each recognizes that his colleagues are participating freely—will they contribute, and so ensure, the success of the program.

After the ideas are presented and noted, the usual careful analysis must be given to each of them. The executive assigned to this task will select the ideas that seem to him the most viable and apply to them the analytical and judgmental techniques which will be discussed in the next chapter to determine which of the alternative solutions suggested is to be adopted.

5

MAKING
THE DECISION

One often hears the comment that managers are paid to make decisions. It is probably this requirement of the management job that gives it the status and the salary level it commands.

Decision-making takes place at many points in the management process. It involves not only decisions on choice of alternative plans, which we are now considering, but also decisions as to organization, direction, coordination and control. The techniques of making the decision are the same in each of these areas.

Many people make their decisions purely on hunch. They trust their intuition—often backed by previous experience—to guide them to the correct decision. The scientific orientation of many modern managers inclines them to scoff at this type of thinking. Yet we cannot deny that many intuitive decisions have been correct ones. Actually there is a place for intuition in decision-making. Intuition has as its foundation considerable knowledge and background about a subject—and this works subconsciously in aiding the manager to make a reasonable decision.

The modern manager does not, however, depend on hunches. He collects as much information about his problem as possible. On the basis of this information, several alternatives are projected; the decision that must be made is really a choice among these alternatives.

In order to make a decision about alternatives, it is necessary to evaluate each of the options on the basis of how it meets the objectives, what problems may arise as a result of the choice, and what risks will be incurred.

An evaluation can be arrived at by making a comparison of each of the alternatives, preferably on a side-by-side basis so that the advantages and limitations can be easily noted. This can be illustrated by the following example:

The Apex Printing and Duplicating Service has been in the downtown area of their city for several years. They recognize the expansion of the city to suburban areas and one of their long-term objectives is to open branch operations in several suburban shopping centers. The immediate objective is to open their first branch. They have chosen a site in "Suburban Mall." Now they are faced with two alternatives: 1. to open this branch as a company-owned facility, or 2. to open this branch as a franchised facility.

Management has to compare the two alternatives in light of a variety of factors, giving major consideration to how each alternative will effect both the short- and long-term objectives.

On the accompanying chart, the company listed in the left hand column the pertinent factors that must be considered. In the adjacent columns they listed the relevant information. It now becomes much easier to compare the way each alternative relates to each of the key factors separately, and how *in toto* to immediate and long-range objectives.

In this case management decided on Alternative 2, opening a franchised office. Although there would be a greater profit over several years in operating their own office, it would have taken a large portion of their capital and a great deal of managerial time. The franchised office would bring them some immediate capital from the sale of the franchise; it would take less supervision because the franchisee would have a vested interest in the business and would not require the same type of supervision as an employee. The immediate objective of opening an office in Suburban Mall would be at once accomplished. The long-run objective would be expedited, because through franchising the company could open offices in several shopping centers with a

Long-range objective: To open several branch operations in suburban shopping centers over the next five years.

Short-range objective: To open first branch in "Suburban Mall."

	Alternative 1.		Alternative 2.	
	To open branch as a company-owned facility		*To open branch as a franchised facility*	
Concept	Company will purchase equipment, arrange financing, invest total capital, provide working capital, employ staff and furnish management. Company will benefit from total profits and risk any loss.		Company will sell franchise to franchisee. Franchisee will buy or lease the equipment, provide working capital, employ staff and furnish management. Company will train franchisee in operating and managing unit, will provide all systems and procedures, include branch address in its area-wide advertising, and give continuing training and counsel to franchisee.	
Est. Sales				
1st year	$ 75,000		$ 75,000	
5 yr. period	450,000		450,000	
Costs	Equip. lease	$ 3,500	Cost of selling	
First	Rent	7,500	franchise	$5,000
year	Materials	5,000	Cost of training	5,000
	Payroll	30,000	Misc. costs	5,000
	Misc.	10,000		
	Total	$56,000	Total	$15,000
Profit			Return from franchise	
first yr.	$19,000		based on franchise	
			fee	$10,000
			royalties (5% of	
			gross sales)	3,500
				$13,500
Projected 5 year earnings	$114,000		$32,500	

	Alternative 1.	Alternative 2.
	To open branch as a company-owned facility	*To open branch as a franchised facility*
Managerial time	Manager will have to spend much of his time supervising new office to the neglect of home office. As branch mgr. will be an employee, he will require close supervision.	Manager will train franchisee and be available for consultation. This should take little time after first three months. Franchisee as owner-manager will have more reliability than employed-manager.
Risk	It will take 6 months to determine whether branch will be success. Risk is about $30,000, plus managerial time, and loss of business or profit in home office due to time and effort spent in branch.	Little financial risk, as franchisee puts up all money. Failure would only risk loss of managerial time in selling and training.
Intangibles	Company-owned office will give opportunity for advancement to current employees.	Franchisees can bring new contacts into operation. They usually will know people and businesses in area.
	Quality of work will be better supervised.	Proper training should alleviate quality problems.
	Customers from suburban area can be serviced at home office as well as at the branch.	
Timing	4 to 6 weeks after decision is made, branch can be open. As home-office manager and staff will provide initial work force, production goals should be reached in 2 months.	Franchise must be sold first. This may take considerable time. Once franchise is sold, 4 to 6 weeks needed to open. As franchisee must be trained, it will take 2 to 4 months to reach production goals.

	Alternative 1.	Alternative 2.
	To open branch as a company-owned facility	*To open branch as a franchised facility*
Effect on Long-Range Goals	Company will not be able to open additional offices until this one has paid for itself and generated capital for more expansion. This might take several years.	Once first franchise is sold and under way, company could sell additional franchises. It is easier to sell these and get new branches started, once the first office is established. It would be possible to open 5 more offices the first year.

Summary

Advantages:	Higher immediate return. Can open branch sooner. Higher morale of staff. Higher control of quality. Risk of loss much lower.	Franchise fee provides new capital. Company capital investment small. Little managerial time needed after training. Capital and time available for opening additional franchises.
Disadvantages:	Higher investment of capital. More managerial time needed. Long run growth limited. Long run return on capital investment lower. Ties capital up so long-range goal must be deferred. Home office may suffer because of time and effort devoted to branch.	Profit from branch much lower when franchised. May take time to sell franchise. Once sold, takes longer to open and make productive.

minimum investment of capital and time. The franchise fees and royalties received from the franchisees would be less per unit than the profits from operations, but because the company could open several units, the return on investment would be much higher.

The process used in making this decision is referred to as *rational analysis*. The first step in making this rational analysis was to have a clear understanding of the objectives. This was indicated on the top line of the chart. Unless this is done, management might lose sight of the objectives when comparing the alternatives.

The next step is to examine the consequences of each alternative in each of the areas that are relevant. To do this a list of relevant factors must be made. These will always include tangibles: the cost of getting the project started, the cost of keeping it going, the facilities available, personnel available, managerial attention needed, etc. Also to be considered are intangibles: how each alternative might affect customer good-will, public image, employee morale; what the effect might be on other aspects of the business, etc.

In making the comparisons, focus on the aspects where there are differences rather than working on all of the items equally. It is easiest to note first the areas where there is no difference between the alternatives and disregard those areas in making the decision. In the example, there is little difference between the alternatives as to the time it would take to open the new outlet, the cost of equipment, the service to be provided to customers, and projected sales. These, then, will not have to be considered.

The differences arise in the areas of operating costs, profit from the unit over a period of five years, managerial time and attention, and capital investment. It is to these factors management must address itself.

This should not be interpreted to mean the areas of similarity are not important, or that they may not have some weight in the decision, but they are much less important in the choice between the alternatives than the areas of difference.

Where the differences can be quantified—as in costs, capital investment, projected earnings, etc.—it is easier to make comparisons. Where possible, try to convert figures into the common denominator of money. For example, instead of comparing units of production stated in pieces with sales stated in dollars, convert the units into their dollar value so that the comparison will be more easily understood.

When comparing costs, a helpful rule to keep in mind is to identify the difference between those costs that will be involved if the alternative is adopted, and those that would exist even if the alternative were not adopted. In the example of the printing company, the managers did not take into consideration the cost of running the home office, as that would be the same no matter which of the two alternatives were selected.

One of the self-deceptions that often occurs in decision-making is failing to recognize that certain costs will not really bear on the decision and including them in the problem-solving process. A typical example is that of the company that has invested a good sum of money in developing a new product. A different approach to manufacturing the product is under consideration. A common reaction is "We have already invested so much in the original process that we should continue with it." This is throwing good money after bad. In making the decision, what has already been spent should not be considered. This is a "sunk cost." The decision should be made on the basis of what future costs will be, starting from the present, plus the other factors involved.

As the intangible factors often are as important as, or even more important than, cost factors, they must be carefully analyzed. Some intangibles can be projected into future costs, thus making comparison easier.

For example the effect of reduction in employee morale as a result of a decision can be quantified somewhat by projecting the possible labor-turnover caused by it. A company may have to choose between hiring an outsider or promoting someone from within. Management knows that the "insider" will not quit if bypassed because he is close to retirement, but feels others lower in the hierarchy may be discouraged and leave. If management is willing to take that alternative, it may be able to compute that the replacement of certain personnel would cost a specific amount and use this figure as a means of measuring its effect.

In recent years there have been many aids developed to assist management in making decisions. Most of these are quantitative in nature; they often require knowledge of complex mathematical techniques.

There is a place for this type of analysis, and managers should be aware of the various methods used. However, it takes some mathematical training and skill to use these techniques. Managers should carefully note that quantitative decision-making techniques are not a cure-all for management ills. They only aid in evaluating quantitative matters and cannot be substituted for good judgment. Have the results of the mathematical analysis interpreted by specialists, and use them as one of the tools available to help make the best possible decision.

The Computer as a Decision-Making Tool

Since the advent of computers in business, there has been a reliance upon data processing to provide business managers with information and often with solutions to problems. Data processing has aided many managers in making decisions; it can actually make minor decisions for management when all the aspects of a problem can be programmed into the equipment.

As most problems, however, cannot be pre-programmed, the computer becomes a tool that is best used for preparation of details so that the human manager can have adequate information on which to base a decision. The use of the computer enables managers to make some decisions earlier than they had previously been able to do because data comes to them more rapidly. It allows them to consider more thorough analysis of a situation that requires quantitative analysis. The computer can review several courses of action by simulating them using mathematical models; it can thus enable management to project possible results from each of several alternatives. It can also spot missing material so that managers will be able to know when it is necessary to dig deeper before making a decision.

In the future it is likely that as computers become more sophisticated and smaller computers become available, their use will become practical for smaller companies, and more use of data processing will be available to the decision-makers.

Panel Decisions

Group decision-making is utilized in many organizations. In some instances it is carried out by committees, in others by special task-forces, and in still others by informal discussion among the management people concerned.

The key to group decision-making is consensus. The objective is to get all of the concerned parties to agree on the appropriate decision. If all of the people who are responsible for implementing the decision are in agreement, they will be highly motivated to assure its success.

A more formalized approach to group decision-making is the panel technique. Based on the concept of brainstorming to create alternatives, it carries the process into the determination of the choice of alternatives.

Basically this technique is a method by which many—or perhaps just a few—ideas can be processed by successive comparison, analysis, evaluation and judgment to achieve consensus in solving a problem. The panel consists of experts and managers who will be involved with the problem.

The ideas presented are rated on a score sheet on a 1 to 5 scale. The average score of each idea is then determined by the group leader, and the best ideas are passed on to another panel at a higher level.

The higher panel also rates the ideas. Duplicates are analyzed and combined where appropriate. The lower-scored ideas are eliminated, and the more viable ones passed on to a final panel, which is staffed with top managers of the organization. This group reviews the screened ideas and the justification statements which the lower panels provide with each item passed up to the top. In some organizations, the panel is given a limited number of hours to reach a decision. This is done to avoid debates on matters which should have been covered in the earlier discussions and presented in the justification statements. If the panel cannot decide, the proposal is returned to lower panels for further consideration. If a decision is agreed upon, it is sent to the appropriate administrator for action.

This approach is more suitable to a large organization than to a small one. It formalizes group decision-making and forces choices that are more objective by calling for rating and justification. It carries the brainstorming concept beyond the creative aspect, which is non-judgmental, to the evaluative phrase.

On the negative side, this technique is time-consuming and therefore expensive. It is suitable only to large organizations where the expertise of staff is available, and where there are adequate management personnel to provide members for the several panels that are required.

Some of the concepts of this type of technique, however, can be applied to smaller groups—particularly the rating of alternatives by several people and the use of justifying statements to back up recommendations.

The Human Element in Decision-Making

Whether the decision is made by a panel of specialists or by one person, the human aspect of the decision-making process has to be considered. In the group situation, the human factor is less pronounced because areas of difference among the members tend to be neutralized by the group itself. Nevertheless, each of the members of the group is influenced by his or her own orientation.

In individual decision-making the human element is more significant. Each person has certain personal objectives in his job and in his life as a whole. These objectives plus his general perception of the situation affect the decisions he will make.

To be really objective as a decision-maker, the manager must understand his own prejudices, orientation and personal goals, and compensate for them in reaching a decision that is for the best good of the company. It is not true in every circumstance that the manager's goals and those of the company coincide.

Recently a New York City-based manufacturer was faced with a decision on relocating the plant from a crowded and dirty section of Manhattan. The alternatives were both in new industrial parks—one in New Jersey, the other in Long Island. Although the New Jersey location had many advantages, the president chose the Long Island site because it was easier for him to reach it. This very human choice was not a good business decision. He allowed his personal desires to overly influence the selection.

Some managers, particularly in the middle levels of the hierarchy, become so imbued with the specific objectives of their own departments, that they fail to take in the whole picture. Decisions in which they participate are often so colored by narrow individual perspective that they are inconsistent with corporate goals. This sometimes continues when such people move into top management: they still act and react as they did when they were specialists, and their decisions may reflect this.

Another human aspect of decision-making is the fear many people have of making decisions. This often arises from having been criticized and rebuffed in their early days, and sometimes carries over into management responsibilities. There are times when not making a decision is the best decision, but in most instances the buck must stop somewhere, and that is as a rule at the desk of the manager of the appropriate department or organization. The effective manager will recognize that he cannot always be right, but also that it is better to be wrong some of the time than to fail to make needed decisions and so get nothing done. A manager can afford a good number of bad decisions so long as the good ones outweigh them. If a man utilizes the tools available to him and evaluates the alternatives with objective views, it is more likely than not that the decision will be a good one.

Effecting Compromises

It is rare that a decision that is made will be satisfactory to everybody. Some of the participants will have agreed to it reluctantly, others may agree in principle, but differ on details. There is rarely a perfect decision. As management always should strive for consensus, the result may not please anybody, but be just acceptable to all. Compromises have probably been made all through the deliberations leading to the decision.

The main factor should be *what is right* rather than *who is right*. Yet very often compromises are made to appease a strong faction or an individual rather than for the best interests of the company. This is seen in the public sector when one examines how bills pass in Congress. Compromises and trade-offs are determined by political interests rather than by intrinsic factors. The result has been a great deal of ambiguous and ineffective legislation.

However, it is important to take political factors into consideration in decision-making. Sometimes it is wise to trade-off certain aspects of a proposal in order to get the entire proposal's major aspects accepted.

In making the compromise, it is essential not to sacrifice the key objective to appease opponents, nor to accept an unworkable solution for political reasons. Some compromises, like Solomon's proposal to cut the baby in half, may appear to satisfy both sides, but would also kill the baby.

A good compromise takes into consideration what is negotiable and what is not negotiable, makes trade-offs on the negotiable factors and sticks closely to the non-negotiable ones.

Often conflicts stem from obstinacy on the part of some members of the management group; they resist any change in what they have always done. This is sometimes based on lethargy, and sometimes on fear that change is implied criticism of their previous activities. An understanding of the reason for resistance to a proposal will enable the manager to know what compromises he must make and what ones he should not make. There are other methods of overcoming resistance to change than giving in to them. These will be discussed later in this book.

When a Decision Should Not be Made

Many managers are overimpressed by the importance and often urgency of making a decision. There are many instances where it is not wise to make any decision *at the time*. Often stalling for time may make the decision unnecessary. This is particularly true when the manager is under pressure.

A good rule for managers to remember is to not be forced into making decisions without proper deliberation. Once in a while, emergency decisions will require shooting from the hip, but this is rare in most business situations.

Interim decisions which do not solve the problem but alleviate the immediate conflict are often expedient. An example comes from the time when college students were protesting our involvement in the Viet Nam war. At one college in a small midwestern town the students demanded that the American flag be removed from the flag pole. The college, fearing a violent demonstration, complied. The student group then called on the manager of a hamburger outlet across from the college and demanded that he remove his American flag; if he refused, they said, they would boycott his store. As half of his business came from the college, and the other half from the townspeople, who would resent compliance with the students' demands, the manager was in a quandary. He called the home office for counsel. After some deliberation he was given this interim decision: When the delivery truck came the next morning, the driver would hit the flagpole and knock it down. Thus the students couldn't complain—the flag was not flying; the townspeople couldn't complain because the pole was down. By the time the pole could be replaced, the school session would be over, and by the fall when college reopened, the situation would have calmed down, and there would be no necessity for a decision on the question.

On the other hand, there are times when stalling only aggravates the situation. A delay in determining whether prices should be reduced to meet competition might cost a significant loss of business; a delay in settling a union grievance might cause a work stoppage. Managers should evaluate the real urgency of a situation to determine what effect delay will have, how long a decision can be put off, what factors have to be dealt with immediately and what ones can be deferred until more deliberate consideration can be given to them.

Testing the Decision

It is not always possible to test a decision to be sure it works, but there are times and situations where this can be done.

In the marketing field, it is quite common to use test markets to check whether the marketing decisions were right and how they can be improved. A company may test the package they have chosen for a product by packaging the product in two or more types of box and selling them in the same market. It can check the effectiveness of an advertising program in a local market before using it nationally.

In manufacturing, too, decisions on production methods can be tested on a small scale before being adapted to the entire line.

As noted earlier, some organizations reduce decisions to mathematical terms, and by use of simulation and computer technology project possible results of their decisions. This form of testing is becoming more effective and useful as the sophistication of computer science increases.

Decisions should be tested where possible. Unforeseen problems often are brought to light, and mistakes can be corrected before implementation of the decision on a broader scale. Testing also prepares management for difficulties it may meet in carrying out a program and in the type of reception and acceptance it will find among those concerned with it.

Feedback

The finalization of a decision does not mean that management can sit back and expect that what has been decided upon has been carried out. It is important to build into the solution to any problem a feedback mechanism that will keep management informed of the results.

Feedback is a continuing test of the decision. By providing for reports, computer print-outs, periodic review and other means of determining what is actually happening, management can make sure that the decision was correct, and that if there is any need for revision such revision can be made rapidly and effectively.

Managers often have staff assistants who spend much of their time checking on the effects of decisions. Often managers themselves visit the people in the field who are working on the projects affected by the decisions they have made to see how things are going. Personal observation can be an important means of feedback.

The ultimate feedback, of course, is the determination of how well the decision made achieves the objectives. How this can be done and what steps can be taken to correct deviations will be discussed in Part V of this book.

Decision-making—the choice of a solution from among possible alternatives—is a key factor in the management process. It is not and can never be purely mechanical—despite the use of mathematics and computers. It requires intelligent, innovative insight into problems by managers and the ability to bring together all the facets of a problem, foresee problems that may arise, and then take the risk of making the decision.

6

FINALIZING
THE PLAN

Reaching a decision as to which alternative will be accepted and incorporated into the plan is not the end of the planning process. The details of the plan have to be worked out and presented in a form that is understandable to all concerned. Usually this is a written statement of the policy, procedure or strategy.

There are many advantages in reducing the approved plan to writing. Managers who must do the writing are required to really think through the meaning of what they have decided; they have to be able to make it clear both to themselves and to those who will read the statement. A written statement also provides a permanent record of what is expected of persons following the plan and usually indicates who will be responsible for each aspect of the plan. In addition, it will enable all persons who use the plan to have an authoritative source to which they can refer in the future.

It is best to write policies in a simple, direct style rather than in legalistic or bureaucratic language. The tone should not be condescending. The statement should encourage the reader to follow the plan and show how it benefits the participants by helping to meet the objectives of the department, the company and the individual himself.

The examples of written plans in Chapter 3 will give some idea of how a plan or procedure is presented. However, many aspects of a plan must be left to the judgment of the manager responsible for it, as it is almost impossible to cover all contingencies. The plan should give adequate guidelines to assure consistency in the actions of any person who refers to it.

There are, however some disadvantages in committing a plan to writing. Sometimes particular aspects of a plan should not be given wide circulation because of the confidential nature of the subject. Anything in writing tends to be seen by eyes that should not see it, even when security measures are taken. Another problem is that it is sometimes difficult to state a policy accurately and completely so that there is no misunderstanding. We often know just what we mean to say, but find that a reader interprets it differently. If the written material is not checked on to make sure that the reader understands it exactly as intended and accepts it, we may have a worse situation than if it were not in writing at all.

As previously stated, there is a natural inclination to accept the written word as immutable. This tends to make written policies inflexible and may inhibit creative approaches to the areas covered in the plan. Management must make provision to overcome this by building into each written policy or procedure some degree of flexibility and provision for revision. More on this subject later in this chapter.

The single-use plan also should be put into writing. Even though it does not have the repetitive feature that standing plans have, it is helpful to be able to refer to it and use it as a guide in checking progress. Refer to the "Plan for Introducing a New Product Into the Market" in Chapter 3 for an example of this.

Long-range plans present a different problem when they are put into writing. In many instances the plan can be broken down into segments, usually by organizational breakdown (Manufacturing, Marketing, etc.), or by profit centers or geographic areas. It can be further broken down by years, so that the five-year plan would have a sub-plan for each of the five years.

Objectives for each segment and for each year should be clearly stated, and an indication should be given as to what phases of the program are to be completed by the end of each year, and what ones at the end of the total period.

A long-range plan should start with the objectives clearly stated, as in this five-year plan of a publishing company:

Objectives: Over the next five years we plan to change the emphasis of our magazine from one of specializing in news of interest to marketing and sales executives to one with articles and features aimed at the overall business executive readership.

This should enable us to increase our circulation from the current 100,000 to 125,000 over this period.

As circulation increases our advertising rates can be increased according to ABC (Audit Bureau of Circulation) rules and increase our profits by 15%.

The plan goes on to detail specific strategies for reaching the general management market, and letting executives know about the change in policy. This includes advertising and sales promotion strategy, circulation planning, editorial programming, and all of the other aspects of the long-run strategy.

Next the publisher breaks down this plan into annual segments, showing just what is to be done each year of the plan.

Lastly, he sets up a five-year budget—*a quantified statement of the plan.* It is this aspect of the planning that will probably be the key tool in the plan. Although it is not useful in every phase of planning—for example, it cannot specify details of advertising and editorial content—it is significant in bringing together the cost and projected income figures which govern the whole operation. Even the advertising can be "quantified" as to how much money will be spent on it.

Budgets

Budgets serve a dual purpose in management. Budgeting is both a planning and a controlling medium. In this chapter we will examine the budget as a planning device. Later in the book we will show how the same budget can be used in management control.

All budgets are estimates of income and expense, predicated on how much money is expected to be available for meeting the organization's objectives. In business available funds are usually determined by the sales forecast; in non-business organizations, they are based on appropriations, estimates of funds to be raised or other appropriate figures.

Budgeting can be used for either the entire organization or any segment of it. It need not be limited to financial matters. Although the most common types of budget are expressed in dollars and cents, some industries have budgets of production in physical units or of labor in terms of hours worked.

Most budgets are set on an annual basis. Budgets can also be broken down into smaller time periods (quarters or months) or planned for longer periods (2- 3- 4- 5-year budgets, etc.).

The types of budget most frequently used are:

Sales budgets: Estimates on sales expected, broken down by territory, product, month (or quarter), salesman, etc. In addition a sales budget should specify the cost of sales, including advertising and promotion expenses, salesmen's salaries and commissions, travel expenses, share of overhead and any other expenses that are to be incurred to make the sales.

Production budgets: Often the production budget is expressed in units of production (number of cases of the item produced, number of yards, pounds, etc.). It indicates when the products must be completed to meet the production schedule. It also indicates what equipment is to be utilized and how much production can be expected from each machine. Cost of production of each item is frequently added to this type of budget so that it can be used later as a control to ensure that items are not being sold at too low a price.

Cash budgets: The cash budget, which is based on anticipated income is the key budget used by most companies. It shows anticipated receipts of cash and planned expenditures to ensure that working capital will be available when needed. A company can tell from the cash-flow figures when temporary outside financing may be required and can note rapidly when financial problems may be looming.

Master or Consolidated budgets: As the name implies, this type of budget is the sum of all the specialized or departmental budgets. It is the chief tool with which top management works. In it the total picture of the company's activities can be seen. Details of specific phases of the operation are left to the operating department's budgets.

Preparing the Budget

Although some companies have specialists to prepare budgets, the most effective way of preparing a budget is calling on the people who are responsible for working with it once it is completed. In people-oriented managements, the people themselves will work up their unit budgets.

A member of top management should coordinate the departmental budgets, advise the department heads of the parameters of their budgets and act as coordinator to resolve conflicts among departments. It is his responsibility to make sure that all the interests of all departments are in balance.

Managers should of course draw on the expertise of their own staffs in preparing the budget. The persons closest to the operation are likely to be of great value in furnishing realistic information which will assist in determining budget requests. If the people involved are consulted as the budget is framed, it is more likely that when the budget is finally approved, they will understand and accept it.

There is a tendency on the part of many managers to pad their budget requests on the logical assumption that as requests are going to be pared down, they might as well ask for more and so, perhaps, get what they need. As the budget is a plan for accomplishing an objective, this should not be necessary. A sensible budget policy would not require automatic paring down of budgetary requests, but would set specific targets; if all the participants recognize that their requests are to be measured against these targets, they will present figures in line with them.

Budget targets are usually established on the basis of past performance and experience. With this as base, consideration is given to general business conditions: trends of prices, availability of similar products in the market, the competitive situation, growth of the market served, etc. To this are added plans for increasing or decreasing advertising, production capacity, company plans for expansion, etc.

Using all the techniques available for forecasting and planning (as discussed in Chapter 4), each participant in the budgeting process will contribute ideas and pertinent information for the first proposals to be considered.

In many companies these first proposals are handled by a committee which works out tentative estimates based on the recommendations made by the department heads. When this work is completed, a first-draft budget is submitted to top management or in some companies, to a budget director. Usually several meetings are held with the various department heads to discuss their estimates, and in due course, a final budget is adopted. In people-oriented companies the final proposals are gone over by the persons who will have to live with them to make sure that they understand any changes made in the original suggestions. If a major problem is uncovered by this review, the budget will be restudied, and an adjustment will be made, if it is warranted.

Manpower Planning

In large companies or organizations, it is essential that plans be made to ensure that there will be adequate staffing of personnel to meet company objectives. Manpower plans are quantifications of the personnel projections for both short- and long-range periods.

On a short-term basis, the company should always know how many people in each job category it will need to meet production demands. A typical manning table for a factory is shown below. This represents a one-year projection for a seasonal business. The same form can later be used as a control sheet to indicate how many persons are actually employed in each category. That figure is shown in this example in italics.

Long-range manpower plans are more complex than mere quantification of personnel needs. They should also include

MANPOWER PROJECTIONS

Month	Punch Press Operators Req.	On P/R	Drill Press Operators Req.	On P/R	Assemblers Req.	On P/R	Packers Req.	On P/R	Inspectors Req.	On P/R
Jan.	4	4	6	6	20	18	12	11	4	4
Feb.	4	4	6	6	20	20	12	11	4	4
Mar.	4	4	6	6	20	20	12	12	4	4
Apr.	6	5	8	8	25	22	14	12	5	4
May	6		8		30		16		6	
Jun.	7		9		35		17		8	
Jul.	7		9		40		20		8	
Aug.	5		7		40		20		8	
Sep.	4		6		30		20		8	
Oct.	4		6		20		15		5	
Nov.	4		6		20		12		4	
Dec.	4		6		20		12		4	

Req. = estimated number of employees in job category required for month.

On P/R = number of employees on payroll in each category at beginning of month. This is entered by Personnel Dept. on first of month. *(completed in this example as of April 1.)*

needs that may develop because of normal attrition, retirements, expansion and other factors. A long-range manpower plan is really a complete organizational plan. It includes the prediction of the numbers of people the company will have to hire, train or promote over the period covered. It takes into consideration the interrelationships among various personnel policies and programs.

Using the past experience of the company, estimates can be made as to how many people in various categories will retire, quit, be terminated, be transferred, be promoted, etc. On the basis of this information the company can plan how many people will be needed to replace them, and where they will come from. It can be ascertained that a certain percentage will come from the ranks of employees and that another percentage will have to be recruited from outside. Plans can be made to employ trainees from colleges, trade schools or other sources to be a cadet corps for future supervisors and managers. Training and management development programs can be worked out to aid currently employed personnel in learning the skills needed for upgrading and the assumption of greater responsibility.

Care should be taken to keep abreast of changes in the skills and talents needed. It cannot be assumed that because we currently have thirty accountants, we will need at least thirty accountants at all times. The introduction of computers may reduce the need for so many accountants and increase the need for computer specialists. Other technological changes will affect the types of personnel required. Manpower planners have to be alert to all of this.

Another factor in this area is the changing supply of labor available for the kind of work performed. Personnel in some job categories are in short supply, and good manpower planning would consider finding substitutes if possible. A company that has always employed a good number of secretary-stenographers and now recognizes that such people are in short supply might shift to new word-processing systems which reduce the need for stenographers. Pressures from government and other sources to employ minority-group members in a variety of capacities in which they were not previously employed must also be taken into consideration in manpower planning. In times of economic slowdown, manpower planning should also include lay-off priorities and transferability of high-seniority employees to other jobs. The methods by which these plans are to be implemented will be discussed in Chapter 10.

Setting Timetables

In finalizing the plan, a definite timetable should be established so that the persons assigned to fulfil the plan will have prearranged dates by which the successive phases of the operation are to be completed.

The use of deadlines provides the plan with a sense of urgency. Without deadlines people tend to procrastinate. The job does not appear to them as important if there is no specific time by which it must be completed.

Timing the plan starts with the division of the plan into logical phases. Each phase covers a specific aspect of the plan and should be set up in its order of priority, so that a prerequisite phase is completed in time for the succeeding phase to commence. Once the phases and their order have been determined, the time for starting and completing each phase should be established.

Here participative planning becomes advisable. The men and women who are assigned the responsibility for carrying out the plan should be involved in the determination of the deadlines that they have to meet. If the people who are to do the job set the timetable, there is much greater likelihood that deadlines will be met.

An advantage of breaking down the plan into segments and setting a deadline for each segment is that it becomes easier to control. Management can note when a phase has fallen behind and make adjustments at the time, rather than discover at the last moment that the entire project is behind schedule. Another advantage is that as the participants complete each phase, they have a chance to evaluate it and to make any alterations that are called for before the next phase starts. Of course, the satisfaction of completing a segment gives each of those responsible that special feeling of fulfillment which comes from seeing the conclusion of a job well done.

Another advantage is that it is much easier to reach a goal by taking one step at a time. Breaking the plan into "bite-sized pieces" makes completing each piece appear much less formidable than trying to encompass the entire project at once. Participants are much more comfortable working with a plan segment by segment.

Building In Flexibility

Because we are always unsure of the future, good planners attempt to build flexibility into the plan itself. This is done so that with only slight adjustments the plan can be made to fit changing conditions.

One effective way of doing this is to have what is called "a moving plan." The "moving plan" is never considered a finished document, but is reviewed and revised at the end of each time segment. For example, a five-year plan would not be limited to a specific five-year period (1976–1980, for example), but would change each year so that when the 1976 plan was completed, the 1981 plan would be added. As this new unit is worked out, adjustments in each of the years before it will be made to accommodate changing conditions.

In situations where experience has shown that there is a smaller degree of stability, the plans should be drawn broadly—more as guidelines—so that the manager can use discretion in adjusting to immediate situations. With this broader discretion managers can react within definite parameters to rapid changes in the situation. For example, the marketing plan calls for introducing a new product over a period of several months—one region at a time. After the second month, however, the marketing manager notes that the public is accepting the product and that competitors are going to introduce a similar line. He should now have the flexibility to accelerate the introduction of the product into the rest of the country in order to beat the competition.

In much planning, funds are appropriated in advance to cover the projects. Often these funds are earmarked to implement the plan and cannot be used for other purposes. However, the executive responsible for this plan should remain flexible and avoid actually committing the funds until necessary. A company planning to build a new plant three years hence must start its planning now. However, if circumstances change between the onset of the planning and the actual planned starting date, the project may have to be modified or even cancelled. Management should set up certain key points at which the plan should be reviewed before each successive step is taken. Unfortunately, once certain points are passed, it sometimes seems impossible to change, and the plan must be completed even if it is no longer desirable. In some cases, nonetheless, it may be better to lose the time and money already allocated than to pursue the original plan, if circumstances have made it less desirable.

Another type of flexibility is the development of alternative plans. A company planning to build a plant in Community A is not sure it will get the zoning changes needed. To protect itself, it develops an alternative plan to build the plant in Community B, and takes an option on land there. If Community A refuses to grant the zoning change, the alternative plan will be used and the plant built in Community B. Although the alternative adds to the cost of the project (options must be paid for), it does ensure that the construction will not be delayed.

Some firms set up a plan for "normal" operation for the ensuing period with alternative plans based on sales volume. If sales are higher or lower than specified figures, the alternative plan is put into effect. This gives them flexibility to handle their operations on the basis of their original forecasts or under changed circumstances, as the case requires.

Once a plan is adopted it should be frequently reviewed to make sure that it is being followed, and that it is accomplishing the objectives of the company. Regular evaluation, and revision where necessary, will make planning a dynamic and meaningful aspect of management, and this will lead to better control and a healthier overall organization.

PART III

Organizing

The way to achieve success is first to have a definite, clear, practical ideal—a goal, an objective. Second, have the necessary means to achieve your ends—wisdom, money, materials, and methods. Third, adjust all your means to that end.

Aristotle

7

THE ORGANIZATIONAL
STRUCTURE

The second step in the "PLORDICOCO" approach to manage
ment is organizing the resources of the company to achieve the
results which have been planned for.

To be an effective manager it is essential that the manager
know what activities he or she is to manage, who is to work
with him, to whom he reports and who reports to him. In addition, he must be aware of the entire corporate structure, his
place in it and the official channels of communication which he
must utilize. All of this must be directed toward reaching the
goals of the department and the company. It is best to state these
goals in terms of the results which are expected.

Unfortunately, many companies build their organizations
around the people currently on the staff rather than determining
what results they seek and fitting people who can do the job
into the positions required. Often there is no real organizational
structure in a small company; certain people are assigned to
perform certain jobs; if they succeed, they become the nucleus
of a department. Soon additional personnel are hired and assigned to the various departments, and a jerry-built structure
begins to form. There is little relationship to the real needs of
the company. This type of structure works so long as things go
along smoothly. The moment a crisis develops, the whole structure falls apart. Often a poorly structured organization will survive for years because of an unusually dynamic leader or because

a high margin of profit (due to the nature of the business) compensates for poor management. However, such companies often fail to grow as they should.

In order for most businesses to be successful, it is necessary to structure the organization on a results-oriented basis. The goals should be clear and realistic, and the management should always be aiming toward the achievement of those goals. The structure is established solely on the basis of the results expected, and each position is established and staffed with the specific purpose of meeting its specific aspect of the goals. Instead of the job's being built around a manager, the manager is hired because he is the man who can do the job most effectively.

Since the organization structure will be a determining factor in the achievement of company objectives, it should be carefully and logically tailored to meet the needs of the organization. To do this a number of sequential steps need to be taken:

The first step is to make a careful analysis of the resources available—human, physical, financial. Such analysis should take into consideration the factors both within the organization and outside it that may help, and those that may hinder, in goal achievement.

The next step is to ask and answer the question: "In the light of the resources at our command, what would be logical, reasonable, attainable objectives for the company, both long-range and short-range?"

When objectives have been formulated, we are ready for a third step—the framing of an organization structure to achieve company objectives. That can best be accomplished by asking and answering the following questions:

1. What are the *key result areas* where time and attention need to be concentrated to ensure achievement of company objectives?

2. What major functions are needed in these key result areas to ensure achievement of expected results? The correct answer to this question will ensure that only those major functions which are actually needed to achieve desired results will be structured into the organization.

3. Exactly what results are required of each of these major functions? If the exact results required of major functions are not clearly defined, the people performing these functions will very likely be working at activities rather than for results.

4. What are the "critical activity" areas in each of these major functions which require concentration of time and attention to ensure achievement of desired results?

5. What major jobs are needed in each of these major functional areas to ensure achievement of desired results? Asking and properly answering this question will ensure that only those major jobs which are essential to goal achievement will be structured into the organization.

6. How can these major jobs be structured on a results-oriented basis? A great number of job descriptions existent today are not serving their intended purposes because they are "task-oriented"—not "results-oriented." They tell the manager what he is to do, but they do not clearly identify the results he is expected to achieve. In order to create a "results-oriented" environment in major job areas, the jobs should be structured so that managers clearly understand the major and supporting goals to be achieved. There should also be built-in performance standards which clearly indicate what constitutes satisfactory performance. How to construct results-oriented job descriptions will be discussed later in this chapter.

7. What back-up (supporting) functions are needed to ensure achievement of company objectives? What results are needed from these back-up (supporting) functions? What are the critical-activity areas in these back-up functions where time and attention need to be concentrated to ensure achievement of desired results? What jobs are essential to goal achievement in these back-up functional areas? How can these back-up jobs be best structured for results?

8. How can we best delegate on a "results-oriented" basis? All too often delegating assignments to subordinates is done by telling people what to do and how to do it, and this simply creates and perpetuates a "task-oriented" situation. People need to be "tuned in" on what results are expected, and they need to be involved in the ideas and decisions essential to goal achieve-

ment if they are to be "results-oriented" instead of "task-oriented."

9. How can an effective control and information system be structured into the organization which will keep people on target in the key-result and critical-activity areas? Failure to ask and properly answer this question may very likely cause all of our carefully laid plans to misfire. It is one thing to plan for results. It is quite another to control results. Good planning in structuring an organization will include a built-in information and control system which will help those upon whom results depend to stay effectively on target.

10. What related activities can be grouped into units so that similar or closely connected activities will be under the same control? For each activity to be performed, define clearly the duties required. Assign the resources of the company—human, physical, financial—to enable the staff to achieve the expected results.

11. Who are the best qualified personnel to assign to each job? Fit the people to the function rather than the function to the people. If incumbents are not highly qualified, arrange for their training and development if possible; if not, phase them out and replace them with people who can get results. Delegate the necessary authority to the persons assigned to accomplish the job. Let each person know what is expected of him, and how he will be measured. Establish and maintain proper relationships and interrelationships to assure teamwork and unified effort. These relationships should be coordinated, but established in such a way that each manager will have the flexibility to translate the goals into concrete plans and then into action.

Unity of Control

To ensure that an organization functions effectively, it is essential that there be no confusion or ambiguity concerning who is in authority over each area of activity. There should be one boss. When two or more people try to share the job of immediate supervisor, their actions are likely to be inconsistent. One may give a subordinate an order, and the other may countermand it. One may interpret a policy in one way, the other entirely differently. This leads to conflict.

There should then be singleness of authority. Each individual should have only one superior to whom he is responsible. Each individual knows who reports to him, and to whom he reports.

Unity of control, however, is not necessarily infringed upon if the control is shared by two persons who have a very close working relationship and tend to act and think as one person. In some companies this *alter ego* relationship works out very well, but it can only succeed when both parties have a clear understanding of the objectives to be attained and have a uniform policy in dealing with the subordinates involved.

Span of Control

How many subordinates can a manager manage effectively? Too wide or too narrow a span of responsibility can weaken the management structure. To assure optimum competence, the organizational structure must take this question into consideration. To make a determination, the manager must ask these questions:

1. How much time will the manager devote to supervision? Inasmuch as most supervisors are engaged in technical, administrative and other activities in addition to supervising their staffs, it is essential to understand how much of the time is actually utilized in working with their people. If the work is mostly supervisory, the manager can have a broader span of management responsibility; if the manager devotes considerable time to other work, he will not be able to give adequate attention to a large staff, so his span should be narrower.

2. How complex are the problems the manager deals with? If they are of a highly technical nature or at a high level of management, it is better to have fewer people reporting to him. One should differentiate between executive supervision and operative supervision. The executive makes decisions which are often

precedent-setting and affect many areas of the organization; the supervisor usually is only concerned with his own department and follows predetermined policies. Operating supervisors can have a broader span than executives.

3. Are the problems and activities managed repetitive or unusual? Managers working chiefly with repetitive situations can supervise more people than those who handle a more varied type of activity.

4. How well-trained and capable are the subordinates? A manager with a very competent team can control more people than one who has to spend considerable time training and checking his people.

5. Over how wide an area are the subordinates spread? If the people being managed are spread over too wide an area, the manager cannot maintain effective person-to-person contact. Communication is difficult, and motivation suffers. It is better to have a superior close to those he supervises. On the other hand, too close physical proximity, with the boss right on top of his people, may stifle initiative.

6. What staff assistance is provided? If subordinates can seek aid from technical staff personnel as well as from their boss, and if the organization has an active staff support team, the supervisor will have less direct contact with his people on the matters the staff handles, allowing him to handle more subordinates.

The trend in span of authority in recent years has been toward larger numbers. At one time a span of six to eight persons was considered optimum. With the improvement in communications and data gathering and the routinization of many operations, a supervisor can handle a much larger span with ease. The wider span also allows a reduction in the number of layers of the organization, making communication within the company easier, with less chance for incomplete or distorted information to move through channels. The more layers information must pass through, the greater the chance of misinterpretation and inaccuracy.

A wider span also gives the manager a greater challenge. It enables him to make more important decisions and fits the new management philosophies of "management by objectives" and participative management more closely. It also offers the subordinates an opportunity to take on more responsibility, and this gives them excellent training and experience in preparing them for growth within the company.

Departmentation

There are a number of ways in which a company's activities can be divided in the organizational structure. The most common way is to group them into departments or divisions. Very large organizations may set up their structures according to product lines, services rendered, geography or some other appropriate way. However, in most firms the department is the basic group. The department consists of several "positions" or "jobs" which are coordinated and work toward a common objective.

In determining how to departmentalize, certain factors should be taken into consideration:

1. What are the key results that are expected? The key result areas are the vital areas where individuals and the department as a unit should concentrate their efforts. For example, the key result area to which the Inventory Control Department aims is the maintenance of adequate inventory to meet sales demands. All jobs related to this should be coordinated by this department.

2. When a function is not directly related to a key result area, where should it be placed? Most effective placement of support functions is with the department having the most use for their activity. For example, the office duplicating section in an engineering-oriented company would be more effective if placed under the engineering department which uses it a great part of the time, rather than in the more traditional "office services" department.

3. Can we take advantage of specialization? If we have a group of persons who are specialists in an area of importance to the company, it may be expedient to establish them as a special department. For example, instead of spreading the several statisticians employed by the company among functional

departments, it might give the company better control over utilizing this skill to create a statistical department.

4. Will the departmentation aid coordination? Even though certain functions are dissimilar, they might be placed under one executive because they require close coordination. This is particularly helpful when the key results areas are closely intertwined. For example, in a hotel the registration desk and the cashier's office are often supervised by the same manager. In a factory, shipping and receiving—two related but really opposite functions—frequently fall under the same department head.

5. Can the departmentation be so set up as to facilitate control? There are several techniques that can be built into an organization which will make control easier. One of these is to structure activities so that each may serve as an independent check on other activities. For example, quality control should be separate from production. In that way the "Q.C." people will not be inhibited in checking production by reporting to the same boss as the production people. Another example is the internal audit department; it should never report to the same manager as the departments it audits.

Try to build into the departmentation *clean breaks* between the duties of one department and those of others. If there is no confusion as to which department has the responsibility of performing certain tasks, it is easier to measure how well the tasks are being done and to determine where corrections or adjustments have to be made.

In some companies competition between departments is deliberately built in. The purpose is not only to stimulate greater achievement in each department, but to enable top management to compare results of similar departments. This is commonly done in the sales field where territories are structured in such a manner that results, as well as costs and methods, are easily comparable.

6. Can the supervisor of the department give adequate attention to all of his subordinates? If this cannot be done, the department might better be divided into more than one unit. Keep in mind the unity of control rule and the problem of span of supervision in making this decision. Sometimes the use of

staff assistants can augment management's ability to provide adequate attention.

7. What will it cost to departmentalize? The more departments, the more personnel will be needed to staff them. Not only are managers required, but each manager must be provided with a secretary and staff. A department needs office space, telephone and other services to function effectively. Specialists are often required to perform the function of the department. This adds the cost of salaries, travel, etc. It is much less costly to have fewer departments.

8. Does the company have managerial and technical personnel to perform the functions assigned to the department? Unless this personnel is available, it would not be expedient to set up a department. To staff from scratch adds many problems which may negate the entire departmentation program. Of course a new company must do this, but if it is avoidable it may be better to add duties to existing departments rather than start new ones.

9. Will the proposed departmentation achieve harmony and cooperation within the organization? Consider the people who will staff the departments. Are their goals being taken into account? Do all of those affected by the change understand the reasons for it, and are they committed to it? In the last analysis, the major goal is obtaining results—and if this must be done at the expense of creating some personnel dissatisfaction, the two elements must be weighed accordingly. Companies which overemphasize "harmony" may create the danger of encouraging a sycophantic management group or a staff of non-achievers whose only interest is making everybody happy, with no consideration of accomplishing the company's real objectives.

Line and Staff Relationships

The concept of organization through line and staff channels originated in the military. It was adopted by business as a seemingly logical approach to the intricate problems of growing hierarchical structures.

Line Authority is direct operative authority. All positions report directly to a higher position. Each line manager is responsible for all activities within his unit. In a pure line organization, the line manager will schedule work, supervise the personnel, check quality and make all decisions related to his department. This works well in a small organization, but it becomes awkward as the organization grows. It has the advantages of getting things done with a minimum of red tape and of eliminating the problems of poor communications inherent in a more complex organizational structure. Its obvious disadvantages: managers tend to become overloaded with too many duties; if a manager is absent from work or leaves the company, it is difficult to train a new man to replace him. Moreover, in this age of specialization, it is unlikely that any one manager can master all of the complicated aspects of the job and have adequate time to give to each of them.

The term *staff* usually refers to a supporting activity. In management circles, the term *line* is used to describe those functions of the organization that actually provide income for the company. In a manufacturing company, this would be the production department and the sales department. All others which provide support to these activities *have staff functions.*

Among the various staff functions in a manufacturing company are the marketing department which provides the sales department with the tools it needs to sell the merchandise, the finance department which accounts for the money received and spent, the personnel department which watches over the manpower aspects of the company, etc. Staff managers do not usually have any direct relationship with the line workers, but they do advise and support the line managers on matters concerning their specialty.

Most organizations today have a combination line and staff management. The staff people relieve the line managers of those aspects of their duties which they can do better and so allow the line manager more time to devote to work directly related to his own department's activities.

It is important to note that although a function may in itself be of a staff type in its relation to the entire organizational structure, it can within itself operate as a line activity. For example the Personnel Department in its function of recruiting and screening applicants is performing a line activity. It actually does the interviewing and hiring. However, in its function in employee relations, it advises and supports line managers in how to handle morale and discipline problems—a staff function. The personnel manager has line authority in dealing with his interviewers, personnel assistants and others of his staff, but staff authority in dealing with all other persons in the organization.

There is often conflict between line and staff managers within an organization. Line people complain that staff people take credit for successes in which they have played only a minor role and shift blame to the line on failures based on what line managers attribute to staff recommendations. Another complaint is that staff people assume line authority when they should not and so confuse the line worker and disrupt the unity of control in the department. This occurs when a staff specialist, in his anxiety to put his ideas into effect, ignores line management and goes directly to the workers.

The staff managers' major complaint is that line managers resist new ideas, that they do not call on staff when needed and do not follow the recommendations of the staff when given. Another common charge is that staff managers are not given adequate authority—after all, they argue, they are experts in their fields and should be given sufficient power to enforce their decisions.

To overcome these problems, management has attempted several approaches. One of the most important of these is to clarify the basic relationships between line and staff. This involves careful training of all concerned in what their responsibilities and powers are. Clear, concise job descriptions and a distinct understanding of authority channels are essential. Both line and staff managers should be involved in setting goals and should be committed to the key results areas that have been determined. Team work rather than competition between line and staff must be indicated.

There are two kinds of staff activity: personal and specialist.

The former is best illustrated by the "assistant to" position; the latter by experts in such categories as law, public relations, market research, etc.

The personal staffer's duties may vary from those of a "gopher" (go for coffee, go for cigarettes) to that of an executor of the manager's decisions. In many organizations the administrative assistant to an executive digs up information on matters under consideration, assists in formulating plans, interprets his boss's orders to subordinates and peers, works on special projects for his boss and may even make decisions on minor matters. In rare cases the job may develop into "chief-of-staff," with considerable influence and power. President Eisenhower's use of Sherman Adams and Nixon's relationship with Alexander Haig are examples of this.

The specialist staff is concerned only with matters within its expertise. Specialists operate in four different ways: 1. as an advisory group 2. as a service to the line 3. as a control staff and 4. as a functional staff.

1. *As an advisory group,* the staff involved studies problems, offers suggestions and may actually develop plans for the line managers, who have the authority to accept or reject all or part of their recommendations. As the accountability for the success of an action always rests with the line manager, it is necessary for him to have veto power. However, as recommendations from experts are usually supported by top management, the line manager is more likely to accept their advice than reject it. Good staff work will save the line manager time, money and effort and enable him to make sounder decisions.

2. *As a service to line managers,* the staff department actually performs a specific function rather than just advise. An example is the personnel department, which actually hires people, writes job descriptions, etc., or the purchasing department, which accepts requisitions for materials and equipment from line managers, but does the actual purchasing itself.

3. *As a control unit,* the staff exercises certain controls to ensure that line departments meet the key results criteria. An example of this is the quality control department.

4. *As a functional staff:* in certain instances the specialty of a *staff* department is needed to expedite the success of a project. The usual authority exercised by the line manager is delegated to a staff specialist who is better equipped to handle the project. An example of this is the introduction of a new product. The product manager may be given functional authority over the salesmen (who normally report to the Sales Manager) to ensure that the new product is properly launched. Note that the product manager is given this authority *only* for this one product, and only for a specified period of time. Functional authority must be limited in this way, or the line manager's position would be severely undermined.

New Types of Organizational Structure

In recent years several new developments have been introduced to handle special problems in organization. One of these, the position of *product manager,* has just been mentioned. The product manager is a staff executive with a very special responsibility. His function is applicable to companies where many products are made and sold, such as Proctor and Gamble, where the product manager concept originated.

The product manager is responsible for the entire process of handling his product, from research and development through manufacturing, marketing, sales and distribution. Once the product is developed and becomes part of the regular product line of the company, his job is to manage its maintenance and growth.

His main work is to coordinate the efforts of line people in promoting his product. For example, the sales force of a toiletry company sells ten different items. The product manager of each of these items makes sure that his particular product is not ignored, that it gets adequate attention from the salesmen and that any problems arising in connection with that product are properly handled. Product managers work with production people and quality control people to make sure that merchandise is available and of standard quality, with advertising people on the marketing programs, and with the sales force when applicable. They do not usually assume line responsibility, but stimulate each of the appropriate departments to do its job more effectively.

The equivalent of the product manager in technical organizations is the *project manager*. He is responsible for a specific project, such as the design and manufacture of an electronic system. This executive will coordinate the work of engineers, production supervisors and contract administrators to make sure the project is completed properly and on time.

A variation of the project-manager function is the *matrix organization*. This is used in highly complex situations where many uncertainties may affect an activity. Most companies that engage in such projects have a store of talent spread throughout the company whose assistance is needed to complete the project. The matrix organization utilizes these talents by appointing a project manager for the specific mission and then assigning to him from each of the functional departments the talent needed to complete the mission. During the time the specialist works on this project, he is on loan to the project manager. Upon completion of the project, he returns to his usual department. This enables a company to draw talent from any department in its organization to meet a special program, rather than try to assign the program to an already established department. The problems in this are obvious. It may cause some disruption in other activities of the company if personnel are removed from their regular duties. However, matrix organizations are formed only when a particular project is essential to the overall goals of the company, and the cost is clearly specified. The project is usually geared to a deadline so the "borrowed" specialists know when they will return to their regular assignments.

The matrix organization is sometimes known as a "temporary project team." During assignment to the team, members are relieved of duties and responsibilities in their regular departments. For the duration of the project, they report to the Project Manager—not to their usual bosses.

The advantage of a matrix organization is that it is very flexible. As no member is permanent, specialists can be dropped and new ones added as the need occurs. Its impermanent nature makes the team more receptive to correction of project problems, as they do not have a vested interest in the status quo. As the lines of authority are not permanent, there is less concern about pleasing a particular boss and more attention to the results desired.

Among the limitations of this structure is the fact that accountability is sometimes difficult to fix. Coordination is necessary, but because of the transient nature of the project, it may be difficult to achieve. Line managers find the matrix situation upsetting as it takes key men away from them—sometimes when they are needed in their regular work—and it blurs the lines of communication.

Here is a diagram of how a matrix organization is structured.

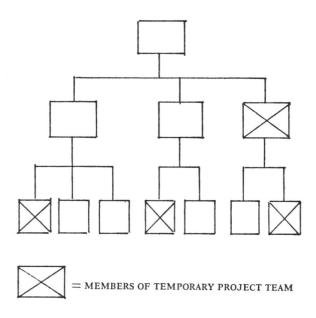

= MEMBERS OF TEMPORARY PROJECT TEAM

At the top level of management a recent innovation is the creation in some companies of an *"Office of the President"* instead of a one-man presidency. A group of senior executives share the overall responsibilities of the presidency, each contributing his own expertise in his field, in addition to their combined brain-power in making decisions.

The success of this arrangement depends on the personalities of the executives involved. As many top executives are basically strong men, they may resent having to share the presidency with others. On the other hand, many persons brought up in a team atmosphere are more comfortable with this setup.

Variations of this system may use a one-man president with a very active Executive Committee or a Board of Directors which is more than the usual purely advisory group.

Results-Oriented Job Descriptions

Whether the job is that of first-line supervisor or president of a company, the manner in which the incumbent pursues his functions depends on how he perceives his position.

In the organizational structure of a company, each position is described in some detail. It is this job description which determines just what the holder of the position will do and what others within the organization—both higher and lower in the hierarchy—expect of him.

Unfortunately, a great number of job descriptions are "task-oriented" rather than "result-oriented." They indicate how a job should be done—often step by step—instead of focusing on the results expected. Modern management thinkers agree that if people are not guided to think in terms of results, their work will not only suffer but will have little purpose or meaning for them.

In structuring an organization for results, we must structure the key jobs for results. The job description should emphasize what results are expected not what should be performed.

Each job description should include a statement of the major goal (why the job exists), the key result areas (where the incumbent needs to focus attention), supporting goals (which will assist in achieving the key results) and realistic performance standards (specific, quantitative and measurable).

Here is a job description of a Sales Manager. Note how the characteristics discussed in this chapter are included. Of course, the job will probably cover many more factors, but for this example only a few key areas are shown. The same principles will apply to other key result areas. The same type of job description can be used for all management jobs.

Note: This represents only a few of the key result areas a Sales Manager would be required to meet. A total job description would cover every phase of the job and the performance standards on which they can be measured.

JOB DESCRIPTION

Sales Manager

MAJOR GOAL: To achieve a predetermined volume of sales within allowable sales costs.

Key Result Area

To maintain a balanced salable inventory.

Performance Standards

The job of Sales Manager in the area of balanced salable inventory will have been satisfactorily performed when:

1. Surplus of needed inventory items shall not have at any time exceeded 4 percent of the total inventory.
2. There shall not have been at any time evidence of lost sales due to shortages of needed inventory items.
3. There shall have been no evidence of lost sales due to inadequate inventory items.

Key Result Area

To maintain sales force productivity at a level which will ensure achievement of major goal.

Performance Standards

The job of Sales Manager in the area of sales force productivity will have been satisfactorily performed when:

1. All salesmen have met the quotas established for their territories.
2. Sales of all product lines meet established goals.

Key Result Area

To create and maintain strong, continuing demand for company products and services.

Performance Standards

The job of Sales Manager in the area of continuous demand for product or service will have been satisfactorily performed when:

1. The number of new accounts increases at rate of 10% per year.
2. The loss of old accounts is kept to less than 5% per year.
3. The volume of business from established accounts increases by at least 8% per year.

By indicating results expected and performance standards by which these goals can be measured, the manager is here given not only a standard against which he can measure his performance, but a motivational instrument impelling action which will lead to the desired results.

To make these results-areas even more meaningful, it is necessary to develop them in cooperation with the manager instead of superimposing them. If he helps to create the objectives and develop the performance standards, he will accept them as realistic and reachable. Too often unilateral goals dictated to subordinate managers by their bosses are not fully supported by the subordinates, and therefore are frequently not achieved. If the manager is competent—and he shouldn't have the job if he is not—his superordinates should have enough confidence in him to bring him into the picture early in the planning stage. With their assistance in determining key results areas and performance standards, there is a far higher degree of assurance that the objectives will be reached.

If managers fail to achieve the results, as outlined in the job descriptions, they can be assisted in analyzing the reasons for the failure, and suggestions for corrective action should be elicited from them. These recommendations, together with the opinions of staff experts and senior managers, should be incorporated in the solution. In some cases it may be that the job description was improperly designed. If this is true, corrections should be made to make the description more accurate.

Organization Charts and Manuals

The organization chart is a schematic representation of the structure of the organization. It indicates the major functions, the relationships among them, the channels of supervision and the relative authority of the people in charge of each function.

Looking at an organization chart, one at once sees clearly the skeleton of the organization. However, one must keep in mind that what is seen is only the skeleton. There is much more to the organization than any chart can show.

The chart serves a useful purpose in enabling one to determine at what level of management any one position is placed, and which higher position each department reports to.

In the following chart, it is easily seen that the District Managers report to the Central Manager, who in turn reports to the Vice President in charge of Marketing, who in his turn reports to the President.

The major disadvantage of depending on organization charts to convey an understanding of the power structure of a company is that they do not portray the real situation. As we have pointed out, there is much more to the organization than the chart can show. For example, this chart shows the vice-presidents for Finance, Production, Marketing and Research and Development all at the same level and all reporting to the President. This, of course, is the formal organizational structure. However, in reality, any one of these positions may be significantly more important than the others and carry much more weight in the company. If this company is an engineering-oriented firm it is likely that the VP for Research and Development will be more important than the other vice presidents. In a

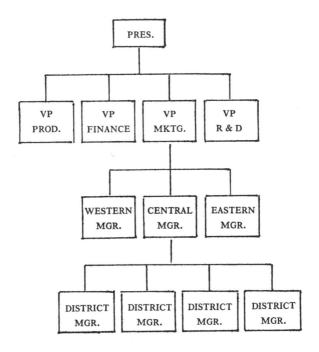

sales-oriented company, where manufacturing, finance and R & D play less of a role than the marketing department, the most important job in the VP level would be the VP Marketing. This is manifested in the power he has in management decisions, in his salary (which may be considerably higher than those of his "equals") and in the manner in which he is looked upon by everyone in the company. Although shown on the same level on the chart, it would be a serious mistake to interpret these positions as equal in power.

Another dimension must be taken into consideration when evaluating the organizational structure. The chart cannot show one of the most important factors in the real analysis of the company—the personalities of the managers holding each of the positions listed on the chart. In many organizations there are one or more executives who have far more influence than their job title or place on the chart would suggest. This may be due to any number of factors. Often it is the strength of the manager's personality which enables him to dominate situations and have his ideas and opinions given more weight than those of less forceful colleagues. It is important to know who these people are and what influence they have, if one is to understand the true picture of the company.

There is no way these added factors can be portrayed in an organization chart. Some chart-makers have tried to express them by unconventional charts such as the circular organization chart which shows the chief executive officer as the center of a series of concentric circles and the other executives placed as satellites close to or far from the center, depending on their position and power. Such a chart is more difficult to read and work with and really does not show much more than the traditional hierarchical one. The best way to use an organization chart is to consider it as the skeleton it is and to flesh out the real structure by observation and discussions with the people within the company.

To supplement the organization chart, most companies develop organization manuals. These provide additional details, including specific job descriptions and indications of the limitations of responsibility and authority of each of the positions.

Manuals are helpful in getting to understand the nature of the jobs in a company because the title of the job on the chart often is not enough to clarify the real function. Titles can mean different things to different people and often have varying meanings. A "Plant Manager," for example, in one company may be nothing more than a general foreman; in another company, he may really be the equivalent of a vice president for manufacturing. Only by reading the details of the job description in the manual can one determine the status of the position. Even officer-titles such as vice president may not have real significance. Some companies grant titles instead of increases in salary. One must examine the total responsibilities and the authority of each job, compare it with others on the chart and consider the real relationships before one can really understand the organization.

Organizing is never finished; it is a continuing task. A major misconception is to accept the organization chart and manual as the end-all in organizational development. Organizational changes must be made as situations change, for organization is a dynamic procedure and can never be completed.

Why do organizational changes take place? Often the reasons are external. Business increases or falls off, requiring more or less manpower. When this occurs, the company's original organization is no longer viable. A change must be made to reflect the new conditions. Another external reason may be government requirements. Any major government regulation may involve redesigning the organizational structure of a company. When Congress passed the Equal Employment Opportunities section of the Civil Rights Act of 1964, personnel departments had to be restructured to include facilities for recruitment and training of minority personnel. Passage of the Occupational Safety and Health Act precipitated the creation of Safety Departments where none had existed; the wage and price controls set by the Nixon Administration caused many firms to set up departments or sections to deal with these special problems.

Technological change too has an effect on organizational structure. The advent of the computer probably caused more reorganization of accounting departments than any other recent innovation—and as well, of many other functions.

Internally, changes become necessary when new products are developed, when old lines are changed and, often, when a dynamic individual leaves the company.

As organizations grow, the structure must change to fit the growth pattern. Growth occurs vertically and horizontally. On a vertical basis a company changes its structure as volume of business increases. When it was a small organization, one or two managers could handle much of the managerial work; as it gets larger, additional management people—often specialists—are added to the staff. Still more growth adds more managers, and with them the hierarchical structure of managers over managers, the multilayered prototype of the large corporation.

Horizontal growth takes place when a department within the organization requires added staff to accomplish its objective. For example, in the early days of a company, two salesmen were able to cover the entire market; as the company grew the sales department required several more salesmen, so they set up regional offices. It then required sales support, and so staff departments such as Market Research, Sales Promotion and Customer Service were added.

The organizational structure of a company should be re-evaluated periodically to make sure that it is still meeting the objectives it was established to achieve. Unless the organization is well-structured, the planning that preceded its development will have been futile: the company will not be geared up to actuate its operations, and the leadership of the company will not obtain optimum results from their direction and will be limited in coordinating and controlling the entire management function.

8

DELEGATION AND DECENTRALIZATION

The effective manager recognizes the talents of his subordinates. He uses these talents to their greatest advantage and in doing so hones the skills and professionalism of his people to their greatest acuity. One of the best ways of doing this is by delegation.

To delegate means to assign to someone else a duty, a task, a power, an authority, which the executive himself may possess. In its simplest form, a busy manager may delegate the clerical detail of his job to an assistant. But this represents a low-level aspect of this important managerial method. The real strength of management develops when the executive passes authority—power—to his subordinates.

Yet, despite lip service to this facet of delegation, there are countless managers and administrators who refuse to delegate anything but the most menial of tasks to subordinates. Often, those who do pass on authority tie so many strings to the delegation that it becomes meaningless.

Why should this be so? To understand why we must recognize that when a manager delegates authority, he does not divest himself of it. He still has his power, and even more significantly, he retains the accountability that is the reverse side of the coin of authority.

Because the manager will be held responsible for failure, he often fears to give the necessary authority to his subordinates. Until he overcomes his fear, delegation is a farce.

The result of this fear is that the manager refuses to trust his subordinate to do the job. He rationalizes this lack of trust by saying, "I can do it better myself." Indeed, he may be able to perform some tasks more efficiently than a subordinate, but his job is to manage, not to do lesser jobs. If no authority is delegated, the work of the company or department will be bottlenecked at the desk of the fearful manager.

Another reason some managers refuse to delegate authority is their lack of self-confidence. They worry that a subordinate may be able to do the job better than they can, and that the manager's own position may be put in jeopardy. Such managers have to be aided in developing self-confidence, or they really will become as inadequate in their positions as they fear.

Some managers do not know how to delegate. They have to be taught. A detailed discussion of how to delegate effectively will be found later in this chapter.

A serious problem with some executives is that they are enamored of the power they have. They are reluctant to relinquish any of it to others. This is really another manifestation of their fear of bearing the responsibility of decisions made by others.

In some instances managers think they are delegating authority when they actually are only delegating duties, and perhaps a modicum of authority on minor matters. They keep the real powers themselves and then wonder why their "delegation" does not succeed.

The counterpart of this type of manager is the manager who delegates authority to persons who are not capable of handling it. The process of delegation assumes that the subordinate is well-trained and is capable of bearing the responsibility. To delegate without the assurance that the subordinate can really do the assigned job is poor management. Certain powers cannot be delegated. If the matter involved requires decisions that affect areas outside of the purview of the subordinate, or requires judgments which can only be made by the boss, authority should not be delegated.

Making Delegation of Authority More Effective

By following the ten principles outlined here, managers can expect a much higher degree of success in delegation:

1. Make the person who must delegate some of his authority feel secure about his position with the company. Often the "delegator" is insecure about his job and fears to give any of his authority to his subordinates. This can be overcome by helping him develop self-confidence. Praise him for his successes. Grant recognition to him by giving him a title or special privileges. Encourage him to take the Dale Carnegie Course in *Effective Speaking and Human Relations.* Make sure he understands that by asking him to delegate some of his authority the company is not depreciating his value but enhancing his worth to the firm. Assure him that by delegating part of his authority, he opens up time and energy so that his boss can give him part of *his* authority.

2. Help him understand the need for delegation. As long as a manager is limited to what he can do himself, he can never reach his own true potential. Managers should be measured not only by their skill in their own personal specialties, but by how well they bring their subordinates along. This can only be accomplished by proper delegation.

3. The climate of the company should encourage innovation. It should be people-oriented. Management should exude confidence in all their people. Fear and frustration should not be allowed to develop and should be curtailed whenever they begin to appear.

4. Management should really believe in delegation. It should be practiced from top management all the way down the line. Managers at all levels should accept the fact that in order to grow, subordinates must be allowed to make decisions, and also, as a matter of course, to make mistakes. For delegation to suc-

ceed, the company must be prepared to absorb the cost of such mistakes, and charge it up to the development of the staff. Experience has shown that if a budding manager is allowed to make mistakes at a low level in his development, he will learn from them and perhaps make fewer costly mistakes when he reaches higher levels in the corporate hierarchy.

5. The manager delegating the assignment must do it in such a way that the person accepting the assignment sees and accepts it as a forward step in his own progress. Delegation is one of the most effective ways to train people. They should be clearly shown how this added authority and its concomitant responsibility will make them better managers.

6. The subordinate should know what results he is expected to achieve. He should be asked to provide a plan of action to show how he expects to accomplish the results expected, and what support he will need.

7. The manager must know the capabilities of each of his subordinates and be assured that the subordinate to whom he delegates a job has not only the skills but the motivation to reach the objective he has been assigned. Studies show that a high percentage of managers do not utilize their full potential in performing their normal duties. Seek out these hidden abilities and delegate assignments to subordinates which will make them stretch their minds and use talents that have been ignored or underused in the past.

8. Performance standards should be established to help both the subordinate and his boss measure actions taken against results attained. In the people-oriented company, these standards are not superimposed on subordinates by the senior manager, but are developed participatively with the team that is responsible for achieving the objectives. The operating manager should be given added freedom to measure his own progress and to make corrections in his plan and its implementation as needed; of course, he is accountable for the results.

9. Management must give the subordinate sufficient authority to make the decisions necessary to achieving the expected results and to assemble the resources needed to do this. He should

be given access to staff departments which can help him and be encouraged to make his own decisions on all matters within his scope.

10. Management should be available to give the subordinate whatever assistance is required. Delegation should not be a "sink or swim" process. The delegating manager has a definite responsibility to make sure that the subordinate can meet the objectives. He will take an active role in providing the subordinate with whatever aid is called for. He will make sure the subordinate knows the company's policies and rules and regulations concerning the matters involved. He makes himself available for counseling, discussions and practical help, if the circumstances warrant it. Although he is available and the subordinate is aware of it, the effective manager does not intervene. Even if he sees a problem arising, it is better to give the subordinate a chance to identify and solve it.

Many managers *believe* they are delegating authority to their people when in fact they are only assigning them chores to perform which are secondary in importance. Even when they do give a subordinate authority, they supplement it with so many rules and regulations, procedures and methods, warnings and suggestions, that the subordinate is really stifled—prevented from using his own thinking or initiative.

True delegation involves three actions—all interrelated like the three sides of a triangle:

1. Assignment of duties
2. Granting of authority
3. Creating an obligation.

The manner in which these three actions are conveyed to the subordinate determines how really effective the delegation will be. In assigning duties, a common approach is to specify every phase of the actions expected. Either in writing or verbally, we give the subordinate a list of *"by's"*:

"You are assigned to sell to department stores in the counties of . . ., . . . and . . . and will do this

1. *BY* making 20 calls each day on regular customers
2. *BY* prospecting for new customers
3. *BY* working with retailer's salesmen to push our products.
4. *BY* . . .
5. *BY* . . . , etc., etc."

These *"by's"* structure every move every day of the subordinate's work-life and give him no chance to use the innate creativity, initiative, and common sense he could personally contribute to the job.

A better way of delegating duties is by *results*. Instead of detailing *how* a job should be done, the manager and subordinate reach an understanding of what result is expected, and the methods are left to the subordinate.

A results-delegation of the assignment given above would read:

"Your territory is the counties of . . ., . . . and . . . .

Results expected:

1. Increase in sales volume of 7%
2. Addition of three new customers each month.
3. Increase in sales of Lines A and B by 15%.
   etc., etc."

There are no *"by's"* in this assignment. The expected results are stated. How these are to be achieved is in the hands of the delegatee.

In order for a subordinate to carry out all but the most routine duties, he must be given authority to take whatever action is needed. This may involve expenditure of funds, assembling of resources from within or outside the company, committing the company to purchase materials or equipment, and directing others in the company to perform certain work.

Authority is essential to effective delegation. However, this sort of authority should not be confused with unlimited power.

All authority is limited by the customs and practices of the industry, as well as by legal restrictions, the capabilities of the delegatees and company policies.

Each person in a management position has certain parameters of authority beyond which he cannot go. A department head may have the authority to purchase raw materials for his department—up to a specific dollar volume; to make changes in production-scheduling—within limits; to authorize overtime or grant pay raises to employees—with approval from above required if his costs exceed a predetermined amount. When a union contract exists, the power over employees is further curtailed. A supervisor may be given the authority to hire and fire people, but in reality he would have to follow personnel practices set by the personnel department to hire a person for his staff, and he could not fire anyone unless he complied with company and union policy. Because these restrictions exist, it is important that when a delegation is made, the rights and powers associated with it should be made clear.

The third leg of the delegation triangle is the creation of an obligation. Often this obligation is called a "responsibility" or "accountability." However, this factor involves much more than just the determination of who should be blamed for failure or credited with success. An obligation is a moral compulsion felt by the subordinate to accomplish the duties assigned to him. This obligation is implicit in every aspect of delegation. When a subordinate accepts an assignment, it is understood and expected that he will carry it out. Without this understanding no delegation could take place.

Most people to whom work is delegated desire the assignment and are committed to do their best to fulfil their obligation. Management creates the climate in which this feeling of obligation can be nurtured.

Also essential to effective delegation is the assurance that the delegatee is competent to handle the assignment. Companies make a practice of carefully selecting and training their managers before authority is delegated to them.

There is a much quoted axiom in management circles: "Responsibility without authority is hell." It is true that to put a manager in a position where he will be held accountable for results and not give him the power to do what is necessary to achieve the results is poor management. For example, a manager obligated to meet a deadline on a rush project, but not given the authority to order his men to work overtime or to hire additional personnel is in an untenable situation.

However, an obligation cannot really be delegated. The superior who delegates an assignment to a subordinate still is obligated to meet the objective expected.

If the company president delegates a task to a vice president who in turn redelegates it to a department head who redelegates it to one of his subordinates, both the department head and the vice president retain the obligation and accountability for the task. To say "It's not my fault that it was not done—the section head fell behind" satisfies no one.

Decentralization

The logical step beyond delegation is decentralization. Most companies start as highly centralized organizations. All direction comes from the top and filters down the chain of command to the operating units. As the company grows, it becomes more and more difficult for ideas and innovations to radiate out from the center. The people on the firing line cannot react fast enough to the dynamics of their situations if they have to depend on the center to receive, absorb and then respond to their problems.

To overcome this, companies have decentralized—that is, they have given significant authority to the operating units to make decisions on their own. In some organizations this decentralization has become unit autonomy. The unit operates almost as an independent business with its own profit-and-loss responsibility. Although its managers may call upon the parent company for help and counsel when needed, they make their own plans, develop their own organization, direct, coordinate and control their activities. This is known as *profit decentralization*.

The autonomous units may be chosen on the basis of product, customers served, geography or any other logical breakdown.

There are advantages to both centralization and decentralization. In determining which type of setup is applicable to any specific company, one must take the following facts into consideration:

In a centralized organization, the chief executive and his staff have considerable power and the prestige that goes with it. They make the decisions and are ready to take the consequences— good or bad.

In the decentralized organization, the top manager does not have as much power, for some power is delegated to subordinates, and they in turn delegate some to their subordinates. This relieves the top management of considerable direct work. However, as previously pointed out, top management still has the accountability. To decentralize, the chief executive officers must have enough confidence in their people to allow them to make key decisions.

Centralized companies promote uniformity as to policies and practices. They tend to stifle creativity, particularly if it is cumbersome to obtain permission to vary actions in order to meet changing situations.

In decentralized companies, initiative is encouraged. Practices are established to assure uniformity of basic policy, but the decentralized unit manager can alter them where required.

Centralization utilizes the central office staff specialists to a great degree because they are close to the top managers both physically and organizationally. Because the scope and volume of their work warrants it, the company can support highly qualified (and therefore expensive) technical experts. Together with the line executives at the apex of the corporate hierarchy, staff and line are developed into a strong management team.

In the decentralized organization, top management and its staff become less important. Each division develops generalists who are responsible for many aspects of the work. This has the advantage of grooming them for later promotion into general management. One of the limitations of centralized management is the emphasis on developing specialists, who become so specialized that they are not equipped to move up into general management when the need arises.

Because of the distance between the top and bottom layers of the organization in centralized companies, there is little real feeling on the part of either for the other. The more remote the connection, the less sense of kinship exists. The decentralized group, by reason of its more intimate personal relationships, engenders greater commitment to the work and more enthusiastic subordinates.

Centralization fosters greater control, and this helps in the elimination of inefficient practices and of deviations from company policy. Indeed, with centralization automatic controls are easily built into an organization, for the proximity of top management to the operating managers makes control easy.

On the other hand, the decentralized company has the advantage of being on top of local situations and can react rapidly to them. Since the decentralized organization works chiefly for clearly defined objectives, it sets its own controls to ensure that they are met.

A significant added advantage of decentralization is that it gives a company a testing ground for experiment and exploration. New ideas can be tried in one unit and, if successful, be adopted by others. That also spreads the risks. One unit can sustain a loss without its affecting other units of the organization.

An aspect of profit decentralization which has been criticized in many firms is the heavy emphasis on profit. Decentralized units and their managers are measured on the basis of the bottom line. The credit—with its concomitant financial rewards—and the blame are both often determined by short-run financial statements. Managers are, either subtly or overtly, pressured into sacrificing long-run gains for short-run profits. A research and development project may be postponed or dropped entirely to show a higher quarterly or annual profit. Had the project been instituted, a larger profit might have resulted in future years, but the manager's current performance would not have looked as good this year.

Another negative factor in decentralization is that undue competition among divisions often occurs. One division might hurt the growth of another division in its fight for a higher profit and thereby reduce total corporate profits instead of augmenting them.

In the past one of the reasons many companies chose to decentralize was their inability to obtain adequate information rapidly from their diverse units. The advent of the computer has made the information-gathering phase of control much easier. Objective data can now be transmitted, analyzed and retransmitted very rapidly.

However, this development may work to improve decentralization rather than to encourage recentralization of organizations. The decentralized units can do a more effective job by utilizing central facilities and making their decisions on more complete data just as the centralized organization can help control its arms by the same means.

Profit decentralization usually reduces the size of the unit to a manageable capacity. Fewer people are involved, so they can communicate more effectively without the distortion that broad channels of command incur. The decentralized unit is "bite-sized." The executive can easily handle it. However, to counteract this advantage, there is the limitation that not all companies can be divided neatly into self-contained bite-sized units. Sometimes technology makes it impossible for a large organization to be broken into several smaller ones. A significant limitation on the profit decentralization process is that the operations of the organization must be divisible into autonomous, self-sufficient units of manageable size.

Smaller autonomous units are more likely to receive adequate attention when decentralized than when part of a larger centralized organization, for such units are then more easily coordinated and controlled, and accountability is more readily placed.

Some of the other limitations of profit decentralization concern auxiliary service activities that the parent company must perform for its operating divisions. Often a single central service unit is not responsive enough to the needs of the various operating divisions. There have been situations where it was less expensive for the operating unit to buy its services from outside sources. This may reduce the cost to the decentralized unit and increase *its* profit, but how will it affect the profit of the total corporation?

To make profit decentralization most effective, here are some guidelines. The central office should:

1. Set long-range objectives and annual goals which include not only quantitative matters but such intangibles as improvement of corporate image, higher employee morale and the development of the people in the unit.

2. Establish the broad policies within which the decentralized units should operate. These should be comprehensive enough to provide a basis for managers to make consistent decisions, and flexible enough to allow them to use their initiative and react to local conditions.

3. Make sure that the key executive within each unit is the best possible manager for the job. This can be done by aiding the division in recruiting and selecting management personnel from outside the company, and by establishing management development programs and executive appraisal systems within the company.

4. Make financing available to the company's subsidiaries so that (with company approval) expansion can take place.

5. Have facilities for review of transactions that may affect the profit-or-loss of the division so that corrective action if needed can be suggested in time to prevent undue loss.

6. Establish facilities to provide needed technical service and staff counsel to divisions at reasonable cost.

7. Establish standardized accounting, personnel, purchasing and other procedures to ensure consistency throughout the company.

9

THE INFORMAL
ORGANIZATION

When we look at the organizational chart of a company, we see only the formal structure of the establishment. We do not see, nor can we even guess at, the unofficial interactions that are constantly taking place. It is like looking at a drop of water with the naked eye—it looks completely clear and placid. Put that same drop under a microscope, and we see countless microorganisms scurrying back and forth.

This "informal" structure must be detected, understood and considered by management if it is to be properly channeled to meet the company's objectives.

The behavioral scientists advise us that in order to fully appreciate the influences of informal groups on the behavior of their members, we must look at the development of customs and work mores in the organization at large and in the informal social groups that develop among employees.

Customs and cultural attitudes develop in every type of human social relationship, whether on the job or in the personal lives of individuals. They are often influenced by national and ethnic factors, educational levels, loyalties to certain people or ideals, and identification with specific "classes" or philosophies.

If the employees of a company identify themselves with their peers as "workers" vis-a-vis their supervisors as "bosses," there is a built-in potential for conflict. Similar problem areas exist when groups of employees think of themselves as members of an ethnic or racial group first and as part of the company second. In many situations there is an automatic segregation by national or racial background. This leads to rivalries and often to conflict. Other types of group and sub-group breakdowns arise from distinctions based on skills or education: the college graduates don't mingle with the non-college types; the skilled craftsmen are aloof from the less skilled, etc.

Groups are formed not only because of personal considerations, but also often because of the position or role the members assume in the organization. People tend to behave according to their preconceived idea of what is expected of them. A shipping-room helper is promoted to supervisor of a section. He immediately changes his manner, his attitudes and often even the way he dresses, taking on the manner, attitude and dress of his fellow-supervisors. He moves from the "rank-and-file group" to the supervisor group.

Not only does the individual thus identify with a group—he or she also plays the role that the job calls for. If the company has an authoritarian management climate, the new supervisor will take on an authoritarian demeanor. A person not only follows the job description of the position which he fills, but fills the established role he feels is expected of him.

This is important because it makes his attitude and approach predictable. If we know what our associates will most likely do under a variety of circumstances—because that has been the usual practice in the company—we will not be taken by surprise, and can depend on this attitude or action in dealing with the circumstances related to it.

We run into difficulty, however, when there is not a full understanding as to all the features of a role. Top management may think of a job in terms of the formal organization plan, but the incumbent may have a different point of view, one based on the way he perceives his role. His subordinates may view their roles differently from either top management or their immediate boss. A good example of this is the role of the foreman. Top management assumes the foreman sees the job as it does, namely, getting quality production at low cost at the time it is required.

The foreman's subordinates, however, may view his role as being there to help them in their relations with the higher levels of management, to be sympathetic to their specific work problems. If the foreman accepts either of these views, he will not be acceptable to the other group and will experience pressures from both sides. To overcome this, he takes on his own role, which may lean in either direction. If he takes no role, but vacillates between roles, he becomes unpredictable and therefore ineffective.

Informal Groups

Whenever people work together, informal groups form. The members of these groups tend to socialize with each other, to eat lunch together, etc. They usually have common interests and often come from similar backgrounds.

Human beings are social animals. They need to belong to a group, and having "friends" on the job makes them feel more comfortable in the work situation. They seek social satisfactions from their work, and these are more likely to come from their informal group than from the formal structure in which they find themselves. Also the group gives them support if there is unreasonable pressure from the boss.

Were it not for the social satisfactions offered by the informal groups, many of the dull, routine, boring jobs that make up much of the industrial picture would be intolerable. But even in challenging positions, the small informal group has a significant place in the behavior of its members.

Groups are formed on the basis of many common denominators. Many are completely non-job-oriented, such as a common interest in bowling or living in the same neighborhood or attending the same church. Others are job- or career-oriented, such as membership in a professional association or sharing a management philosophy—for example, the advocates of participative management as against authoritarian management.

Social groups, either consciously or subconsciously, tend to put pressure on their members to conform to the group's standards or ideals. These standards may or may not conform to what management desires. The most frequent cause of conflict between the informal group and management is the establishment of production quotas. Whether it be the number of pieces a group of workers will machine in one day, or the number of claims a group of insurance clerks will process, the informal group sets its own "bogie." If one of its members exceeds this, he will be subjected to pressure to "slow down." The nonconformist is pressured in many ways, the pressures finally culminating in ostracism by the group.

Another major influence the informal group has on its members is the sharing of attitudes and values. A new member of the group automatically assumes the attitudes of his peers. If they feel the supervisor is unfair, the new member will believe this, even if his own relationship with the supervisor indicates the contrary. If the group centers about people from one ethnic background, they will project definite ideas about how the company treats people of that ethnic group, and despite some obvious exceptions in the company, the member will believe what the group believes. If the members say: "We Ruritarians have to stick together because the company is prejudiced against us," the new member of the group who has a Ruritarian background accepts this, even though he knows the new vice president happens to be a Ruritarian.

Groups also tend to resist change if it will upset normal activities. Even if the change seems likely to benefit them, they may resent it. Managers should be prepared to face this type of resistance when changes are contemplated.

Understanding Group Behavior

Membership in a group, both formal and informal, provides its members with a certain status. In the formal group, such as bank officers as opposed to the non-officer group, there is an officially recognized status. In the informal group, the status is unofficial, but it is nevertheless recognized by both members and outsiders.

If the group has a high status in the company, there is a great desire on the part of non-members to be accepted into the group and a high degree of loyalty of the members to the group. On the other hand, if the group has little status, members consider their affiliation with the group as a temporary measure and have less loyalty to it. For example, in one hospital the higher-status group among the nurses was the group assigned to operating-room duties. These nurses were looked upon by their peers and by the other hospital personnel as an elite group. Operating room nurses had a strong loyalty to their group, kept themselves aloof from the other nurses and took a united stand on most issues facing the hospital. Other nurses also had their informal groups, but they envied the OR nurses and vied to be promoted to the operating room so they could join this group, even though other nursing specialties which paid the same salaries were open to them.

The effective group is a cohesive one. If there is dissension within the group, there is less influence of the group on the total business situation. Groups tend to keep their people cohesive. They tolerate differences of opinion on minor matters and allow expression of differences on major matters, but they expect all their members to reach a consensus on significant attitudes and approaches to the organization. If a member is recalcitrant, they pressure him to conform. Groups do not tolerate deviants. Deviation is a major crime in group behavior, and the individual who puts his own personal feelings above those of the group on any regular basis will soon find himself on the outside looking in.

When outside pressure is put on a group, as when it is threatened by a common danger, the members forget their personal differences and close ranks against the outsider. If a new supervisor introduces a series of changes in the way the job should be done, the informal groups in his department will unite to fight it. Often such group activity will defeat progressive innovations that management wishes to introduce. Managers must recognize this and take it into account when making changes.

Another type of group often found in business companies is the "clique." The clique differs from other informal groups in that its members are spread throughout several different departments. What unifies them is a common interest in a special cause. These causes differ; they may range from temporary projects, such as working for the promotion of a popular executive, to long-term concepts, such as developing a feeling of social responsibility in the organization.

The clique can be either loosely or tightly formed. At one extreme it may be a small group of people with mutual interest on an issue who see each other occasionally for mutual encouragement. Such a clique is not as powerful as a tightly knit group that is well organized and politically astute.

Cliques can be created to push a worthy cause that will benefit the company. However, the objectives of a powerful clique often do not tie in with company objectives and may disrupt rather than help reach them. As the clique is spread throughout the organization, its effect is likely to be much more devastating than that of other informal groups. It may break down communications and interfere with the integrated actions needed to run a successful operation.

When a manager discovers that there is an active clique in his company, he should determine what the clique stands for. Often he may find that there is little difference between the goals of the clique and those of the company—only a divergent view on how to reach the goals. In. this case, management and clique leaders can usually iron out their differences. Management should attempt to gain the support of the clique, and both together put all the effort needed into meeting the goal.

On the other hand, management may find that the clique's aims are incompatible with those of the company. This presents a delicate problem to management. If it can, it should try to reach the clique leaders and convert them to the company view. This is not easily done; it takes thorough knowledge of the people in the clique and much persuasive power to change their ideas. Recently a large retail office-supply firm made a decision to convert their accounting and inventory control systems to a new computer program. A strong clique within the organization, one spread throughout several states, opposed this move.

The company either failed to recognize the clique's existence or chose to ignore it. The computer system was installed, but it never succeeded because the clique's members never gave the system their full support.

Whether the group be a localized informal group or a clique spread throughout the organization, it develops its own leadership. It is these leaders who determine the militancy of the group and the direction the group will take.

Group leaders emerge in each group. Most often they are "natural" leaders, individuals who by virtue of personality attract the support and win the confidence of the members. In an old established organization, group leaders may come from among the older employees who are chosen because they were there first. Occasionally a newcomer may vie for leadership and win it by his personal charm, wit, strength or persuasiveness. Informal groups have no elections of leaders. The person who is acknowledged as leader reaches his position in an informal manner.

An interesting experiment in choosing leaders can be made when any group of people who have never met before get together for some type of meeting. Within a half hour or less, one of them will be recognized by the others as the natural leader. In some of the Dale Carnegie programs, groups are arbitrarily formed, and after a discussion session of 20 to 30 minutes, each group is asked to point at the man or woman they would select as the group leader. Invariably most participants point to the same person.

Leadership, of course, can change. Another member of the group takes a more active role in the discussions or actions of the group, and gradually the original leader defers to him. A new member challenges the old leader, and a contest for the leadership ensues. No vote is ever taken, but in due course, one or the other "wins" by being accepted by the others. Sometimes a deposed leader leaves the group and forms a new group. In other cases he accepts his new role and cooperates with the successor.

The leader functions by circulating through the group to urge a united front in dealing with problems. He takes the initiative in proposing ideas and in persuading others to go along with them. He may devise punishment for deviants. However, he functions chiefly by developing consensus on what must be done. The successful leader sounds out his members and suggests compromises where necessary. He may also serve as liaison with other groups, the management or the union.

In many groups there is no *one* leader. Leadership may be shared by several people, each functioning in an area where his expertise or special talents are most useful. It may be that the most vocal member of the group appears to management to be the leader, but he may just be the best "spokesman" and the real leadership may lie somewhere else. The manager must keep alert to this and recognize who really has the most influence when he deals with the group.

Seeking Consensus

In every group sooner or later a decision-making formula must be determined. In some instances it is pure majority rule, but in many groups, particularly informal ones where no official rules for decision-making hold, it is by obtaining a consensus. Everybody must agree with the group's decision.

If the group has some formal structure, a vote might be taken to determine the issue at hand. A six to two vote certainly is decisive, but the group might want to determine why the minority is opposing the decision, and might try to convert them to their way of thinking. As stated earlier, consensus is important because if the individual is not allowed to express his feelings and his reasons for voting against the majority, he will either overtly or subconsciously resist implementation of the decision. If he feels he has had his say, however, even if he is not converted to the majority's viewpoint, he will be less likely to resist the will of the group.

One of the traits of a good leader is to be able to spot disagreement even when it is not overtly expressed, so that he can bring it out into the open. It is important that objections be expressed; the leader must see to it that disagreements are uncovered, and that the objector has the chance to state his ideas.

Another aspect of the group that must be understood to work effectively with it is the relationship of the group members to the leader. Where there is a titular leader who formally heads the group, it is not unusual for the members to have ambivalent feelings toward him: As the official authority, they may have positive feelings toward him because of his position, his expertise, his previous experience in dealing with the group and his personal status. Yet there is at the same time an opposite feeling of resentment against his authority because of his power. These negative feelings are usually not expressed because people recognize that their jobs may be in jeopardy if they are openly antagonistic.

Hostility may, however, be expressed subliminally by such minor rebellious acts as coming late to meetings, making big issues of minor points (because of fear to fight the boss on the big points) or picking on a scapegoat—a weaker character in the group on whom the other members project their negative feelings.

The effective group leader recognizes this and understands that there is nothing really wrong with the presence of some hostility. He tackles it head-on, taking a positive step by acknowledging the hostility, and sometimes even accepting the blame for it. By bringing it into the open, he dilutes its effect on the members of the group and channels it away from internal dissension. The energy that had been directed against the leader or the scapegoat can now be funneled into the constructive action needed to accomplish the group's mission.

Problem Members of the Group

Another common problem in group dynamics is the presence in a group of a problem member. There are two types of problem members: the overactive person and the underactive person.

The overactive person tries to dominate the group's attention far more than his abilities warrant. He may be a loquacious person who has little to say but says it in a great many words, or he may be an insecure person who tries to assert himself by constantly trying to express some thought on every subject under discussion. Soon the other members of the group begin to resent this person and tune him out as soon as he opens his mouth. This distracts them from their responsibility to the group and sometimes even causes the other members to lose their tempers and engage in bitter arguments with or about him.

The best way to handle this problem is for the leader to take the problem person aside and tell him that his contributions to the meetings are valuable, but that, because of his frequent and long discussions, he is not giving the others a chance to express themselves. If this fails, he should be told he will not be recognized by the chair for more than a limited number of minutes at any meeting. Often the other members of the group pressure him to stop attempting to dominate the meetings.

His opposite number is the underactive person who rarely contributes anything to the subjects under discussion. If this member has knowledge or capabilities that are important to the group's objectives, he must be encouraged to take his part. The leader should determine the reason for his lack of activity. If it is shyness, he should be encouraged to participate by asking his opinion, commending his ideas (if they deserve commendation) and showing him by the actions of the entire group that he is an accepted member of the team. If this does not work, he may need psychological counseling or perhaps some training in self-confidence and self-expression such as is given in the Dale Carnegie course.

The problems discussed in the preceding paragraphs apply equally to formal and informal groups. In the formal group, the leader has been designated by management and is a committee chairman or department head or the like. It may be that although he has the official status of group leader, a *real* leader who is officially just another member of the group is tacitly accepted by the members. This may not be because of any lack of regard for the competence of the official leader, but only because he does represent management, and the group feel their interests are best served by having a leader of their own. This informal leader expresses his leadership by acting as the chief spokesman in the group. Often the members will have thrashed out the problems before the formal meeting under the leadership of this individual and have reached some decisions. When new ideas come up, they will often defer to their informal leader before commenting on the subject.

A good formal leader recognizes this. He acknowledges the informal leader as his counterpart in the group. Although he makes no official abdication of his position, he accepts the informal leader as a partner. Together they work toward meeting the objectives of the group and in the long run those of the organization.

Developing Group Support

A different approach can be used to foster the development of informal groups which will be sympathetic to management policies. One way this can be done is using the matrix system of organization (see Chapter 7). This system involves the assignment of special people to temporary projects. They are thus removed from their base unit for the duration of the project. In some instances, the nature of the project requires removal from base group for only short periods of time.

In selecting the matrix team—that is, the personnel who will be assigned to the project—management can keep in mind its need to create a group with goals compatible with its own. The group will not only function as an official project team, but by the nature of its work its members will become closely involved with each other and act in the same manner as informal groups.

Management should keep in mind the human aspects of the situation and select personnel on the basis of their own goals, their previous actions and reactions in relation to the organization, rather than just the technical skills each possesses. A danger in this practice is that some managements will only select teams of "yes-men" who are tried-and-true company loyalists. This may stifle creative approaches to problems. To overcome this danger, personnel should be selected on the basis of their individual capabilities and goals and be given scope to express themselves without fear of criticism or reprisal. But they must be people who can reasonably be expected to reach consensus. Problem people of the type discussed above should be kept off such teams.

Once a project team is selected, it should be given guidelines and a clear-cut picture of the objectives of the team. If a meaningful project is assigned to a team, it is likely that a social group will be formed around the project. Behavioral scientists have shown that when people are enthusiastic about a project, they will work to achieve its objectives with greater effort than when it is just a job to be done.

Often, as we have seen, the informal group is focused on an area of common interest, which may be either job-related or otherwise. In setting up a project team, a common interest is automatically created—the success of the project. To increase the possibility of this success, the team members should be given as much autonomy as possible to develop the plan of action for the project. As the concept of the project incubates, even persons who were strangers to one another before meeting as members of the team interact in their work, and a social relationship cannot help but develop.

In setting up this type of situation, various levels of management and support personnel are encouraged to work together, to share ideas and to form a warm working relationship. This can be abetted by management's giving the group the authority to take the necessary steps to do the job.

If the formal job descriptions of the team members do not account for the new work they will be doing in the project, the job descriptions should be modified or special descriptions written for the project itself. For example, in his regular assignment the "marketing administrative assistant" is responsible for detail work in the marketing department. On the team he may be asked to perform research or creative tasks unrelated to his usual work. This should be made known to all concerned, so he will get the support needed to do the job without having to face bureaucrats who tell him, "That's not part of your job."

To summarize: the manager must take cognizance of both

formal and informal organizational structure to achieve his objectives. By understanding how the informal group operates both internally—in its interactions within the group—and externally—in the relation of the group as a whole to the total organization—the manager will be able to use both structures effectively.

PART IV

Directing

The best executive is the one who has sense enough to pick good men to do what he wants done, and self-restraint enough to keep from meddling with them while they do it.

Theodore Roosevelt

10

OBTAINING
THE RIGHT PERSONNEL

The key to managing through people is to have the best possible people through whom to manage. Good people are not easy to identify, locate and develop, yet personnel is the most important ingredient in the recipe for successful management.

Improved technology has accentuated the need for specially trained and educated personnel. In many levels of the business hierarchy the demand for qualified manpower exceeds the supply even in times of business slowdown. While automation may well have reduced the number of unskilled persons required by industry, the demand for technicians and professionally trained people has increased in geometric proportion.

Management must look at its employment policies from both short- and long-range perspectives. It must obtain the people it needs, not only the men and women needed now at all levels to fill the positions currently available, but also the people it will need for the future, the corps of younger men and women it must train for management jobs for the years ahead.

Internal promotion cannot be depended upon exclusively to fill management jobs. The company which hires an office boy when the chairman dies is in serious trouble. The managers and potential managers who are expected to wait for such promotion are likely to be enticed away from their current jobs by opportunities available elsewhere. True, managers must be prepared for growth in their own jobs and made responsible for training subordinates to move up the ladder at all times. But because it is not as likely as it used to be that a person will remain in one company from the time he or she graduates from school until retirement, companies must always be on the alert to seek managerial personnel from outside as well as inside the company. The person groomed to move up in your company may not be patient enough to wait for his opportunity.

Companies must also examine their personnel policies carefully to make sure that they are realistic in today's economy. Some common problems can be overcome by changes in archaic policies. An example is the firm that will not promote people unless they have held their current jobs for a specified period of time. This may be short-sighted—time does not necessarily measure competence. Other policies that should be reevaluated are salary scales for management jobs, benefits programs, interdepartmental transfers, and the realism of the job specifications on which persons are chosen.

Job Analysis

Most companies have a formal job-analysis program to evaluate each of the jobs in the organization and determine what the duties, responsibilities and other factors are that make up the job. This *job description* has already been discussed in Chapter 7.

The second part of the job analysis is called the *job specification*. It details the skills and aptitudes needed to perform the job. This includes education, previous training and experience, as well as the physical, mental and psychological traits required. It is this aspect of the job analysis that concerns management when choosing staff.

If these specifications are accurate representations of what it requires to be successful on a job, they can be of valuable aid in screening candidates to fill it. Unfortunately, many job specifications are not at all realistic. They have often been in the files for years and have little bearing on the current emphasis of the position. Jobs change with the people who fill them, with changes in technology and with the problems faced in different periods of time. Often these specifications were unrealistic even at the time when they were written—idealized versions of a job far removed from the actual requirements.

All jobs should be reevaluated at regular intervals. It is particularly important to reexamine a job which has become vacant after having been held by the same person for a long time. Individuals usually leave their imprint on a job. In replacing a long-tenure incumbent, it is a common practice to look for his exact image. This can be a serious mistake from the viewpoint of the job itself and the possibility of finding the best replacement. A new study of the job would enable the company to obtain accurate and up-to-date specifications, free from the influence of the past incumbent's personality.

Too often the chief source of a job specification is the immediate supervisor, whose whims, prejudices and personal feelings may color his view of the job. His desires should be given fair consideration, but should be kept in proper perspective. Other guidelines include observation of the job, study of the relationship between this job and its counterparts within the company and an understanding of related jobs in other companies. The main criteria should be the essential characteristics of the job.

In selecting new managers, company executives often tend to seek mirror-images of themselves, or individuals who fit a preconceived specific physical, personality or sometimes ethnic pattern. This not only is short-sighted in that it may eliminate excellent potential staff members, but tends to create an "organization man" climate which often stifles creativity and fosters a "yes-man" atmosphere. The opening of a management position may also open up a window to new ideas and bring fresh vigor to a company. Take advantage of the opportunity instead of just perpetuating what always has been.

Internal Sources of Management Talent

The opportunity to fill a management job, however, should also be an opportunity to bring people up from lower positions in your company. If qualified people are available within the organization, they should be the first persons to be given consideration. Good planning on the part of management should make provision for training persons to meet the growth opportunities provided by the firm.

Many companies have formally developed manpower planning projects, as discussed in Chapter 6. In addition to listing how many people will be needed in each job category over a period of years, they have charts showing who within the organization is being considered for various promotions, and when it is likely these people will be reached. These charts are developed on the basis of estimated dates of retirement and normal attrition.

To supplement these charts, which are at best no more than good guesses, companies maintain skill banks. These are rosters which break down the various skills and jobs factors the company uses, or plans to use, and list the employees who have these skills. For example, if a market research manager leaves and his assistant moves up into his job, the company will check the skill bank and may discover there is a salesman or a person from another department with the education or experience that qualifies him or her for the new vacancy.

In promoting people from other jobs within the company, several factors must be considered to determine whether the "logical" successor is the best qualified person for the promotion. When the purchasing manager of a large manufacturer was ready for retirement, his assistant of many years was the obvious successor. Yet this person did not have many of the qualities that make for good managing. He had always been a specialist in one aspect of the job and was not strong enough for the top spot. The company may have been at fault for not training him —or he may not have had the capacity for the training—but it would have been a major error to promote him just because that was expected.

Another factor which must be taken into account when a person is promoted from one department to another—when, for example, to fill the purchasing-manager job discussed above, the company transfers a man from the marketing department—

is what the loss of the promoted man may mean to his old department. Often department heads hold a person back from transfer or promotion because they need him. This is very short-sighted. The capable individual will not stay on a job if he is overlooked when the chance for promotion comes.

Whether the position is filled from within the company or with an outsider, if the person who is "in line" is bypassed, some provision must be made to handle the situation that then arises. If the bypassed person is to remain with the company, he has to be dealt with, or his position within the organization will become intolerable. If the company is large enough to absorb him, he may be given a different job where his capabilities will be utilized. In some companies an old time employee in these circumstances is given a special title and a raise to allow him to save face. It is better to do this, even though it is sure to cause some resentment, than to promote a person to a job he cannot handle.

Sometimes this type of problem can be avoided if management-development programs are provided to train potential managers to move up within the company. These programs will be discussed later in this chapter.

Recruiting Personnel from Outside the Company

When a company promotes from *within* the organization it gives all the people on the staff the feeling that advancement is available, and that is a great boost to morale. It also assures the company it is getting persons with proven records for their management positions. The company has had the opportunity to observe them at first hand. These people know the company, its policies and procedures, its hidden assets and faults, and can quickly take over their new jobs. Why then do so many companies go to the outside to fill their management openings?

Often there is no one within the organization who is really qualified to move up to the newly vacated position. This may be because of lack of training or because of poor selection of the subordinates. It may also be caused by changes in the job specifications, which may require somebody with technical or managerial skills that do not exist within the company. This frequently occurs when new technologies are introduced into a firm.

Management should always try to find the best possible candidate for any opening. Often "the best candidate" is not to be found in the company, and management must look outside. Companies make a practice of seeking managerial personnel from both inside and outside to give themselves a wider choice of candidates before making a final selection.

Outside personnel have the advantage of bringing into the organization new ideas and concepts which come from their exposure to other businesses. This can prevent the company from becoming too inbred. Although the persons within the company who expect promotion may resent an outsider's coming in, the knowledge that promotion is not automatic and that they must prove themselves worthy of it can be an incentive for them to keep abreast of current developments in their field and to work hard to merit the promotion when it becomes available.

There are many sources for locating management personnel. Many are similar to the sources used to find lower level people, but should be used differently.

Advertising: Most advertisements for personnel appear in the "help-wanted" columns of the local newspapers. Although this is a good source for most job openings, it is less than satisfactory for management positions. The manager a company seeks may not be an active job seeker, but a person who would respond to an interesting ad if he happened to see it. One is more likely to attract this type of person with an ad in the business section of the local paper than with one in the classified pages.

For persons with specific technical or specialized backgrounds, the trade magazines or professional journals may be a better source than local papers. Every field has a publication that deals with its problems. Most of these carry personnel ads. If the job calls for a person with background in a particular specialty, it is more likely to attract him via a trade journal ad than any other medium. The negative factor in using trade papers is that they often are published only once a month. If the job must be filled in a rush, this becomes a major drawback.

Similar to the trade publications are such general business publications as *The Wall Street Journal*. This daily has both regional and national coverage and is very effective in reaching management personnel who are interested in career changes. There are similar regional business publications in various parts of the United States. Such regular newspapers as *The New York Times, Chicago Tribune, Los Angeles Times* and other major city papers have business sections, particularly on Sundays, which have broad-scope readership and are excellent for advertising management positions.

Writing the best ad to attract the applicants you want takes some skill. Go over the ad with the person to whom this job reports to make sure it covers the specifications. Have your advertising agency help in writing it to make sure it is an attractive ad.*

Employment Agencies: Many managers only think of employment agencies in terms of locating clerical or lower-level managerial personnel. They are not entirely right in this view. Many agencies specialize in dealing with executive personnel. In choosing an agency, be sure it is one that deals with the type of job you seek to fill. This can be ascertained by checking the kind of job openings they advertise, by asking other managers in your community about agencies which handle these jobs and, of course, by speaking to the agency people to assure yourself that they know their business.

Employment agencies are particularly helpful because they can give the job almost immediate attention. They usually have available a number of qualified applicants, and they screen them to make sure they meet the specifications. This saves considerable time in interviewing candidates, for the obviously unqualified are eliminated. The final choice is, of course, made by the company.

The speed of service and the pre-screening of the applicants usually makes the use of agencies well worth the fees they

* For a detailed treatment of writing advertising for personnel, see Arthur R. Pell, *Recruiting and Selecting Personnel*. New York: Simon and Schuster, 1969, pp. 16–33.

charge. Fees for finding management personnel are usually borne by the company—not the applicant. These fees range from about 10 percent to 20 percent of the annual salary paid the person employed.

If the job that is open is a difficult job to fill, it may be advantageous to use agencies in cities other than the one where the job is located. Many agencies have correspondent agencies or branches in other cities which can locate persons who are qualified for the job and willing to relocate. A good number of management people will move wherever the opportunity may be, so a company is never limited to just the local market.

Executive Recruiters: The executive recruiter works quite differently from an employment agency, even one which specializes in executive placement. The agency obtains its applicants chiefly through advertising; the recruiter actually searches them out.

The chief advantage of using an executive search organization is that it will uncover candidates for a job who are not actively seeking job change. They research the field to locate the type of applicant sought by their client—they do not wait for the candidate to take the initiative, but actually go directly after him.

This is effective because the best qualified person for any specific job may not be looking for a job. He does not read the want-ads, does not register with employment agencies, and even if he sees an ad in the business section of a paper, may be reluctant to answer it because he may not have a resume available and is unlikely to dictate this kind of letter to his secretary.

The executive recruiter spends considerable time in studying the open position, getting to know not only the job specifications, but also the personality factors needed for success in the company. He helps the management formulate a realistic concept of what is needed and determines where suitable people can be located. After researching the field, the recruiter usually telephones prospects, arouses their interest and then invites them for a detailed interview. After very careful screening, reference checks and sometimes testing, one or two candidates are presented to the management for a final choice. Some of the top positions in business today have been filled by executive recruiters.

Recruiters are not usually retained for jobs that pay less than $25,000 per year. The fee charged by most recruiters averages about 25 percent of the annual salary plus reimbursement of out-of-pocket expenses. Unlike the agency which is paid only if it fills a job, the recruiter gets all or part of his fee whether or not he succeeds. The actual formula on which a fee is based differs from one recruiter to another.

College Recruiting: At the other end of the management scale is the need for young men and women to train and develop for future management positions with an organization. Later in this chapter we will discuss some of the programs geared to train these people.

Large firms often send special college recruiters to campuses in their area or around the country to select graduates who fit their needs. Smaller firms cannot afford to go on extended tours of colleges, but it is usually feasible to visit schools in the area where the company is situated.

The college placement offices have the facilities to arrange interviews with interested students. The company should send to the college a person who has sufficient knowledge of the company's opportunities, programs, long-range plans, and any other material that might be of interest to a prospective employee.

The recruiter screens out those students in whom there is no interest and invites those who appear to qualify to visit the company at a later date. After this second go-around with the applicant, a decision is made whether or not to employ him or her.

It is not essential to visit colleges to recruit the new graduates. Those companies which cannot physically go to the college can send a statement of their requirements to the college placement office with literature about the company. The placement officer will select interested students and forward their resumes to the company. Company personnel people can then invite likely prospects for further screening.

The same procedure is used in dealing with graduate schools for advanced-degree students or with community colleges for their graduates. Usually no fee is charged by the college to the company for this service.

Other Sources of Management Personnel: In addition to the formal sources already discussed, there are a number of informal means of locating people for executive jobs.

The most common is personal recommendation. Every executive has personal contacts who know other management people who may be interested in a career switch. If the search for an executive is not confidential—and sometimes confidentiality is essential in executive recruitment—it is advantageous to let people know what type of person is being sought.

From this "grapevine" excellent leads have developed. The big negative is that an organization may waste considerable time interviewing unqualified people whom some friend or customer thought to be qualified, but who has no real possibility. Not only must a courtesy interview be given in such a case, but an explanation must be made to the referrer as to why the applicant was rejected.

Other sources are banks, accounting firms and other business services. These organizations know of many executives who are seeking a change. They are usually glad to refer them as a favor to both the applicant and the company. However, the same negative applies as to any other personal referrals. Although usually no cost is incurred if the applicant is employed, the cost of the manager's time in interviewing unqualified people is a significant expense.

Trade associations and professional groups often have placement committees. They are useful when a position is open in their particular field. For example, if a company needs a personnel executive, the placement committee of the American Society for Personnel Administration would be a good source. In most instances, however, the committees do not screen applicants, but only refer resumes. As in responses to newspaper ads, the company must make its first judgment on the basis of the resumes and select from them the applicants to be interviewed.

Selecting the Right Candidate

There are four steps in the selection process which are used in some form, whether one is employing a member of the office staff or a senior executive. They are:

1. Review of the application form
2. The interview
3. Testing
4. Verification.

Except for the very top positions in a company, applicants are usually requested to complete a biographical summary form, called, at the lower levels, an "application."

The application gives the company a concise picture of the applicant's background. It usually covers personal data, education, experience and special skills.

Many applicants, when applying for a job submit resumes which they have written themselves. Managers should always request that the applicant complete the company's own form even if a resume is submitted. Resumes are written to emphasize the applicant's strengths and minimize his weaknesses. By using a standard form, the company can spot problem areas and compare one applicant with another more easily.

The application form also serves as a reminder to the manager of who each applicant is. If the person is employed, it can become the source of information needed for the permanent employee files.

Most companies interview a potential employee in some depth before making the employment decision. The interview can be most helpful in determining whether a person is qualified for the job sought.

Interviewing, if properly conducted, can be a significant screening tool. The interviewer must recognize that he is not engaged in just a pleasant conversation between two people, but rather in a structured approach to obtaining information about the applicant, evaluating the applicant's qualifications, both technical and personal, for the job and also giving the applicant information about the company and the position for which he has applied. No one should attempt an employment interview without some training in the techniques of interviewing.

Many books have been written on this subject,* and courses in the field are given in most colleges and adult education programs.

For selecting clerical and other sub-management personnel, a variety of tests are available which measure intelligence, clerical aptitudes, office skills, etc. Less significant are tests which purportedly measure personality factors. There has been much controversy over these personality tests, and caution is advised in using them.

In selecting managerial personnel, testing is not as commonly used. For managerial selection some organizations refer the applicants to psychologists who use psychological interviews, and sometimes very sophisticated testing, to evaluate the applicant. Such assessments are usually expensive and should be reserved for applicants for high-level positions where there is some need to learn more about the candidate than just his ability to do the job.

Personnel consultants can assist companies who do not have their own personnel experts in determining when testing is appropriate and what types of tests should be used.

One of the best ways to determine the potential of a candidate for a position is a careful check of his or her previous work experience. Shakespeare tells us: "What is past is prologue." If it can be determined what a person has accomplished (or has failed to accomplish) in the past, we can obtain a pretty good estimate of what can be expected of him in a new job.

Although many managers rely on letters to the former employer for information, it is much more effective to telephone.

---

* Some suggested books on interviewing: Richard Fear, *The Evaluation Interview.* New York: McGraw-Hill, 1973; Arthur R. Pell, *Be a Better Employment Interviewer.* Huntington, N.Y.: Personnel Publications, 1974.

A conversation with the reference is much more thorough. Most people are willing to tell more on the phone than they are in writing. Telephoning also enables the caller to ask specific questions which may develop out of the conversation and could not have been anticipated in a letter. Of course, in listening to a telephone reference, one can often pick up implications from voice-tone that may not be overtly stated. These can be followed through to obtain deeper insight into the applicant's background.

In making a telephone reference check, it is advisable to write out in advance a list of the questions to be asked. In this way the employer can be assured that no area of interest will be overlooked. Questions should concern not only ability to perform the job technically, but should also seek information on personality, attitudes, reliability and, where pertinent, ability to make decisions, motivate others and be creative.

Once all of these steps have been completed, the manager can choose the successful candidate. The importance of making the best selection cannot be overemphasized. In order to meet management objectives, the organization must be staffed with the best people available. If such people are chosen, it will be easy to train and develop them, to motivate them and give them the tools necessary to achieve success.

Training and Development

There are several forms of training and development of managerial personnel that are used by various companies.

Cadet Training: A program geared to train potential managers, usually recent college graduates, is called "cadet training" or "executive (or management) trainee program."

Companies using this method assign the new trainee to a formal program, usually consisting of classroom work on the operations of the business, assignment on a rotation basis to each of the departments in the organization, and specialized training in the field of work in which the new employee will function.

These programs range in length from a few months to a year or more. They can be very effective or completely wasteful, depending on how well the program is developed. Successful programs usually involve a real work experience for the trainees, rather than just shuttling between departments. Assigning the trainees to meaningful projects where they can participate in accomplishment is much more effective than having them simply observe the work of others. Examples of this include assigning the trainee to evaluate a manufacturing process, the market for a new product, a clerical process, etc. Combining these projects with seminars and assessment sessions on what has been done has usually resulted in better training and lower turnover among trainees than more passive types of program.

Another successful technique for cadet training is giving the trainee an opportunity to make decisions at a low level as early as possible in his career. Sears, Roebuck and Co. has done this in their retail divisions, assigning their executive trainees to department or small-store management jobs after a relatively short but intensive basic training program. In these jobs trainees are given profit-and-loss responsibility and the authority to make decisions affecting their units. It is assumed they will make some mistakes, but learning to cope with problems at a low level is likely to involve only relatively minor mistakes and will give the trainee the experience and confidence needed to grow with the company.

Supervisory Training: New trainees are not the only people in an organization that require training. Persons being promoted or groomed for promotion to supervisory jobs should be taught the techniques and psychology of dealing with people. Many firms also have ongoing training programs for current supervisors to keep them abreast of the latest developments in human relations and supervisory techniques.

These programs may be conducted by the personnel department of the organization or by outside consultants specializing in leadership training. Many films, tapes, pamphlets and books on this subject are available.

One cannot assume that because a person is a good mechanic he will make a good foreman or that a good salesman can easily become a good sales manager. The qualifications that made the worker a successful worker are not the same as those which would make him a successful supervisor. However, one does not have to be a born leader to become a good supervisor. The techniques of leadership can be learned. Management's responsibility is to provide supervisors with the tools which will enable them to acquire these leadership techniques.

In addition to the in-plant programs conducted by many companies, seminars in leadership and supervision are frequently given by colleges and universities, trade and professional associations, and personnel consulting organizations.

Skill Training: Because of the increasing complexity of most jobs, and the introduction of new machinery and equipment both in factory and office work, companies should have programs on line to train personnel needed to perform the work and use the equipment.

Most manufacturers of equipment provide training for personnel in the companies which purchase the equipment. Companies themselves have training programs to train new employees and re-train old employees when changes are made in the techniques or equipment used.

In recent years the government has encouraged companies to provide skill training for minority and other disadvantaged people. With the aid of government funds, many companies have created programs to train men and women from the ghettoes and slums in the skills needed in their organizations.

Management Development: Probably the most sophisticated type of training is preparing individuals to be managers. Many programs are available for this. Some are on-premises programs run by the company for the specific training of men and women being upgraded within the company. Others are outside seminars run by colleges, associations or consultants. The Dale Carnegie Management Seminar is a good example of this type of program.

Management development differs from supervisory training in that it covers a much wider range of subjects, from planning through control. The participants are persons above the level of the first-line supervisor and may range up to top management of a company.

The objective of management development is not only to train potential managers and help persons about to be promoted, but also to hone the managerial skills of current executives and make them more effective in their work.

Some of the techniques used in management-development programs include lectures and discussions on various aspects of the management field, case studies in which actual problems are considered and solutions developed and discussed, role playing and various visual and audio aids. Some of the more sophisticated techniques used by some organizations are business simulation games in which participants make a series of decisions based on the facts presented to them, and the results are evaluated by comparing the decisions with those of a previously developed computer program.

A very important method of management development is individual coaching by senior people of their subordinates. Every executive should consider it part of his responsibilities to train persons in his department to succeed him. Top management must not only encourage this but demand it. Failure to have a trained group of subordinates able to move up can cause major problems in any organization.

Management development is an area which should never be ignored. It is one of the key factors in the survival of an organization and an essential component of effective management through people.

Specific techniques of training and development are discussed in Chapter 14.

11

COMMUNICATING

One of the most important responsibilities of any manager is to be able to give his subordinates instruction, direction, ideas and suggestions, and to receive from his subordinates their reactions and thinking on matters pertinent to their work.

This flow of thought is called *communication*. We can best understand how the interflow of ideas works by comparing it to a two-way radio. On one side we have a manager who is transmitting, and on the other a subordinate who is receiving. At any time, however, the roles can be reversed, with the subordinate transmitting and the manager receiving.

COMMUNICATION IS A TWO-WAY PROCESS

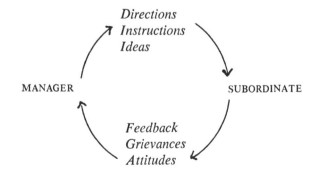

Proper reception of communication means that the receiver not only understands what has been communicated to him but *accepts* it.

As with a radio, interference may distort the communication, causing the receiver to misunderstand what is being sent. The transmitter may not realize that the message is not being received as intended.

The source of the interference may be at the transmitter or at the receiver or between the two. Just as in radio transmission, this interference is referred to as *static* or more commonly as "noise."

The following chart will show some of these barriers to successful communication:

Barriers on part of SENDER	Barriers in between	Barriers on part of RECEIVER
Vocabulary	Channels of communication	Listening
Semantics		Hearing what he expects to hear
Inarticulateness		Prejudice
Attitude		Halo effect
Lack of sensitivity to receiver		Ignoring non-verbal clues
		Emotional set

Now let us look into this problem and examine some ways of overcoming the noise which makes communication often ineffective.

Barriers on the Part of the Sender

Language: Most managers tend to use the vocabulary and idioms familiar to them without considering whether the listener has the same command of the language special to the industry. A manager, in dealing with some employees, might, for example, use technical words which they do not understand, and so the message that is being given may be lost. A block has been created at the transmission point.

People in certain occupations or professions tend to develop their own special language, an "argot" of their own. When dealing with persons not familiar with this language, messages using the argot are meaningless. On the other hand, the use of argot in communicating with persons familiar with it simplifies communication and conveys a feeling of being "on the inside" to the parties concerned, a feeling which improves the communication process.

A more common problem of vocabulary is that certain words have different connotations to different people. A mining engineer and a labor-relations manager from the same mining company were attending a convention in New York when each received the following telegram: "Come back at once. Strike at mine." The mining engineer was elated; the labor-relations man was upset. To the former "strike" meant a discovery of a new vein of ore; to the latter it connoted a labor stoppage.

Some words have emotional connotations to certain people which change their meanings for them. A manager may tell a group of subordinates that a new program will be instituted to increase "efficiency." One reaction might be: "Great, maybe we can put some of those new ideas I have into effect now." But another reaction might be: "Oh, oh, there goes the raise we were supposed to get." The two reactions to the same words stem from the psychological makeup of the hearers and their previous experience with the use of that word.

The study of the meaning of words and their various connotations is called "semantics." It is important to recognize that words may mean one thing to the sender and something quite different to the receiver. What the sender means to say may be interpreted by the receiver in quite a different sense from what was intended.

As most communication is verbal, and in many situations by telephone, it is important that communicators learn to speak clearly and distinctly. Mumbled or slurred instructions or directions are obviously not going to be understood, and as subordinates are frequently reluctant to ask a superior to repeat what he has said, they often fail to get the whole story.

In written communications barriers may arise because of poor grammar or sentence structure. Written instructions and directions will be discussed in some detail later in this chapter.

Non-verbal communication must also be taken into account. The manner in which a person tells somebody something may convey more than words. A supervisor may say: "Do this job when you get a chance," but his eyes, mouth, even posture, may indicate to the subordinate: "This is a rush job" or the opposite: "Do this after everything else."

Another barrier to communication lies within the sender: his attitude toward his job and his subordinates and even his opinion of himself. A manager who is arrogant will convey this feeling in the way he gives directions or information. He may appear to be talking down to his subordinates. This causes resentment, which blocks communication. In order for the message to be received, it must not only be understood, but accepted by the receiver. When resentment develops, acceptance is unlikely. A subordinate who is busy resenting the manager's attitude does not really "hear" what is being said. Good managers avoid such manifestations of arrogance as sarcasm and "pulling rank" when dealing with subordinates.

The sender must always be sensitive to the receiver's acceptance or lack of acceptance of what is being communicated. He should develop an "inner ear" which enables him to pick up the reaction to his messages. This is part of the feedback loop which good communicators develop. By observing the way the subordinate receives instructions or orders, the manager may obtain immediate feedback as to his understanding and acceptance.

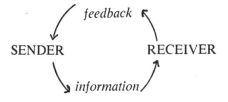

Failure to obtain feedback leads to an open loop. The information goes one way, but as no feedback is returned to the sender, he cannot take the necessary steps to make sure it is being received and accepted.

Good communication requires a closed loop. Information is sent to the receiver, and reaction is immediately fed back to the sender, who makes the corrections or adjustments necessary and revises the message, gets new feedback, etc., until there is assurance that communication is clearly completed.

Managers can obtain this feedback both directly and indirectly. Direct questions to the receiver can elicit at least a partial feedback. However, it may not be accurate by itself. If a manager asks: "Do you understand?" in most cases the answer will be "Yes." But this does not mean that the subordinate *does* understand what is meant. He may be ashamed to say "no" for fear of being considered stupid and so answer "yes" and hope to figure out what is meant later. On the other hand, he may honestly believe he does understand everything said, but actually comprehends only part of it, or he may think he understands the message, but be interpreting it quite otherwise than was intended.

A better approach is to ask the subordinate how he interprets what has been communicated. A diplomatic way to do this may be to say: "So we don't get confused by all this, maybe it would be wise to recap our thoughts. Let's go over it again. Now, how do you see this?" Most of the time neither party will have to go through the entire story again. By asking a few pertinent questions on key points, one can tell how well the message has been received.

Non-verbal clues should be carefully observed. By noting the other person's mannerisms, facial expressions, etc., one can tell if he really understands and accepts what is being communicated.

Barriers in the Receiver

Just as there is sometimes noise or static in the sending apparatus, there are sometimes equivalent barriers at the receiving end. A manager is both a sender and receiver. When he is transmitting (giving directions, information, training, etc.), he must be aware of the problems his subordinates must be having in receiving—that is, in understanding and accepting what is being transmitted. Because communication is a *two-way* process, the manager becomes the receiver when his people are giving him information or airing gripes or grievances, and therefore he must consider himself a receiver as often as a sender.

One of the major barriers to receiving is the failure of most people to really listen. A salesman has been telling his sales manager about his problems for the past fifteen minutes. What has the manager been doing? He started by listening attentively, but then his mind wandered. Instead of listening to the problem (which he may be called upon to solve), he has begun thinking about the meeting he had just had with the Marketing Vice President, or about the golf game he has planned for the weekend. By letting his mind wander thus, he has missed the point his salesman was trying to make.

Why did his mind wander? Psychologists have shown that the human mind thinks many times faster than a person can talk. While a speaker talks, the mind of the listener is racing ahead. He subconsciously completes the sentence before the speaker does, assuming, often incorrectly, that the speaker will say what he expects him to say. In the time that elapses between the "listener's" completion of the speaker's thoughts in his mind, and the actual oral statement of the speaker, the "listener's" mind begins to wander. He thinks of other things because his brain has absorbed the idea at hand and is free to digress.

While these thoughts flow through the mind of the "listener," the speaker is still talking. The sentences that he started and the "listener" completed in his mind have been completed, either as expected or otherwise. He has continued talking, adding new sentences, introducing new ideas. What has happened to the "listener"? He has missed the point! His mind has never caught up with the speaker. He has heard his words, but they did not register. He was not really listening.

What can one do to overcome this tendency not to listen?

First of all, become aware of the problem. Know immediately when you quit listening.

In a conference, the speaker's voice may drone on and on, and our minds may not be following. This is the danger point. *Stop. Listen.*

In a conversation, we often hear words, not ideas. *Stop. Listen.*

In an interview, we have lost the question—or the answer. *Stop. Listen.*

Once we have stopped to listen, the problem is half solved, but we may already have missed a good part of what is being said. A good listener trains himself to *anticipate* the moments when his mind is apt to wander.

Here are some good ideas for improving one's listening habits:

ARE YOU A GOOD LISTENER?

Do You Stop Talking While Someone Is
Trying to Tell You Something?

You should because you cannot listen if you are talking. You cannot really listen if you are poised and ready to burst forth in talk the second your companion reaches a comma, or stops to breathe.

Do You Concentrate on What Your Companion Is Talking
About and Look Him in the Eye Without Appearing
to Be Trying to Hypnotize Him?

It involves conscious effort to listen. This is not easily done because listening is a skill, learned through practice. There are times, too, when you may not be at all interested in what your companion is telling you, but courtesy demands that you give him your full attention.

Do You Listen to a Person's Full Story Without Interrupting
Him Before He Has Had a Chance to Really Tell It?

You won't know what he's trying to tell you unless you give him the chance to tell it all at one time—and at his own pace. General of the Army George C. Marshall had this formula for good listening: "Listen to the other person's story; listen to the other person's full story; listen to the other person's full story first."

Do You Restrain Yourself from Injecting
Your Own Ideas and Opinions and Finishing
Some of Your Companion's Sentences for Him?

This is a most annoying habit many of us have. Listen to your companion carefully and don't try to put words in his mouth or finish his sentences for him.

Do You Always Give Your Companion the Impression
That You Are Interested in What He Has to Say and
Thereby Stimulate Him to His Best Conversation?

You should because many people need the stimulus of an "audience" to bring out their ideas clearly and to warm up to their subject.

At a Business Meeting or Conference, Do You Always Wait
Until the Speaker Has Finished Before You Ask Questions?

Interrupting a speaker is another bad listening habit that should be eliminated. It's possible to throw a speaker off his stride (in addition to annoying him) by coming up with a question in the middle of his talk. Save your questions for the discussion period which usually follows.

And Finally: Do You Remember to Smile When the Speaker
Has Made a Clever Remark? And Do You Give Out
With a Chuckle at the End of a Funny Story?

You should remember to smile when anyone makes a clever remark—it's a nice thing to do and the speaker will appreciate it. And if you can chuckle at the end of a funny (or not so funny) story, the speaker will be convinced that you're the greatest listener of all!

To Sum Up:

We learn from listening. We learn a lot about people by listening to them talk.

Be a good listener—you will be liked by the people you work for and work with. Be a good listener by developing good listen-

ing habits; you will become a better conversationalist and a better speaker. *

Another barrier on the receiver's side is the common tendency to hear only what one expects to hear. What one receives and accepts is often shaped by one's previous experience and background. Many people, instead of actually hearing what others tell them, hear what their own minds tell them has been said.

This is often seen when one has preconceived notions about a person or situation. A manager may expect a factory worker to be uneducated and not too bright, so when the worker makes an intelligent and creative suggestion, he does not "hear" it because he cannot believe a good idea could come from that source.

Similar to this is the tendency to accept only communication that is consistent with one's existing beliefs. Psychologists call this *cognitive dissonance*. Their research suggests that one can predict very strong differences between the receiver's reaction to information he hears which is consistent with what he already believes and his reaction to new information which is inconsistent with his established beliefs.

This means that when one is communicating a message, one must take into account what the receiver of a communication feels about the subject. Often what the receiver feels is dependent on the source of the information. A group of workers who distrust management will take any management statement with a grain of salt. This will show up in the feedback received and have to be compensated for to get the true message across.

Another barrier related to this is prejudice. If a receiver has a prejudice against the sender, he will subconsciously reject his message. This can be easily exemplified in the political context. Often a very cogent and logical argument on the part of the candidate of one party is automatically rejected by members of the opposing party because of their basic distrust of the opposition.

* Reprinted from New York Life NEWS, published by New York Life Insurance Co., March 1966.

The opposite of this is the "halo effect" in which one accepts everything said by a person for whom one has a liking or respect, even if the information or concept is not necessarily good.

Another barrier on the receiving end is the attitude of the parties affected. If a person is secure in himself and has the respect of his managers, he will understand and accept the transmission readily. If his attitude is one of fear of his management or lack of self-confidence, he will tend to block out understanding and acceptance. His fear of misunderstanding will cause him to misunderstand. His fear of asking for clarification (perhaps because he is afraid he will be considered stupid) will compound his lack of understanding.

Barriers Between Sender and Receiver

In addition to the interference within each element of the two-way radio apparatus there is a third source of static—that which comes from the outside.

In communication the major source of interference and distortion is the path the message takes from sender to receiver. In any large organization communication must usually flow through set channels. The more extensive the channels, the more likely it is that distortion will occur. This can be illustrated in the popular party game where one person tells an incident to his neighbor, who repeats it to his neighbor, who in turn repeats it to his neighbor and so on around the room. By the time it is retold to the originator, the story is completely different.

It is not unusual for a piece of information passed orally "through channels" to be distorted at each station, so that what the receiver receives is not at all what the sender sent.

One way to alleviate this difficulty is to use written communications. Writing is more difficult to distort, though interpretation of what is written may vary from station to station in the channel of communications. Still, writing has certain disadvantages: many matters cannot and should not be communicated in writing. Writing is time-consuming. For rush matters and matters of transient interest, writing is unnecessary.

A more effective way to curtail distortion is to shorten channels or allow for bypassing where feasible. The fewer stations along the route from sender to receiver, the less chance for distortion.

Dealing with Barriers to Communication

In addition to the feedback loop discussed above, there are several other ways of improving communications. It is unlikely one can ever have a perfect communication cycle, but much can be done to overcome some of the barriers.

As much of the receiver's static is caused by the way the receiver perceives what is being sent, the sender has to become sensitive to the way his receivers "feel" about the company, the sender himself and the subject involved. The sender must try to predict the impact of what he says and does on the feelings and attitudes of the receiver. This is especially important when there is a significant gap between the sender's background and the receiver's. The sender should try to put himself in the place of the receiver and find a common ground of understanding.

Timing is important. A message will be understood and accepted better at one time than at another. For example, a message sent too early—before the people are ready to deal with it —will not be accepted: A worker may not be ready to accept an instruction about safety on the job before he has been exposed to the dangers of the machine; once he sees the machine, the safety message will be understood and accepted.

One of the most effective means of communication is "face-to-face" dealing with subordinates. By observing how the message is taken, noting the non-verbal as well as immediate verbal reactions and enabling the subordinate to ask and answer questions about the problem at hand, the sender can expedite the communication cycle.

Not only is immediate feedback obtained, but the initial message can be made clearer by the manner in which it is conveyed. Voice control provides emphasis and sincerity that cannot always be expressed in written form. Facial expression and body language also help convey the idea.

Once the message is given, the sender can observe the other person and judge his responses—not only by what he says, but by the total behavioral set projected. He can spot antagonism, discontent and reluctant acceptance or, on the other hand, enthusiasm, high morale and total acceptance.

Communication Within the Informal Group

Thus far we have considered only formal communication. Yet in most large organizations the informal aspect of communication cannot be ignored. These manifest themselves through rumors and "the grapevine."

Rumors are usually based on half-truths or complete falsehoods and circulate all the time in many organizations. Managers must always be alert to rumors and ready to challenge, rebut or quash them when necessary.

Rumors can be misleading and cause considerable damage to the company. A false rumor that the company is in bad financial condition or is planning to close a plant can cause panic in an organization. A rumor that a supervisor is being transferred or that a change is being made in some personnel policy can cause people to quit, grievances to be filed or complaints to be submitted to government agencies.

Managers should be alert to all rumors that are spreading within the company. Rumors cannot be ignored. Immediate action should be taken to verify the truth of the rumor (some of them do have elements of truth in them) and to present the complete and accurate story to the persons involved.

The "grapevine" is the informal channel of communication through which rumors as well as true information spread through an organization. It is fast, spontaneous and flexible. It appears to exist wherever there are people and enjoys a high degree of credibility.

Many managers use the grapevine to reinforce formal communication. Managers often send "trial balloons" via the grapevine to determine what reaction the employees are likely to have to proposals under consideration. Sending material in preparation for a formal communication enables management to obtain feedback concerning the formal communication without putting management in the position of making a commitment as to whether or not it will adjust policies on the basis of the feedback.

Giving Orders

One of the most common aspects of communication is the giving of orders and direction. All managers must give orders from time to time. Most immediate orders are given orally. Long-term orders and detailed directions are given in writing. Written orders will be discussed later in this chapter.

Direct orders: The direct order is best reserved for emergency situations or cases where special emphasis is called for. Direct orders should be enunciated in a slow and deliberate manner, in a voice no louder than is necessary for the subordinate to hear. Shouting and bellowing orders is unnecessary and disturbing.

Requests: More polite than the direct order, the request invites cooperation. In making a request, the manager effectively uses his understanding of the person to whom it is directed. There are few people who will not respond to a request. "Will you please type these letters, Miss Clark" is generally more effective than "Type these letters."

Suggestions: The suggestion plays up to the employee's sense of responsibility. It is frequently used when dealing with oversensitive persons. It implies team work and group benefit. "These letters are important, and it would be helpful if they were out tonight." The suggestion puts the secretary on her own; it tends to develop ability and judgment.

Selling the idea: Give reasons wherever possible. If a person understands what is behind a request or a suggestion, he will respond with greater willingness. Arouse the interest of the person in getting a job done rather than ordering him to do it. "Bill, the deadline for getting that bid in is Friday afternoon. Can you get your people to finish their part of it by Thursday?"

Cooperation: A leader works cooperatively with both those above him and those below him in the organizational structure. Too many managers cater to their superiors and ignore their subordinates. These "apple polishers" lose the respect of their fellow workers and break down the team idea. In dealing with subordinates, the true leader does not talk down to them or act superior. He takes them into his confidence and keeps the team, the "we," spirit.

This attitude is called for also in working with managers on one's own level. Lack of cooperation and good communication among peers breaks down the team spirit and adds complexities to the free flow of ideas and direction within the company. In conveying information and orders to other managers, it is extremely important to keep in mind that they are not subordinates and cannot be pushed. The effective manager "sells" his ideas to them and stimulates their cooperation.

To summarize the techniques of good oral communication, here are a series of guidelines suggested by the American Management Association.

Common Mistakes in Issuing Orders:

1. Speaking indistinctly or selecting words that do not fully convey the desired meaning.
2. Giving orders in a disorderly or haphazard way. (Instructions should be organized in logical sequence.)
3. Assuming that the subordinate understands what is expected of him when frequently, such is not the case.

Suggestions to be Remembered in Giving Orders:

1. Know and understand thoroughly the job to be done.
2. Assign the task to the right man. Some employees are more skilled or adept at certain jobs than others and should be called on to do those things at which they are most proficient.
3. Give orders clearly, concisely, distinctly.
4. Don't assume orders are understood. *Be sure* they are understood. Repeat them if necessary.
5. Keep orders on a high level; avoid sarcasm or other forms of antagonism.

6. If necessary, demonstrate. This is an excellent aid to clear appreciation of the problem.
7. Do not give too many orders at one time. This can be very confusing.
8. If a subordinate is capable, do not nag or stand over him.
9. Allow a reasonable time for the task to be done.
10. Give orders through proper channels. Immediate superiors should not be bypassed or ignored in getting word to an employee to perform a task. The subordinate should be made to realize that his immediate supervisor not only has the responsibility of getting the job done, but has authority to a considerable degree. This functional procedure, this line of authority, should not be disrupted. It is demoralizing to the group and to the immediate superior for a high supervisor to go directly to a member of the group with instructions without clearing through the immediate supervisor.
11. Give adequate details, but do not confuse. Detailed orders are desirable when hazards exist, or where the work is of a special or infrequent nature, or with men of limited experience, or where standard procedure is desired, or in teaching.
12. Follow through. It may be desirable after a reasonable time to check back and be sure that the man has understood and that he is performing his task satisfactorily.*

Written Directions and Orders

In many circumstances written orders are more effective than verbal orders or directions. This is particularly applicable to complex situations where the direction consists of detailed information and will be followed by many people, often in diverse locations.

The Standard Operating Procedures which were discussed in Chapter 3 as a means of planning are also used as formal directions for the persons performing the tasks described. SOPs are also a major tool in training new people to do a job. The details are written for easy study and constant reference when required.

* Dooher, M. J., *Effective Communication on the Job,* New York: American Management Association, 1956, pp. 103–104.

All directions, whether written or oral, should meet the "4 C Criteria": they should be *Complete, Clear, Concise and Capable of Fulfillment.*

The direction should be complete so that all necessary information is provided. It must be clear so that there is no room for misunderstanding. Proper use of words (both from a technical and semantic viewpoint) and good sentence structure help assure clarity. Every order should be read and reread before it is issued to ensure that there is no misleading or vague material in it. Conciseness not only eliminates unnecessary and extraneous matters, but enhances clarity and makes the direction easier to use and follow. The last "C," capability of fulfillment is important because if the receiver does not believe the order can be carried out successfully, he will not make a real effort to achieve it. Giving a person a task which makes him stretch his capabilities can motivate him to work hard to achieve it, but if the task appears to be well beyond achievability, he will give up without even making a real attempt.

Some people who speak effectively seem to lose their effectiveness when putting their ideas into writing. They tend to use pompous language—"corporationese"— or high sounding language, when simplicity would be far more effective. One often finds such orders as: "Upon the receipt of this memorandum, it is requested that action be instituted to . . ." instead of just saying "Take this action now."

One of the drawbacks of written communication is the difficulty of obtaining feedback. In oral communication the feedback is often instantaneous. In written direction one does not always know how the receiver will accept the message.

To overcome this difficulty, some managers have "feedback sessions" after a written communication is promulgated so that questions from the affected parties can be answered, and a testing of the understanding and acceptance of the order by the group can be made by management.

Some companies use written communications for even the most trivial of orders. Memo pads are printed with the slogan "Put It in Writing" or a similar message. One advantage of putting everything in writing is that it does keep a record of what has been ordered. It's great for the JIC * file. It can, however, result in much paper clutter and more confusion than limiting written orders and communications to more weighty types of material.

* "JIC," "Just in Case" someone wants to check who is responsible for taking an action.

12

LEADERSHIP

"Leaders are born—not made" has been a generally accepted statement throughout the ages. Indeed, it was the basis of feudalism and the monarchical system of government.

Even in America where men of humble beginnings have risen to high position, people have said that their qualities of leadership were inborn.

In most business organizations, certain men and women rise from the ranks to positions of supervision and management. Are these men and women natural leaders? Experience has shown that the answer is "Not necessarily."

People have moved into positions of leadership and responsibility for many reasons: seniority, election (in the public sector), nepotism, and promotion due to proficiency in their work or technical skill. Often these people had no real leadership ability or experience, and they had to be taught to be leaders.

In these cases, the reason for promotion had no relationship to ability to lead, nor did the achievement of higher position assure success in leadership. The act of taking off the coveralls and donning a white collar and a tie does not in itself make a man a leader.

Can one learn the skills of leadership? In World War II there were two dramatic examples of success in teaching men to be leaders.

Men in the armed forces, usually quite young and with no military experience, were selected for officer training. By an intensive program they were successfully trained to be leaders in combat. Could all of them have been "natural leaders"? Most unlikely, by virtue of their very number!

Even more significant was the example of the men and women in industry who were trained to be foremen and supervisors. Most of these people had been factory or office workers for many years—skilled in their occupations, but never in a position of leadership. When the war erupted and our defense plants were flooded with work, companies employed additional hundreds of thousands of unskilled men and women. They ranged from older men who had been in all kinds of non-factory occupations before the war to youngsters just out of high school, from experienced factory workers to housewives and grandmothers (Rosie the Riveter and Winnie the Welder) who had never seen the inside of a factory before the war.

Experienced factory workers who had been promoted to the jobs of foremen and supervisors because they had some knowledge of the job to be done had to be trained for leadership. They had to learn how to supervise, direct, control, motivate, guide and train their subordinates.

To teach them all this, the War Manpower Commission developed a program called Training Within Industry (TWI), which was immensely successful in making leaders out of these former rank-and-file people. Not only did TWI accomplish its objective—it also laid the groundwork for training people in leadership during the postwar years. It proved that leadership can be developed—that it is not necessarily inborn.

Many people scoff at the idea that there is anything complex about leadership. "It is nothing more than plain common sense" is a frequent remark.

What is "common sense"? Common sense is based chiefly on inferences developed from one's own experiences. But an individual's experience is never enough to give anything but a limited answer. There is much more to leadership than the necessarily circumscribed experience of any one individual. One must look beyond common sense to the scientific analysis of human behavior to find out what motivates people and how a leader can channel these factors toward good supervision.

A manager would not rely on "common sense" to help him solve financial or manufacturing problems. He would call on the best possible expertise in these areas that was available to him. Why, therefore, should he resort to a less scientific base in handling his human relations problems?

From a practical viewpoint, leadership can be considered simply as a relationship which exists between a certain individual and the other members of a group. This relationship exists at all stages of our lives, among youngsters on a playground, among students in schools and colleges, among workers in government and of course in business.

The common factor in all these different phases of leadership is the factor of authority—an authority which is either earned or vested in a position, or established by some combination of the two.

Most managers are placed in a position over their staffs and given the authority to carry out the objectives of their jobs. This authority does not by itself necessarily qualify the individual who holds it for the name of "leader." On the contrary, there are countless examples of managers who do not lead but who carry out their responsibilities by simply making arbitrary use of their authority.

What do subordinates expect from their leader? First they expect the manager to be competent in his own field of expertise and to demonstrate this in his own conduct and in the standards set for the workers. This does not mean that every leader has to be technically competent in every aspect of his department's work, but only that the leader should have sufficient knowledge to direct, guide and support his people. More important, subordinates expect the manager to be scrupulously just and fair. Since in the final analysis it remains within the province of the subordinates to withhold or confer leadership, it is important that the leader know what is expected of him.

When leadership is effective, its outgrowth and by-products are cooperation and high morale. Without cooperation from his staff, a manager can never meet his objectives. Unless morale is high, he will be plagued by dissension, absenteeism and outright sabotage.

Many things influence and contribute to good morale and organizational spirit, but the basic factor is a feeling of purpose and pride in the organization, its goals and the quality of the leadership of its managers.

Another definition of leadership is the art of imposing one's will upon others in such a manner as to command their respect, their confidence and their wholehearted cooperation. That cannot be accomplished by arbitrary use of the manager's position and authority. It requires a sincere effort on the part of the leader to gain and keep the confidence of his people, to use their strength and expertise optimally and to recognize that they are capable of creative and significant contribution to meeting the company's goals. Leadership of this sort can be developed by studying what the behavioral scientists have learned about human nature and the techniques of helping people give their best efforts by enabling them to achieve self-satisfaction in doing so.

Leadership Styles

Different people use different methods of expressing their leadership. They choose their own "patterns of leadership" often by imitating their own early leaders, or by following the styles used by their current bosses. Sometimes a standard pattern of leadership prevails throughout an organization, but more often the style of leadership which fits the manager, his people and the situation evolves—a style in which all parties concerned are able to work comfortably. However, unless the managers are made aware of the varying styles of leadership that exist, of their advantages and limitations, and of their applicability to specific situations, they may not recognize that there is a choice that can be made.

Robert Tannenbaum and Warren H. Schmidt in a classic article in *Harvard Business Review* summed up the various leadership patterns in a chart showing the continuum of leadership behavior *:

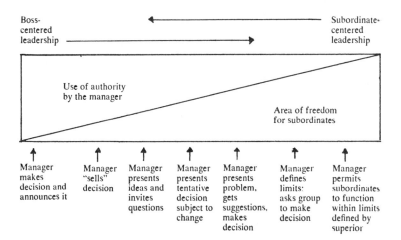

A CONTINUUM OF LEADERSHIP BEHAVIOR

Each of the points along the continuum relates to the degree of authority used by the boss and the amount of freedom allowed the subordinates in reaching decisions. At the extreme left is a pattern of leadership in which the manager is primarily authoritarian, while at the extreme right we have an almost totally democratic style of leadership. Let us examine each of the points in more detail:

1. *Manager makes decision and announces it:* The manager first determines what the problem is. He uses the techniques of decision-making—consciously or subconsciously—which have been previously discussed in this book, makes the decision and announces it to his subordinates. He may or may not give con-

* Robert Tannenbaum and Warren H. Schmidt, "How to Choose a Leadership Pattern," *Harvard Business Review* March–April 1958, pp. 95–101.

sideration to what his subordinates think about the problem or the decision, and gives them no opportunity to participate in the decision-making process. He usually depends on his authority-role to obtain compliance.

2. *Manager "sells" decision:* As in style 1, the manager reaches the decision on his own. However, rather than just announcing it, he takes the additional step of trying to persuade his subordinates to accept it. Recognizing that subordinates may often resist arbitrary decisions, he seeks to reduce this resistance by such sales approaches as showing his staff how the decision will benefit them.

3. *Manager presents ideas and invites questions:* Again the manager has made his decision. At the time he presents this to his staff, he gives them the chance to get a fuller explanation of his thinking and his intentions. The question-and-answer session gives the subordinates an opportunity to express their opinions about the matter, and the manager an opportunity to get feedback as to their understanding, acceptance or lack of acceptance, and possible problems that may arise.

4. *Manager presents tentative decision subject to change:* Here is the first significant move toward more participative decision-making. The subordinates have some influence on the final decision. The manager has thought out the problem, examined the alternatives and come to a tentative conclusion. Before making his decision final, he presents his proposal to his people for their reaction and ideas. He listens to them, but still makes the final decision himself—either accepting or rejecting the views of the group.

5. *Manager presents problem, gets suggestions, makes decision:* Up to this point on the continuum, the manager has made some type of decision before bringing it to the group. Now the subordinates get their first chance to suggest solutions. The manager identifies the problem and asks the group for possible solutions. The purpose is to capitalize on the knowledge and experience of the men and women who are working closely with the matter under discussion. They may present a larger list of alternatives than the manager alone could do.

6. *Manager defines limits; asks group to make decision:* At this point the manager passes to the group the right to make the decisions. He, of course, is a member of the group and participates. Before doing so, he defines the problem to be solved and the parameters within which the decision is to be made. The group comes up with alternatives and then chooses among them. The manager acts only as a member of the group and, where necessary, as the coordinator or chairman.

7. *Manager permits subordinates to function within limits defined by superior:* This represents the extreme degree of democratic management. It rarely occurs in business situations, but is not unusual in professional and research groups where the manager is really "an equal among equals." In this leadership pattern the manager is no more important in the decision-making process than anyone else. There are no limits on what can be decided other than those imposed on the entire organization.

In any participative style of leadership the manager must expect to be held responsible by his superiors for the quality of the decision made, even though these decisions may have been made by the group. Managers who use more participative approaches should be ready to accept whatever risk is involved when they delegate decision-making power to their subordinates.

If the manager's confidence in the capabilities of his subordinates is justified, this risk is minimized, and the possibility of achieving better decisions, better implementation and a more dynamic and stimulating work environment is enhanced.

McGregor's Theory X and Theory Y

No discussion on leadership would be complete without a look at Douglas McGregor's famous theories of human behavior.

McGregor indicates that most management thinking is mistakenly based on the concept that people do not want to work, and that leaders can only get work from them by reward or punishment. This philosophy of leadership he called "Theory X." It holds:

1. Management is responsible for organizing the elements of productive enterprise—money, materials, machines, manpower —in the interests of meeting the company's goals.

2. With respect to people, this is a process of directing their efforts, motivating them, and controlling their actions and behavior to fit the needs of the organization.

3. Unless management intervenes, people would not cooperate and might even resist organizational needs. They must, therefore, be persuaded, rewarded, punished, controlled. This is management's task.

4. The average man is by nature indolent—he works as little as possible.

5. He lacks ambition, dislikes responsibility and prefers to have his bosses think for him.

6. He is self-centered and indifferent to organizational needs.

7. He is by nature resistant to change.

8. He is gullible, not very bright and the ready dupe of the charlatan and the demagogue.

The implied view of human nature may appear harsh, but in practice it underlies the predominant philosophy of employee relations. Theory X uses reward and punishment—the carrot and stick—as its main motivators. If a person is successful, he is given a reward in the form of a raise, a bonus, a promotion or a title. If he does not meet the standards set, he is punished—by losing his job, being transferred to a less important spot or being passed over for promotion.

McGregor proposes that this practice is not valid. It is based on false assumptions. The human being is much more than what Theory X supposes him to be. McGregor counterposes Theory X with Theory Y:

1. Management is responsible for organizing the elements of productive enterprise—money, materials, machines, manpower —in the interests of meeting the company's goals.

2. People are *not* by nature passive or resistant to organizational needs. They have become so only because of their experience in the business world.

3. All people have within them the motivation, the potential for development, the capacity for assuming responsibility, and the ability and willingness to direct their behavior toward organizational goals. Management does not create these traits but it can and should make it possible for people to recognize and develop these human characteristics in themselves.

4. The essential task of management is to arrange organizational conditions and methods of operation so that people can achieve their own goals best by directing their own efforts toward organizational objectives.

McGregor believes people will work because they want to work, and that they will work better if they have a say in how they are to meet their objectives. He feels that if workers are given a chance to decide their own methods and are allowed to use their full capacities, management will get the best results. These are the conditions indicated in the "Continuum of Leadership Behavior Chart" in the leadership styles nearer the right-hand side.*

Management by Objectives (MBO)

One popular leadership style which follows Theory Y and the participative approaches recommended by the behavioral scientists is "Management by Objectives." In this leadership style, the manager and the subordinate together determine the objectives that they wish to achieve in a specified period of time. Performance standards to measure these objectives are developed and committed to writing.

The subordinate is then given complete freedom to do all that he feels necessary to meet these objectives. The boss does not tell him *how* to accomplish his mission but leaves this entirely to the subordinate.

At regular intervals the manager and subordinate evaluate the progress of the program in light of the performance standards and judge how close they are to reaching the goal.

* Douglas McGregor, *The Human Side of Enterprise*. New York: McGraw-Hill, 1960.

The key factor in "management by objectives" is that it is a true participative form of leadership. The manager does not even determine the objectives alone—he does so in conjunction with the subordinate who is responsible for carrying them out. The subordinate is guided and motivated to develop reasonable goals that can be achieved and that will stretch his capabilities. He is then left alone to plan on how to reach the objectives. This takes hard work. Budgets, assembling of resources and all of the other aspects of management are taken into consideration. This type of management pays off in having committed managers working with committed subordinates in a highly motivated environment. This participative approach to management has been successful in many organizations.

However MBO is not a panacea. There are a number of problems in working with MBO which can negate its effectiveness if they are not carefully watched.

1. Lack of balanced planning: Too much emphasis on one part of the picture (for example, sales volume) might cause problems in other areas. Each manager is encouraged to set objectives for *his* department. Unless there is proper balance with other departments, there will be more problems developing than being solved.

2. Improperly trained subordinates: The sub-managers who are asked to set objectives must be thoroughly trained in all aspects of management.

3. Inadequate performance control systems: The success of any management program depends on controls. If performance standards can be measured and corrections made before the problems get out of hand, MBO will work effectively.

4. Overemphasis on quantitative factors: It is easy to measure such items as sales or production volume, costs, profits, etc. But it is often the intangibles that make the difference between success and failure. Methods of measuring how well the managers or sub-managers meet such objectives as employee morale, management development, public image, etc. are difficult to develop, and are therefore often overlooked or ignored.

Leadership Techniques

Managers select a style of leadership which fits their philosophy of management and their own personality. In any case they must always take into consideration the psychology of the people whom they are leading. Although generalizing about human attributes can be dangerous—people do differ from one another—there are some common grounds in getting the most out of one's subordinates. A good leader should try to understand what it is most people want from their managers.

1. *The need for recognition as an individual:* Every person likes to feel that others recognize him for his own qualities. If he is recognized as an individual by his associates, he gets that most satisfying and precious feeling of security in himself. Good managers try to learn about their people, their interests, likes and dislikes, etc. Dale Carnegie's first rule was to take an interest in other people. By taking a sincere interest in his subordinates, the manager has taken the first step toward becoming a better leader.

2. *Pride in work:* Most people have a basic drive to do, to make, to achieve or to improve their environment. Satisfaction of this drive gives one a sense of mastery. If a leader can give his staff a feeling of pride in their jobs, both effort and quality will go up. People without this feeling merely go through the motions of the job with no sense of responsibility for what they do.

A leader can help establish pride in work by:

. . . being proud of his job as a manager

. . . impressing his people with the achievements of the company and of the department which he heads.

. . . showing each person how his job is important to the accomplishment of the company's goals.

. . . always making his people feel that what they are doing is worthwhile and important.

3. *A sense of belonging:* People are happier and consequently more efficient and cooperative when they feel that they are part of a group—belong to a team, especially an effective and successful team. Experiments by behavioral scientists have shown that when a person identifies himself with the entire group, the group gains and the individual will work harder and be happier. Illustrations of group pride may be seen in the "esprit de corps" of a crack military unit, a close-knit athletic team or a successful sales force.

4. *Give people purpose.* All persons in an organization should know the objectives of the firm. It is not enough for them to know the objective of their own little job; they need to see how it all fits together. By bulletins, brochures, personal meetings and direct communication, the manager should let his staff know what they are aiming to accomplish and how well they are doing.

5. *Fair treatment is a must.* A person tends to compare the treatment he gets with that given to others. The man or woman who is always prompt dislikes seeing others getting away with constant tardiness. People respond emotionally, not rationally, to situations when their self-interest is in jeopardy. The need for fair play is deep-seated in the emotional makeup of human beings. Favoritism is the greatest of all demoralizers. It destroys the feeling of security in the non-favored.

6. *A real chance to be heard:* It is always effective to listen to a subordinate's gripes, grievances and complaints. Often there is no basis for them, but the fact that the subordinate feels that there is makes it important that they be heard.

The Easygoing vs. The Tough Supervisor

Two of the major problems of leadership are the manager who is too lenient and his counterpart, the supervisor who is hard-boiled.

The easygoing supervisor tries to please everybody. He is trusting to such a degree that so far as he is concerned everybody is always doing the right thing. Minor errors are over-looked, and the faults of his subordinates are ignored. When a reprimand is necessary, it is frequently put off again and again until the reason for it is forgotten. When it is finally adminis-tered, it is delivered so weakly that it is ineffective. Praise, how-ever, is so common that it too loses significance.

What is the result? The work of the staff becomes sloppy. There is no discipline and little esprit de corps.

Why will a manager be lenient and easygoing to the point where his department will suffer? Basically that can be traced to a deep-seated feeling of insecurity as to the manager's own ability. Insecure persons, to bolster their own egos, act to win approval from others. This weakness can be corrected by build-ing up confidence in the manager and by giving him training in self-development and management techniques.

Sometimes easygoing managers, recognizing the lack of con-trol in their departments, make abrupt about-faces and become tough. As this is not their natural manner, they soon revert to easygoing supervision. This seesawing from one approach to another is even more upsetting to his staff than either of his leadership styles. People tend to adjust to their managers, and it is important that style be consistent and that changes be made gradually.

The tough manager is more common than his opposite num-ber. Many persons given leadership responsibility for the first time assume they have to be tough and dogmatic. They crack the whip and take the attitude: "I am the boss!"

Tough supervision causes a good deal of resentment among the staff. Most workers and sub-managers feel they do not have to accept this treatment. This results in high turnover, absentee-ism and generally poor morale.

The tough supervisor is also an insecure person who hides his insecurity by his rough exterior. Again the answer is developing confidence and strength in the supervisor.

The good leader is neither a wishy-washy hail-fellow-well-met character nor a tyrant. He is neither ignored nor feared by his subordinates. The capable supervisor has inner confidence plus the respect of his staff. Tact in handling people will get and keep their cooperation.

A SIMPLE COMPARISON

The ineffective leader:	The effective leader:
Drives people	Guides people
Instills fear	Inspires enthusiasm
Says "Do"	Says "Let's Do"
Makes work drudgery	Makes work interesting
Relies upon authority	Relies upon cooperation
Says "I," "I," "I"	Says "We"

13

MOTIVATING
YOUR PEOPLE

A manager has the obligation of obtaining the best results from the combination of the resources that he manages. As people are the chief resource of management, motivating them to give their best efforts is a key to success as a manager.

Since the beginning of the modern industrial society, the major motivator used by companies has been money. By paying the workers and sub-managers wages or salaries for the work performed, management expected to get them to produce their best efforts. To encourage increased effort, salary increases were promised, promotions to higher paid jobs were offered and sometimes bonuses were given. The other side of this coin was the withholding of money if the worker did not produce what was expected of him. This might take the form of reduction in pay, failure to be promoted or be given increments in pay, or even, as a last resort, loss of the job itself with total elimination of income.

The basic philosophy behind using money as the major motivator of the work-force was the assumption that people work only for money. Indeed, the Biblical injunction that one must earn one's bread by the sweat of one's brow dominated motivational theory for centuries.

Both in the early days of the industrial revolution and, with more sophisticated modifications, in modern times, direct compensation for production carried the theme of money-motivation to its extreme point. Piece-work in the factory is a form of compensation by which the worker is directly compensated for his production. Salesmen's commissions too are a form of direct incentive, and variations on this type of incentive pay have been adapted to many other work situations. These devices are expected to provide a sound incentive for the worker to produce more; the more he produces, the more money he makes.

If money is the motivator that it is supposed to be, all of these direct incentive plans should be successful in motivating workers to do their best. Experience has shown, however, that money has only a limited value as a motivator. There is no doubt, of course, that money has an important effect on the behavior of workers, but studies by behavioral scientists have shown that money is not as strong a motivator as has usually been assumed.

Experience of production managers has indicated over and over again that just giving the worker an opportunity to earn more by producing more will *not* in fact motivate him to produce more. Sales managers cite countless examples of salesmen who could make considerably more income by working harder, longer or more effectively, but who do not do so. Money alone, then, is not what motivates them.

One reason for this lies in the relationship of the worker with his group. Most factory monetary incentive plans are unsuccessful because the workers do not want to be considered "rate-busters." The group almost always puts a "bogie" on production quotas. Anyone who exceeds this artificial productivity figure is considered a rate-buster and may be ostracized or in other ways made to feel uncomfortable.

The workers will usually meet the established rate, but even though it is possible (often easily) to increase production and make more money, they will not put in extra effort. Group pressure is more important to them than the extra money.

In non-factory situations, similar restrictions occur. In some companies the "eager beaver" is taken aside by his peers and told to take it easy.

Other reasons for the failure of money incentives to really motivate people to do more than necessary are psychological.

After reaching a certain financial level, many people look for other satisfactions in life—satisfactions that mean more to them than money.

In one factory the union negotiated a 20 percent raise for its members. When the raise went into effect, the company found an inordinate number of absences on Fridays or Mondays. The personnel manager asked several of the absentees about it and was told over and over again: "I'm now making in four days what I used to make in five, so if I don't feel like working on Friday, I'm still not losing any money." To these people the extra day off was more important than the extra money.

Commission salesmen often do the same thing. Once they have met their own money goals, they slow down or even stop working.

This does not mean that money should not be used in motivating people. It does mean that it should be used in conjunction with other motivators.

For some people, often people in the management positions in companies where decisions are made, money is indeed a powerful motivator. In providing motivators for them, money should certainly be considered.

One reason why the money-as-motivator myth survives is that monetary incentives become confused with a lot of other motives that have little or even nothing to do with money but are intertwined with it in the minds of the people.

Money's most obvious characteristic is that it is a symbol. Not only is it the means of purchasing what one needs or wants, but also it symbolizes every other value that people are motivated by. Money can represent achievement, prestige, power and security—all of which are major motivators.

To some people money and what it symbolizes dominate life. They make sacrifices, take risks and work long and hard, or apply great creativity and intelligence to their jobs—all for the money the job brings. To others, money has value only for meeting their minimum needs, and the opportunity to earn more by more production will be bypassed in favor of other pursuits.

The attitude of people toward money as a motivator may change over the course of their lives. Some younger people today have no money motivation, yet when they marry and start raising a family, their attitude changes and money becomes a prime motivator. In later years they may again find money no longer an incentive and look to other forces to stimulate their energies.

Frederick Herzberg and his associates in 1966 made a study of what motivates people. On the basis of this study, Herzberg developed his motivation-hygiene theory of worker satisfaction and dissatisfaction.

From his interviews with engineers and accountants in several firms, Herzberg came to the conclusion that certain factors that had been thought of to be motivators actually did little motivating, but were nonetheless essential to worker satisfaction. He called these "hygiene factors." He said that these factors, to the degree that they are absent, increase worker dissatisfaction with their jobs. When present, these factors serve to prevent dissatisfaction, even though they do not result in positive satisfaction and motivation. These factors reflect a need for the avoidance of unpleasantness and are related to the context of the job.

Among hygiene factors, which tend *not* to contribute to motivation but without which there would be considerable dissatisfaction, are salary, working conditions and interpersonal relationships.

If these factors do not motivate, what does? Herzberg defined *motivators* as those job factors which when present to a positive degree, positively increase satisfaction from work and motivate toward superior effort and performance. When absent, these factors do not necessarily lead to dissatisfaction. These factors usually reflect a need for personal growth and are, like the hygiene factors, related to the job.

Herzberg concluded that these motivators are achievement, recognition for achievement, the work itself, responsibility and advancement.

Most criticism of the Herzberg study concerned the place given to salary. Critics claimed that because the participants were accountants and engineers, the study was not a true picture of the entire work population. Perhaps production workers were more influenced by money and less by job satisfaction. Further studies by others tended to confirm the view that job satisfaction, particularly "the work itself," was a major motivator, and that money was only a hygiene factor. True, if the money were not there, and if people felt they were not being paid fairly, nothing would motivate them to work. However, if they were satisfied with the money, more money alone would not motivate them. At that point, the Herzberg motivators took over.*

Out of Herzberg's studies much of the work in job enlargement and job enrichment has developed. It is this new approach to work both at the factory and office-clerical levels that has been used in recent years to relieve the boredom of many jobs by making them more meaningful, and by doing so, to create an opportunity for the worker to obtain job satisfaction. This in turn will allow him to be creative, and so to be open to motivation from "the work itself."

Other types of intrinsic motivation used in many companies are perquisites which accompany many jobs. At one time employee-benefits programs—insurance, pensions, etc.—were installed to motivate employees. Today they are purely hygiene factors. Most workers expect them and are not motivated by them at all. The company car provided to some personnel (other than in sales departments where it is needed to perform the job) has had a motivating effect. But, like all perquisites of this type, it too is taken for granted after a while and loses its incentive value.

In many companies, the higher one moves up the corporate ladder, the more elaborate the office and the furniture provided. This does give one a sense of recognition which is a motivator—and perhaps fear of losing the new office acts as a negative motivator to keep one working.

Studies of what people seek on their jobs almost all show that these extrinsic factors have only limited value in real motivation. Yet we must always consider we are dealing with individual human beings, and that what motivates one person may have no effect at all on another. Some people really work best when

* Frederick Herzberg, *Work and the Nature of Man*. New York: World Publishing Co., 1966.

pressured by the fear of losing a possible promotion or even being fired. Others, faced with the threat of loss of promotion or job, will be demotivated and will not even try.

Many managers feel that "pep talks" and inspirational meetings will motivate their people. Some organizations have regular motivational meetings at which programs are dedicated to uplifting the spirits of the participants and inspiring them to do a more effective job. Films, tapes and often guest speakers are used, as well as readings of articles, poems and short quotes— all aimed at motivating the listeners.

Experience has shown that these do have some value—but only a limited value. A good number of people find these speeches and films stimulating; others gain nothing from them. However, the main problem with any extrinsic motivating program of this type is that it has only a short-term value. The participant leaves the meeting all excited about his hidden potential and how he can unleash it, but in a few days, sometimes a few hours, it has all been forgotten.

This is the real weakness of any extrinsic motivator. It does not have a long-range effect. It must be repeated over and over again, and even then eventually fails. The more exposure one has to such programs, the less effective they become, because the human mind becomes resistant to the same type of stimulus repeated again and again.

If extrinsic motivators have only a limited value, we must seek to develop intrinsic factors to really motivate our people. A churchgoer who does not sincerely believe in what his religion preaches will obtain little inspiration from the sermons he hears; however, if he is a true believer, he doesn't need sermons to inspire him. Management's goal is to help their people truly believe in their jobs and their companies.

Abraham Maslow, a noted psychologist, analyzed what human beings seek in their lives and developed what has been termed a "hierarchy of needs."

Maslow bases his theory on the principle that man is a wanting animal. As soon as one of his needs is satisfied, another appears in its place. A man will work hard to satisfy a need, but once it is satisfied, he will seek to fill a higher need.

Man's needs are organized in a series of levels. At the lowest level are his physiological needs—the need to survive. If a man has to concern himself about basic survival, no other need develops. When one is hungry, he has no interest in anything else. The person who has no bread does live by bread alone.

However, once a man eats regularly and adequately, hunger no longer is an important need. This also holds true for all the other physiological requirements—rest, shelter, warmth, etc.

Once these physiological needs are satisfied, once a man no longer has to concern himself with the basics of life, the next level of needs begins to dominate his behavior. These are called "safety needs," they make up the need to be protected against danger, threat and insecurity. In an industrial environment, such threats may be manifested in the arbitrary actions of a management which creates uncertainty in the minds of its employees and in unfair treatment, such as favoritism to others and discrimination against oneself. Unless the employee, whether worker or vice-president, has the conviction that he has "safety" in the job, other levels of motivation will not work.

The third level of Maslow's hierarchy relates to the social needs of human beings. When man's physiological and safety needs are satisfied, his social needs become important motivators of his behavior. These include belonging to a group, winning acceptance by others and giving and receiving friendship and love.

One of the early experiments in human relations, the Hawthorne studies made in the 1930's, showed that this feeling of belonging and acceptance by the work group was a major factor in high morale and increased worker productivity. Subsequent studies confirmed that the tightly knit, cohesive work group may be far more effective than the same number of individuals working on their own to achieve organizational goals.

This fact is often overlooked, intentionally ignored or even actively opposed by management. Perhaps fear of collusion among workers, of the organization of labor unions or of ganging up by groups of workers in opposition to management has caused this opposition. However, there is a natural urge for people

MASLOW'S HIERARCHY OF NEEDS

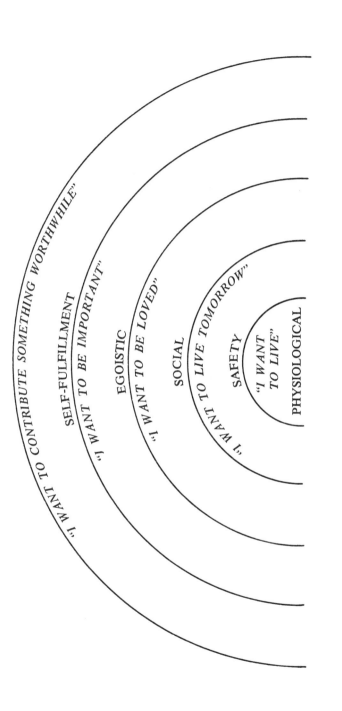

"I WANT TO CONTRIBUTE SOMETHING WORTHWHILE"

SELF-FULFILLMENT

"I WANT TO BE IMPORTANT"

EGOISTIC

"I WANT TO BE LOVED"

SOCIAL

"I WANT TO LIVE TOMORROW"

SAFETY

"I WANT
TO LIVE"

PHYSIOLOGICAL

to group together, and rather than oppose this, management would do better to encourage it. If the social needs are frustrated, the workers will become hostile and uncooperative. The fears of management will be realized as a *result* of its actions, not as a cause of it.

Egoistic needs—the need to be important—are very strong motivators, but they do not begin to take a place in the human being's thinking until his social needs are fulfilled. There are two kinds of ego needs. One type relates to one's self-esteem. This is the need for self-confidence, for independence, for achievement, for competence, for knowledge. The other type relates to one's reputation, one's need for status, for recognition, for appreciation, for the respect of one's peers.

Higher-level members of the corporate hierarchy find a great deal of opportunity to satisfy their ego needs in their work. Lower-ranking employees rarely can do so. In fact, the typical factory worker's job is so unsatisfying that there is no possibility for him to gain any ego satisfaction unless his job is completely restructured. Later in this chapter we will discuss this problem.

Maslow's highest level of need is the need for self-fulfillment or self-actualization. On this level we find the needs for realizing one's own highest potential and for being creative. To many that means contributing something worthwhile in their job, in their profession or in some other aspect of their life.

If a company can give its employees a vehicle through which to achieve this self-fulfillment, that might be the most effective motivator.

The climate of a company is determined by the manner in which top management approaches its human relations activities. If top management strongly believes in motivating their people by applying some of the concepts of the behavioral scientists, that belief will filter through the ranks of middle and lower management.

Now let us look at ways of implementing some of these theories in the day-to-day operation of a business organization. Many companies have applied the methods described here:

Decentralization: In chapter 8 we discussed the areas of decentralization and delegation. These techniques free people from close control and give them some freedom to direct their own activities. This is one way of enabling them to satisfy their egoistic needs.

Job enlargement: This approach is relatively recent and is aimed at making routine jobs more diverse and therefore more satisfying. It tends to expand job content. Instead of a worker's doing only one phase of the work, the job is enlarged so the worker may do his own inspection, make minor repairs on the work or equipment, select his own work methods, etc.

There are two types of job enlargement. Vertical job enlargement (sometimes called *job enrichment*) employs a great variety of skills. The employee becomes more involved in his work; he sets the pace and sequence of work where feasible; he assumes more responsibility, and may modify work methods. Horizontal job enlargement simply adds a larger number of somewhat similar tasks. For example, the assembler who previously put some nuts and bolts together, now assembles several components. This lengthens the job cycle, reduces the repetitiveness of the work and so may reduce the monotony.

Work hours: Some companies have experimented with flexible work hours. This may involve allowing workers to come in when they please and leave when they please, provided they put in a specific number of hours each week. Another variation is to require everybody to be at work during prime work hours (perhaps from 10 A.M. to 4 P.M.), but to allow a choice of starting and closing hours. Still another variation is the four-day, ten-hour per day work-week.

Participative decision making: When dealing with middle managers, first-line supervisors, administrative and professional personnel, many companies have been quite successful in obtaining a highly motivated team by using participative management. In this plan each of the persons who will be involved in carrying out a decision is asked to help make that decision.

The various techniques of participative leadership have been discussed in Chapter 12. Inasmuch as people do want to have more say in the matters which affect their jobs, participation in making decisions about their work has proved to be a significant tool in satisfying both ego and self-fulfillment needs.

A form of participative management which applies to production workers is the Scanlon Plan. As developed by Joseph Scanlon, it consists of two basic parts: 1. a wage formula or incentive and 2. a new form of suggestion system.

The wage formula is designed to distribute the gains of increased productivity proportionally among all employees involved. For example, a typical formula might be: For every one percent increase in productivity, there is a one percent increase in wages and salaries to all employees involved, including clerical force, salesmen, supervisors and even top management, as well as the production workers themselves.

The suggestion system works this way: In each department a production committee consisting of a representative of the union and the foreman is formed. They meet periodically to evaluate suggestions from the employees and to formulate general plans for improvement of productivity. The Scanlon Plan differs from the typical suggestion system in that instead of there being a reward for the individual who suggests the accepted idea, the group as a whole gains through a higher bonus whenever production is increased. The union takes an active part and individuals cooperate with each other in developing suggestions, instead of keeping their ideas to themselves.

In companies which use the Scanlon plan or variations on it, production has generally increased significantly. More and better suggestions have been made, higher profits and therefore higher wages and salaries have resulted, better relations have developed between management and the union, and there has been greater cooperation among work groups and between individuals and their supervisors.*

Utilization of this type of management-worker cooperation requires significant changes in the attitudes of both management and the union, high employee morale and excellent internal communications.

* Douglas McGregor, *The Human Side of Enterprise.* New York: McGraw-Hill, 1960.

Motivating Your People

Up to this point in this chapter we have discussed general methods of motivation. Now let us look at some of the specific things a manager can do to get the best work from his own subordinates.

It is important to know each of the people as individuals. The manager should not only know his staff as employees of the company but as human beings with their own goals, aspirations and ambitions. He should know how a man's family affects his work, both positively and negatively. He should know what aspects of the man's work and life give him the most satisfaction. Some people find their real challenges in outside activities, such as church, civic or social activities. Can some of the needs satisfied by these outlets be fulfilled through the company? Often high-potential employees are lost to an organization because their jobs are not challenging enough, and they channel their creativity and energies into outside activities.

In motivating people, it is important to recognize that people are different and seek different things from their work. No two people respond exactly alike to the same treatment, and often the same person will not respond in the same way at different times. Handling people requires not only an understanding of the psychology of human behavior, but also sensitivity to the emotions and moods of each individual.

Attention to the following guidelines will help managers assist their people to reach peak achievement:

1. Set clear, well-defined reasonable goals. Be sure that they are attainable and that the workers understand and accept them.

2. When discussing goals with subordinates, encourage them to offer ideas and suggestions and review with them the problems that may be encountered. Involve them. Let them share in creating ideas that relate to their goals.

3. Assure the staff that management believes in them and has confidence in them. The need for feeling secure and believed in is an important psychological need.

4. A manager should back up his people when necessary.

Public support of his people by a manager, particularly in the presence of others, gives the staff confidence that they do have the needed authority.

A manager who is genuinely interested in his people can implement these concepts if he will:

1. Get his people to see the end-results of purposeful, dedicated, consistent effort on their part, as it relates to their future and the advancement of their own careers.

2. Provide them with goal-oriented job descriptions.

3. Utilize incentive programs which will have purpose and meaning for them.

4. Show them how they fit into company goals and the related importance of their work.

5. Give them deserved praise and meaningful recognition. However, do not overdo praise, as the praise may then become meaningless. Praise should always be related to specific performance rather than consist of vague comments such as "You're doing OK."

6. Give them the opportunity to achieve. Achievement is in itself a great motivator.

7. Determine what their personal goals are and try to tie these in with the goals of the company.

8. Help them acquire and maintain a spirit of achievement by careful planning and organizing of efforts directed toward the attainment of meaningful results.

9. Help them set and achieve self-improvement goals. We will discuss some of the ways to accomplish this in the next chapter.

10. Acknowledging their accomplishments and publicly recognizing them will meet the key need for recognition and for feeling important.

11. Help them attain the conviction that they are accepted and approved by the company and by their bosses.

12. Show them how and why they are doing useful work.

13. Tell them about their progress. People are always concerned about this. More on this in the next chapter.

14. Listen with interest to their problems, their ideas and

their grievances. Even when these may appear to management to be trivial, they are important to the worker.

15. Show them how they can meet their goals through the company and by their own meritorious performance.

16. Never neglect them, ignore them, forget them. This is one of the worst mistakes a manager can make in handling people.

14

EMPLOYEE APPRAISAL
AND DEVELOPMENT

Human beings like to know how they are doing. Managers have an obligation to their people to keep them advised on their progress or lack of progress on the job. Traditionally bosses have taken the attitude "If I don't criticize you, you know you are doing OK." This is not enough. Modern management leaders build into their organizations a formal method of evaluating performance and counseling employees on their performance.

There are three principal reasons for having a formal evaluation program:

1. It provides a regular period for reviewing work-related behavior. Discussion of past deficiencies can lead to corrections and improved performance; discussions of areas in which the employee showed proficiency can reinforce these areas and help motivate him. Good counseling and coaching can give the employee recognition for past work and help him focus on future improvements.

2. A formal evaluation program provides helpful data for promotion decisions. It makes the evaluation process more objective and makes it easier to compare one employee with another.

3. The analysis can be used as a basis for wage or salary increases, bonuses and other financial incentives.

Formal Methods of Performance Evaluation

In establishing a formal evaluation system, there are four questions that must be considered: 1. Who shall do the evaluating? 2. What criteria should be used in the evaluation process? 3. Who should be evaluated? 4. What techniques should be used to assess the performance criteria chosen?

1. *Who should do the evaluating?* In most companies the subordinate is evaluated by his immediate superior. It is assumed that this person has the greatest opportunity to observe the subordinate's performance and will be able to interpret it in light of the organization's objectives.

Another approach is to use a rating committee of the managers who are most likely to have some contact with the employee. This could have the advantages of offsetting bias on the part of a single supervisor and giving additional scope to the total evaluation.

Some organizations use a peer evaluation, in which people working at the same level evaluate one another. This method, successfully used by the military in officer candidate schools, has limitations in the business world because peers are often either friends or rivals, and either relationship might distort the rating.

Another approach is the use of outside specialists, such as industrial psychologists to do the rating. Still another is allowing the individual to rate himself. Some firms use a combination of several approaches.

2. *What criteria should be used?* The criteria selected should reflect the main purpose of the evaluation. If the purpose is to improve job performance, the criteria should be performance-oriented. If social skills or personality are important on this or future jobs, these should be stressed.

3. *Who is to be evaluated?* Most firms rate all employees from the lowest work group to the people at managerial levels. The approaches used in dealing with workers and with managers are different, of course; the differences will be discussed later in this chapter.

4. *What techniques should be used?* The most widely used performance appraisal system is a graphic rating scale. The rater is asked to mark on a chart how he rates the individual on a series of traits. Such factors as quality of work, quantity of work, knowledge of the job, personal qualities such as cooperativeness, creativity, resourcefulness, etc., are rated. Usually the rater checks a box indicating his evaluation in each trait as excellent, good, satisfactory, fair or unsatisfactory. A sample of such a chart is shown opposite. The traits are assigned a point value and a score is computed for each employee. Usually the supervisor is also asked to explain briefly his overall view of the person being rated.

A more effective variation of the graphic rating scale is the use of a results approach rather than a trait approach. Instead of having the evaluator rate the worker on the basis of his opinion on such traits as quantity of work, initiative, creativity, etc., the rater focuses on specific results attained.

This is the basis of the Management-by-Objectives type of evaluation, but it is not limited to MBO. Results-based rating scales can be used in any type of situation where results are measurable. It is obviously more easily used when quantifiable factors are involved, such as sales volume or production units, but it is also useful in a variety of intangible areas, such as attainment of specific goals in management development, reaching personal goals, etc.

In a results-oriented evaluation system, the evaluator does not have to rely on his judgment of abstract traits, but can focus on what was expected from a subordinate and how close it came to being attained. The standards on which the person is measured are established in one period and measured in the next one. At that time new goals are developed to be used in the subsequent period.

Under an MBO system, the goals are developed according to the principles of Management by Objectives. In other systems the goals may be participatively set or may be unilaterally set by management. A combination of the two is most usual.

TRAIT ORIENTED EVALUATION FORM

PERFORMANCE APPRAISAL-WEEKLY-NON-EXEMPT PERSONNEL

NAME	EMPLOYEE NO.	BIRTH DATE	DATE EMPLOYED	
FSDS-FACILITY	DEPARTMENT	DEPT. SECT. EXP.	OCCUPATIONAL TITLE	OCCUPATION CODE

PERFORMANCE REVIEW PERIOD:
FROM   TO

PART 1. PERFORMANCE APPRAISAL SUMMARY
Summarize your judgement covering the overall performance of the Employee being rated, considering the individuals accomplishments in terms of relative importance of work performed.

APPRAISAL PROFILE

CODE	POINT RATE	RATING SCORE
(A) Inadequate	12-35	
(B) Below Requirements	36-59	
(C) Meets Requirements	60-83	
(D) Exceeds Requirements	84-96	
(E) Outstanding	97-108	

RATING FACTORS	A	B	C	D	E	TOTAL
1. Productivity Amount of work satisfactorily produced. Use of time & facilities. Comments _____	1 2 □ □	3 4 □ □	5 6 □ □	7 8 □ □	9 □	
2. Quality of Work Accuracy, neatness and thoroughness. Percent of error, rejection and rework. Comments _____	1 2 □ □	3 4 □ □	5 6 □ □	7 8 □ □	9 □	
3. Job Knowledge Knowledge of skills required to perform his job. Comments _____	1 2 □ □	3 4 □ □	5 6 □ □	7 8 □ □	9 □	
4. Sense of Responsibility Desire to meet schedules, carry out instructions, be on time with good attendance. Comments _____	1 2 □ □	3 4 □ □	5 6 □ □	7 8 □ □	9 □	
5. Personality Effect on others as a result of disposition, tact, enthusiam, sincerity and appearance. Ability to control emotions. Is not tempermental or dominating. Comments _____	1 2 □ □	3 4 □ □	5 6 □ □	7 8 □ □	9 □	
6. Effort & Initative Basic drive to get things done. Ambition & energy applied to job. Ability to take the lead in starting needed action. Comments _____	1 2 □ □	3 4 □ □	5 6 □ □	7 8 □ □	9 □	
7. Planning Ability Capability to plan & organize his work. Comments _____	1 2 □ □	3 4 □ □	5 6 □ □	7 8 □ □	9 □	
8. Judgement Ability to arrive at logical or rational decisions with due regard for timing, economics, etc. Comments _____	1 2 □ □	3 4 □ □	5 6 □ □	7 8 □ □	9 □	

RESULTS-ORIENTED EVALUATION FORM

PART I ANNUAL OBJECTIVES PLAN FOR DEVELOPMENT ACTION	PART II ANNUAL PERFORMANCE APPRAISAL
Quantitative Objectives	Quantitative Objectives
Qualitative Objectives	Qualitative Objectives
Personal Objectives	Personal Objectives

Another frequently used rating system is ranking. The evaluator is asked to rank employees from highest to lowest on each criterion of measurement. This is usually effective with smaller groups of workers. It is relatively easy to rank the top and bottom people on the scale, but very difficult to rate those in between.

A similar approach is paired comparisons. Each rated person's name is put on a card. Then the rater must compare each person in each measured trait with others in the group. Other systems use weighted scales, forced distributions and other mathematical methods to avoid some of the pitfalls of the simpler systems.

A different approach is the essay type of evaluation. The evaluator is asked to write a brief essay about the strong and weak points of the employee. Often this is geared to specific points on the rating chart, such as results obtained in specific aspects of the work: production, planning and organizing, direction, decision-making and other phases of the job. This type of evaluation is more commonly used with management and sub-management personnel than with rank-and-file workers.

A modification of the essay method is the "critical incident" technique. The supervisor records in a log critical incidents in the work of his subordinates—for example, an especially successful result of action taken by the employee, or a disastrous experience with a customer, etc. These critical incidents become the source for evaluating, coaching and developing employees. In this way, emphasis is placed on facts and actual experiences rather than on vague impressions.

Problems in Appraisal Techniques

The chief problem in any type of evaluation is that it depends on the skill of the appraiser for its success. If the evaluating supervisor or group of evaluators are not carefully trained to do the job, the system, no matter which one is used, becomes meaningless.

Some of the significant problems that arise in evaluation are:

The halo effect: This results from an overall assessment of the person based on overemphasis of one trait. For example, an employee is always punctual and never absent. This so impresses his supervisor that he rates all of his traits high, even though they may not be worthy of the rating.

Central tendency: Some evaluators rate all their personnel within a narrow range. They mark no one superior or unsatisfactory, but tend to mark all personnel down the middle of the rating form.

Recent-behavior emphasis: Supervisors may tend to forget past activity and rate the subordinate only on the basis of his behavior in the period most recent to the time of rating. This distorts the true evaluation. Often employees, knowing that rating time is approaching, are on their best behavior, just like children before Christmas.

Personal bias: As many people tend to be biased in favor of people like themselves and against people who are different, their evaluations may show this prejudice. A Swedish supervisor may, for example, rate his fellow-Swedes higher than Norwegians in the same department. Supervisors should be watched carefully to see if such biases are reflected in the ratings they give.

More Sophisticated Appraisal Methods

Field Review: In this method a specially trained member of the personnel department will go personally to each of the raters with a specific list of questions. The answers are recorded and then converted to a written analysis. The advantage of this is that relying on oral interviews rather than written forms elicits much more information, and that matters which the supervisor may be reluctant to put in writing are often uncovered. Too, the personnel specialist can maintain similar standards over a large number of interviews, and thus eliminate halo effects, biases and other problems often involved in ordinary evaluation processes. On the other hand, however, such procedures are time-consuming and expensive; they may only be practical for evaluating personnel in key positions or persons being considered for promotion or entry into a management development program.

Psychological Appraisal: In addition to evaluation of pure work factors by the individual's supervisor, some companies have an industrial psychologist assess the individual to determine what he can about the intellectual, emotional and motivational characteristics of the employee. On the basis of this study the psychologist prepares an analysis of these factors and predicts anticipated behavior under specific circumstances.

Such evaluations may be helpful when decisions are made concerning promotion or transfer because they provide information about the way the individual might be expected to work under conditions different from those with which he is familiar—conditions where the management has had the opportunity to observe him.

Assessment Centers: Some of the larger companies have developed a highly sophisticated and complex evaluation system in which individuals are brought to a special assessment center for two or three days for intensive observation, interview, testing and counseling.

A team of management specialists and psychologists make the evaluations. The ratings are compiled from a variety of sources. Personal history forms, interviews by management representatives, observed performance on a series of situational exercises, analyses of projective and other psychological tests, peer evaluations of other assessees, and personal impressions derived by the evaluators during the sessions, all are utilized as components of the final appraisal.

Among the techniques used to make the judgments are a series of situational exercises such as case studies, role playing, business games, in-basket performance, and leaderless group discussions. These techniques will be discussed in the section of this chapter on Management Development (page 230). For the moment, let us note that such games, especially when specifically tailored to fit the particular company's environment, have proved to be highly predictive in determining future management performance.

After the sessions, counseling meetings are held with each participant, and he is given an opportunity to discuss his future with the company and how the data developed at the assessment center can be applied to his self-development.

Using the Appraisal Systems for Career Development

In the early days of merit ratings, as appraisal programs were originally called, the rating was solely used for determining whether an employee should be given an increase in salary or a promotion, or even whether he should be retained on the job. Because of this, most companies used to keep the ratings secret. Employees rarely knew officially what their rating was.

Because companies now use personnel evaluation and appraisal as a means of helping the employee help himself in growing with the company, it has become the usual practice of most firms to discuss the evaluation with the employee.

Usually this task is the responsibility of the immediate supervisor. Unfortunately, most supervisors do not know how to convey this sort of information to their people, and because of its very nature, this is a sensitive area. Supervisors must be trained to know the best ways possible to tell their people about their evaluations without incurring resentment.

Norman Maier,* a specialist in the field of appraisal-interviewing, suggests three different approaches to telling the employee about his evaluation.

1. *The Tell and Sell Method:* The objective of this approach is to communicate the employee's evaluation to him as accurately as possible. The supervisor seeks to let the employee know how he is doing, to gain his acceptance of the evaluation and finally to get him to follow the plan outlined for his improvement.

To do this effectively, the supervisor requires considerable skill. He should be able to persuade the employee to change as indicated in the review, but an evaluation of this sort sometimes meets with resistance, or even hostility. If the subordinate dis-

* Norman R. F. Maier. *The Appraisal Interview.* New York: John Wiley & Sons, 1958.

guises his hostility, the supervisor may not recognize it and may assume the evaluation is accepted and will be acted upon.

The supervisor must learn to understand the motivations of his employees and tie in his evaluation with those motives. He can make improvement on the job more attractive to the employee by such extrinsic means as rewards for good work or threats of punishment for poor work or failure to correct undesirable behavior. In that situation, the new behavior is accepted not for its own sake but rather for the reward one gets for changing or out of fear of punishment if one does not change.

This limits the effectiveness of the *Tell and Sell* method. Often the subordinate accepts the evaluation, or at least says he does, in order to get out of the interview situation. After the conference, however, nothing happens.

The *Tell and Sell* method is useful with the type of employee who is inexperienced or insecure and wants the assurance of an authority figure. People who prefer authoritarian leadership are most able to profit from it. It is efficient under favorable circumstances, but there is a tendency for it to develop "yes-men," or worse, to be ignored. It provides little or no opportunity for upward communication, so the supervisor really never gets to know how much of his evaluation is accepted and what problems may arise as a result of it.

2. *The Tell and Listen Method:* A method which overcomes some of these problems is the *Tell and Listen* method. The idea here is to communicate the evaluation to the employee, and then let him respond to it. The first part of the interview covers the strengths and weaknesses as seen by the supervisor. The second part covers a thorough exploration of the subordinate's feelings about the evaluation.

The supervisor needs to develop certain skills to succeed in this approach. They are: *active listening*—accepting and trying to understand what the employee is really feeling and what his attitudes are; *making effective use of pauses*—he must be able to wait patiently for the other person to talk and not put words in his mouth; *reflecting feelings*—he should respond to the other person's feelings to show understanding; and last, *summarizing*

CAUSE AND EFFECT RELATIONS IN MAIER'S THREE TYPES OF APPRAISAL INTERVIEWS *

Method	Tell and sell	Tell and listen	Problem-solving
Role of interviewer	Judge	Judge	Helper
Objective	To communicate evaluation To persuade employee to improve	To communicate evaluation To release defensive feelings	To stimulate growth and development in employee
Assumptions	Employee desires to correct weaknesses if he knows them Any person can improve if he so chooses A superior is qualified to evaluate a subordinate	People will change if defensive feelings are removed	Growth can occur without correcting faults Discussing job problems leads to improved performance
Reactions	Defensive behavior suppressed Attempts to cover hostility	Defensive behavior expressed Employee feels accepted	Problem-solving behavior
Skills	Salesmanship Patience	Listening and reflecting feelings Summarizing	Listening and reflecting feelings Reflecting ideas Using exploratory questions Summarizing

feelings—to indicate progress, show understanding and emphasize certain points.

Such an interview minimizes hostility and resentment because the person being rated has a chance to express himself openly without pressure from his boss. He feels accepted and impor-tant; he is involved in solving his own problems, clarifying any misunderstandings between supervisor and subordinate, and learning from the interview. On the negative side, the employee may dominate the situation and so not benefit from the supervisor's evaluation at all. This method may also encourage the supervisor to overemphasize the desire to make his people like him-

* Ibid., p. 22.

Method	Tell and sell	Tell and listen	Problem-solving
Attitude	People profit from criticism and appreciate help	One can respect the feelings of others if one understands them	Discussion develops new ideas and mutual interests
Motivation	Use of positive or negative incentives or both (Extrinsic in that motivation is added to the job itself)	Resistance to change reduced Positive incentive (Extrinsic and some intrinsic motivation)	Increased freedom Increased responsibility (Intrinsic motivation in that interest is inherent in the task)
Gains	Success most probable when employee respects interviewer	Develops favorable attitude to superior which increases probability of success	Almost assured of improvement in some respect
Risks	Loss of loyalty Inhibition of independent judgment Face-saving problems created	Need for change may not be developed	Employee may lack ideas Change may be other than what superior had in mind
Values	Perpetuates existing practices and values	Permits interviewer to change his views in the light of employee's responses Some upward communication	Both learn since experience and views are pooled Change is facilitated

self rather than simply to improve productivity.

3. *The Problem-Solving Method*: Maier's third method of appraisal is the *Problem-Solving* method. This system takes the reviewer out of the role of judge of his employees and makes him a helper.

Unlike other approaches, this method makes no provision for communicating the appraisal per se. It makes the assumption that the mutual interest of both interviewer and subordinate is to improve the work being done. When the subordinate accepts the fact that the supervisor is there to help rather than criticize him, he is more willing to describe his difficulties. The real objective here is employee development, not praise and/or disapproval.

In this method the function of the supervisor is to discover the subordinate's interests, respond to them and help the employee examine himself and the job. He tries to forget his own viewpoint and tries to see the job as the employee sees it. If the employee's ideas seem impractical, the interviewer should ask questions to learn what the employee really means.

The supervisor does not try to solve the problems presented; he refrains from making suggestions of his own. Even when the employee's ideas are naive and superficial, he tries to make the employee work toward more effective answers, rather than superimpose his own thinking on the employee's.

This approach uses non-directive techniques such as listening, accepting and responding to feelings, just as the *Tell and Listen* method does. However, it goes one step further in that the leadership of the discussion rests with the subordinate rather than the interviewer.

The *Problem-Solving* approach motivates original thinking because it stimulates curiosity. It develops intrinsic motivation because the individual comes up with his own suggestions as to how he can do a better job and is therefore committed to them. He now feels he is in control of his own activity rather being told what he should do by others. This leads to greater effort to achieve the results desired and a strong feeling of job satisfaction when the effort is successful.

Manpower Training and Development

A logical follow-up of an employee appraisal is a program to help the employee develop along the lines that come out of the appraisal interview. This may mean intensive training by the supervisor in special aspects of the job, or special training in new areas that will help the employee acquire skills needed to perfect his work in the current job or to prepare for a better job, or it may mean recommendations for outside education for his long-run development.

Most companies today have some form of training program for both skill training and advancement preparation. They take the form of training and development programs inside the organization and utilization of outside sources in the community for a variety of educational services.

Skill training: The simplest type of training is teaching or reteaching the employee to perform the basic functions of his job. This applies to factory and clerical employees as well as to sales, administrative and supervisory personnel.

Most training of this type is done on the premises and is conducted by company personnel. The most common type of skill training is "on-the-job" training. Often such training is informal —the supervisor trains the worker as he performs the work. This can lead to problems in quality, as the new worker is likely to make errors, and to reduction in production, as a new worker is likely to be slow. However, a systematic approach to on-the-job training can reduce these problems considerably. During World War II, the War Manpower Commission developed, as part of its Training Within Industry (TWI) program, a highly effective method of skill training known as Job Instruction Training (JIT). This method was extremely successful in training the workers in war plants during the war and is still used today in training personnel in factories, offices and service organizations.

JOB INSTRUCTION TRAINING METHODS

First—here's what you must do to get ready to teach a job:

1. Decide what the learner must be taught in order to do the job efficiently, safely, economically and intelligently.
2. Have the right tools, equipment, supplies and material ready.
3. Have the work place properly arranged, just as the worker will be expected to keep it.

Then—you should instruct the learner by following four basic steps:

STEP I. PREPARATION (of the learner)
1. Put the learner at ease.
2. Find out what he already knows about the job.
3. Get him interested in the job and desirous of learning it.

STEP II. PRESENTATION (of the operations and knowledge)

1. *Tell, Show, Illustrate* and *Question* in order to put over the new knowledge and operations.
2. Instruct slowly, clearly, completely and patiently, one point at a time.
3. Check, question and repeat.
4. Make sure the learner really knows.

STEP III—PERFORMANCE TRY-OUT

1. Test learner by having him perform the job.
2. Ask questions beginning with *why, how, when* or *where.*
3. Observe performance, correct errors and repeat instructions if necessary.
4. Continue until you *know he knows.*

STEP IV—FOLLOW UP

1. Put the learner "on his own."
2. Check frequently to be sure he follows instructions.
3. Taper off extra supervision and close follow-up until he is qualified to work with normal supervision.

REMEMBER—If the learner hasn't learned, the teacher hasn't taught.

Another form of skill training is *vestibule training.* Rather than teach the trainee at the work place with all of the problems that involves, a simulated work environment is used. The worker is trained on machines and under conditions similar to those on the factory floor, but in a different location and without the pressures of a production situation. This method of training can be very expensive to develop and operate, and is not recommended unless a large number of trainees are involved.

Apprenticeship training fits into the pattern of skill training. This is the oldest type of training known and requires a long period of time (two to five years usually). It is used to train young people in various skills, and many companies have such programs to assure they will have skilled craftsmen in the future.

In addition to on-the-job programs in the company, a good number of firms utilize the facilities of local trade schools, community colleges and other schools to train their people.

Management development: Since the end of the Second World War most of the large companies and many smaller organizations have instituted management development programs. Today over one million managers and supervisors attend some form of management development activity each year.

Seminars, special conferences, individually tailored courses, regular college curricula, all play a part in management training. Companies send their people to outside courses such as the Dale Carnegie programs, American Management Association seminars and special conferences in professions or industries, as well as developing their own programs.

However, management development is not limited to taking courses. It starts with an on-the-job program geared to make the manager more effective in his present job as well as preparing him to move up the corporate ladder.

Coaching and Counseling: This is probably the most frequently used method of management training. The senior manager works with his subordinate and "shows him the ropes." A manager who is a good teacher can accomplish a great deal by good coaching. However, many managers are impatient or are too busy doing their jobs to give the necessary time and attention to working with subordinates. Another problem with the coaching method is the tendency of the manager to perpetuate his own concepts, which may not be the most effective, or may not fit the personality and management style of his subordinate. He also may consider his subordinate a rival and hesitate to develop his talents.

Project Assignments: Another technique of developing managers is to provide them with transitory experiences in areas other than their own specialty. This can be done by putting them in charge of projects which will expose them to a variety of experiences.

Rotation: This is more frequently used with new management trainees than with experienced managers. The trainee is assigned to a number of departments to give him some knowledge and experience in each.

The Training and Development Departments of the many companies and organizations that have their own management development programs use a number of techniques to help their people develop managerial skills.

Lectures and Conferences: Lectures by specialists are often used to keep people informed of the latest developments in various fields. Lectures are the least effective type of training, as people retain only a small part of what they hear in a lecture. The situation can be improved somewhat by the use of such training aids as charts, films, workbooks and demonstrations. Conferences which encourage participation by the conferees are more effective than straight lectures.

Case Studies: A problem is given in written form to a group. Enough detail is provided to enable the members of the group to analyze the problem and come up with alternatives to solve it. The group works together to reach a solution. The responses are criticized and discussed by the entire group and by the manager in charge of the program. This procedure is appropriate when participants are sufficiently knowledgeable in the subject areas involved. It is useful as a basis for development of the general principles that may be used in solving actual on-the-job problems. This technique—like role playing, business games, and in-basket exercises—is a situational exercise; the use of these methods as evaluation devices is discussed on page 221.

The Incident Process: This is a modification of the case study procedure. It attempts to simplify that method and bring it closer to reality. The class is given a brief written account of the incident to be studied. The total case is developed by means of a question-and-answer process. The leader supplies information only as the trainees ask for it. Each participant comes up with a solution. The group discusses these solutions, and may debate the validity of the various approaches to solving the problem. As these incidents are usually true situations, the leader then tells the group what actually happened and what the consequences were.

Role Playing: Individuals play the roles of parties involved in interpersonal situations. These may involve the relationship between a supervisor and his subordinate, between a salesman and a customer, or any other type of episode in which people must relate to others. Specific applications have included handling appraisal interviews, reprimands and other discipline problems, management-union negotiations, etc. After the role-playing session, sessions of criticism are held. In some instances the participants are asked to interchange the roles they have been playing, and the group is asked to compare the two approaches.

Business Games: This is a variation of the case method in which a case with a large number of variables is spread out over a period of time. Each competing team organizes itself, studies the available information and makes an initial set of decisions. Each decision period equals a unit of time—10 minutes may represent a day, a week, a month, etc. After the first decisions are submitted, the trainers calculate what would occur, usually with the aid of a computer. They feed this back to the teams. More decisions are made and the game continues. At the end, the trainers show each team how their management resulted in success or failure of the "company."

In-Basket Exercise: The participants are presented with a series of papers which might appear in their in-baskets on a typical day. They are asked to determine the priority they would assign to each item (memos, letters, telephone messages, etc.) and what action they would take on each one. This is particularly valuable in training managers in time management and in helping them evaluate real life situations they may face in their regular jobs. Each individual is given the opportunity to explain his reasons for his action and to compare it with those of the other participants.

In addition to these and many other individualized programs offered by organizations, correspondence courses and regular college graduate school programs are made available to managers who want to improve themselves or are being encouraged to take special training. Usually these courses are paid for by the company, either directly or by a tuition reimbursement program.

As real management development means self-development, all personnel who have the drive and desire to move ahead should be given every opportunity to learn the techniques and acquire the knowledge needed to help them meet their needs through growth in the company.

15

DEALING WITH
PEOPLE PROBLEMS

Even when the employee or subordinate manager is carefully selected and properly trained to do his job, the manager still must provide assistance in helping him accomplish his mission. This can be best achieved by using this four-step formula:

1. *Set up definite goals:* Unless the individual is fully aware of what management expects him to achieve, it is not likely that he will achieve it. The goals may be developed with the subordinates who are expected to carry them out. Usually a goal set participatively is more effective than an objective unilaterally set by senior management and dictated to the subordinate.

2. *Set and define the rules and limitations to observe in reaching these goals:* Unless the individual is given a clear understanding of what he can and cannot do in his efforts to meet the goals, he may not make the necessary plans and so fail to take the steps required to achieve the desired results.

3. *Determine and establish the method to achieve the goals:* It is often better to allow the people responsible for the operations to determine the methods they feel are most effective. The management team can and should be called upon for their expertise. However, the plan of action should come from the operating people, and they should be held responsible for it. Operating methods should be clearly laid out before starting the

operation, and management must make sure that both the operating team and the management are familiar with it.

4. *Follow up, control, and where needed, improve the methods:* Perhaps the greatest reason for failure to achieve desired results is failure to follow up. Without definite follow-up procedures to check and control results only partial success can be expected.

In order to ensure that the action taken leads to goal achievement, the manager should focus his attention on the expected results rather than on the methods used to achieve these results. This can be implemented by letting the staff know exactly what results they are expected to produce, what limitations, if any, are placed on their activity in achieving these results, and finally, the performance standards by which their performance will be measured.

All too often managers supervise subordinates by merely issuing directives, orders, instructions, policies, etc. In so doing, they simply tell their subordinates what to do and how to do it, but fail to tell them why it is important for the work to be performed satisfactorily—important not only to the company, but to their own personal careers.

Helping People Meet Management's Standards

If the performance standards are set cooperatively with the people involved, it is much easier to achieve the objectives set. When people voluntarily cooperate, management's job is made much easier.

The following chart helps illustrate this. The first box shows the basic prerequisites for effective leadership. The center of the chart indicates the major types of leadership activity that a manager can use and the last section indicates the major leadership functions of a manager.*

* W. H. Newman, C. E. Sumner, and E. K. Warren, *The Process of Management,* Englewood Cliffs, N.J.: Prentice-Hall, Inc., Third Edition, 1972, p. 501.

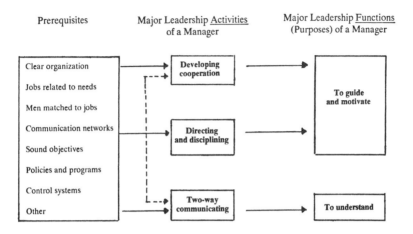

Prerequisites	Major Leadership <u>Activities</u> of a Manager	Major Leadership <u>Functions</u> (Purposes) of a Manager
Clear organization	**Developing cooperation**	**To guide and motivate**
Jobs related to needs		
Men matched to jobs		
Communication networks	**Directing and disciplining**	
Sound objectives		
Policies and programs		
Control systems	**Two-way communicating**	**To understand**
Other		

How can management develop a spirit of cooperation in its people? The desire to cooperate is usually emotional and is based largely on the feelings a subordinate has toward his boss and his company. If the subordinate believes that the company is a good place to work, that his treatment by management is usually fair and that his interests and goals are always taken into consideration, it is most likely his cooperation can be consistently maintained.

There are many ways of constructing organizations which will engender a higher degree of cooperation and a feeling of esprit de corps. Some of these are described below:

Building on-the-job satisfactions into the job calls for designing a job so as to provide the person who fills it with direct personal satisfaction through job enrichment or job enlargement and so a greater utilization of his capabilities. As noted in Chapter 13, this result can also be achieved by setting up committees and task-teams, and by decentralization and delegation.

Matching the person assigned to the job will also help to utilize his best abilities. Persons working on assignments well above their capabilities become discouraged and often defensive because they cannot meet their obligations. Persons working below their capabilities become frustrated, bored and unhappy.

Clarify the duties and corresponding authority of a person's job so he can develop pride in his work and gain status from it. Knowing what is expected of one, what results are anticipated from one's work, gives one a sense of security. Nothing is more disturbing to morale than not knowing what is expected from a job.

Good communications networks are essential. Each person should be provided with the information he needs promptly and accurately, so that his work can proceed smoothly and he can take pride in his accomplishment. Poor communication can only lead to confusion, frustration and negative attitudes toward meeting the organization's goals.

Sound objectives, too, are essential. Broad goals should be translated into specific aims that are meaningful to each employee. Reasonable levels of achievement should be agreed upon. Such specific goals can become the basis of a sense of cooperation, for achieving them gives the worker a significant feeling of accomplishment.

Policies and programs should be developed to cover the handling of repetitive problems. As we said earlier in this book, standard operating procedures do away with the necessity to make individual decisions on minor matters. This eases the performance tasks, gives the worker a sense of security and frees his mind to tackle the exceptions.

Balanced control systems can be designed in such a way as to minimize negative reaction to controls and provide constructive aid to persons in meeting their own goals. To do this, management must select the right criteria of performance, set reasonable standards, measure these standards reliably and provide prompt and direct feedback. A poorly designed system causes discontent and inhibits the development of voluntary cooperation.

Much has been written in management literature about how management should go about developing a good climate and high morale in the people it supervises. In other parts of this book, this problem has been touched upon in a variety of ways. Managing through people requires knowing what people expect from management. As this chapter concerns itself with "people problems," it may be helpful to restate some of the guidelines to dealing with people we have already presented:

1. Show sincere friendliness and approval. Simple courtesy is to be taken for granted. A subordinate seeks more than this. He is dependent upon his boss for all of his activities in the organization, and he needs assurance of approval. This can be shown by taking a personal interest in the subordinate, asking about his family and off-the-job activities, and letting him know that he is considered by his boss as a total person, not just a cog in the company machine.

2. Be consistent. A boss who is inconsistent causes his subordinates to feel insecure. On the other hand, circumstances do change, and patterns of behavior may have to be changed to meet them. If a change becomes necessary, the manager should let his subordinates know that a change is being made and what the reason for it is.

3. Be fair. Even more important than consistency in developing a spirit of cooperation is fairness. A boss who plays favorites will gain no cooperation from the non-favored persons in his group. Fairness does not necessarily mean that all people must be treated exactly alike, but it does mean that in making decisions about individuals all of the factors concerning the problem must be given proper weight, and the decision be equitable.

For example, Bill Taylor and Jud Falk are seriously hurt in the same automobile accident. Neither will be able to return to work for at least six months. The company lays Bill off with the right to reapply when he is able to work, but gives Jud an indefinite leave of absence with a guarantee that his job is waiting for him with no loss of seniority. Is this fair?

If we look at all the facts, we see that these actions are not as unfair as they seem at first. Bill Taylor has been with the company for only six months; Jud Falk has a twenty-year record with the firm. Under these circumstances, nobody in the company will consider this unfair treatment; indeed, if both had been treated alike, it would have been considered unfair.

4. Emphasize a desired action. Accentuate the positive. Instead of constantly calling attention to deficiencies in a subordinate's work, praise him for his accomplishments. The psychological school of operant conditioning teaches us that people learn more effectively if they are rewarded for their merits instead of being punished for their demerits. In business the subordinate should know just what he is expected to achieve, and when he succeeds in achieving what is expected of him, he should be praised. When he does more than is expected, he should be given special recognition.

5. Support your subordinates. Management should give its people all of the help they need to do the job properly. A subordinate should know that he can get help from his boss if and when he needs it. This builds a feeling of security and confidence in him.

But support means more than just giving aid when it is needed. It involves vigorous support for one's people in getting them better treatment from top management, standing up for them in interdepartmental disputes, seeing that all matters concerning them are handled effectively.

In addition, an effective supervisor supports his people with information. He keeps them advised on what is being planned and on any changes that may affect them.

6. Consult the staff on decisions. Whenever possible, let the facts of a situation determine what should be done rather than depend on the power of management to impose solutions. If a group of intelligent and dedicated workers are faced with a problem situation, they often come up with valid solutions.

7. Standard grievance procedures should be available. If good management techniques are used, major grievances should not develop. However, under any type of circumstances, problems arise that may take on major proportions in the mind of the aggrieved. Good management encourages the airing of these gripes, because if they are kept hidden, they fester in the minds of the subordinate and inhibit his desire to be cooperative. If

some type of procedure is established to enable employees to bring their grievances to the supervisor and expect immediate and fair treatment, this problem is alleviated. Inasmuch as many of these grievances may concern the subordinate's relationship with his immediate supervisor, some arrangement should be made for bypassing the immediate boss in these cases. In some companies personnel department specialists handle such problems; in others, more formalized grievance procedures, perhaps similar to those set up in union contracts, may be used. In any case, good supervisors try to solve such problems before they reach the stage where formal action has to be taken. For this type of grievance handling to be effective, managers must recognize that in order to keep the department's morale high, they must sometimes accept decisions which go against them, and not let that influence their attitude toward the person or persons who instituted the action.

8. Lastly, an easy flow of communication should exist between subordinates and managers at all times. (See Chapter 11.) Just as the supervisor lets his people know what he expects from them, so he should always know what they expect from him.

Analyzing Performance

Unfortunately it occasionally happens that a subordinate does not perform up to the standards expected. When this occurs, it is the responsibility of the manager to determine the cause and take corrective action.

The simplest solution may appear to be to terminate the employment of the subordinate and start over with a new person who is either better qualified or can be more effectively motivated to do the job efficiently.

But termination as a solution to personnel problems is too simplistic. It is not always possible, and even where it is possible, it may not be the best solution. After all, termination is the capital punishment of industrial life. It should be used with restraint, and every other possible solution should be explored before it is used.

Termination is costly. It is expensive to recruit, select and train a replacement. There may be a period of time before a replacement can be found and made productive. During this time the work will not be done, or the overtime work of others may be required. If a company terminates the employment of a number of people, its unemployment insurance rate will be increased.

In addition to the cost factors, termination causes morale problems within the company, especially if the terminated employee is popular with his peers. If a union is involved, the termination may cause grievance hearings and possible work stoppages. If the employee is a member of a minority group, he may claim his termination was due to discrimination, and the company will have to prove otherwise.

It is to the best interests of the company, then, to investigate the reasons for poor performance and try to correct the situation rather than fire the employee.

There are a large number of possible causes for poor performance. Some are individual matters—that is, they lie within the person concerned. Others are organizational—they develop from the actions or attitudes of the company or the manager himself.

Individual factors:

1. Insufficient capability to cope with the job: The employee may not have sufficient verbal skill, clerical aptitude, mechanical dexterity or some other major personal attribute that is essential for successful job performance. This reflects poor selection or placement of the individual. The best solution is to transfer the person to a job which can use the capabilities he possesses.

2. Lack of job knowledge: The individual has the capacity to learn the job, but has not been given adequate training. Often proper training can overcome this and make the worker more effective.

3. Emotional problems: Persons with emotional problems often express them in the way they do their jobs. Emotional problems range all the way from a temporary upsetting condition to deep-seated neuroses and even psychoses. The manager can do little about serious emotional illnesses other than

suggest that the employee seek professional help. He should be able to recognize that some emotional problem exists, for such problems can have severe impact on the level of work performance and result in large numbers of errors, inability to concentrate so that output is slowed, a tendency to be constantly engaged in controversy, and an inordinate number of gripes and complaints about the work or working conditions.

4. Individual motivation to work: One of the most common types of motivationally caused performance failure occurs when an individual wants something from his job but is unable to attain it. It may be recognition, social acceptance or other egoistic needs. If these needs cannot be met by his job, he may become demotivated and make no effort to perform effectively. Such people often leave the job and seek positions where their needs can be met. Others remain on the job, put in the hours, but do not really achieve anything.

Some persons have a low level of motivation and set very low work standards for themselves. They are meeting their own goals within their jobs, but the goals are so low that they do not reach the standards set by the company. Some of these people obtain their real needs-satisfaction from sources outside the company. They will do only what they minimally must do to keep their jobs, but give their all to their outside activities.

In other sections of this book we have discussed some of the ways to increase the level of motivation for people of this type and how to help people realize their goals through the organization (See Chapters 12 and 13).

5. Personal problems: Everybody is affected by problems which develop within their families and in their personal lives. Major problems, such as a death in the family, divorce, illness, trouble with children, etc., occur from time to time in the lives of employees of every company. Normally these are transitory situations, but on occasion a problem may affect the work of a normally excellent employee for a considerable period of time. Managers should be aware of these problems and be empathetic with the involved subordinates. Patience and sympathetic attention may carry them over the crisis and back to normal activity.

Company Factors

1. Ineffective management: Differences in managerial styles influence performance in different ways. Managers who are inconsiderate of their subordinates and managers who fail to provide structure often have low-producing staffs. Sometimes specific subordinates will produce well no matter how poor the manager, but more often the work of the department reflects the efficiency of the manager.

2. Unrealistic standards: Sometimes the standards or criteria set by management are out of line with what can realistically be expected. In this case the "failure" may only be in the mind of the too-demanding manager but not out of line with appropriately set goals.

3. Inadequate corrective action: Failure to perform may occur because the company does not take the proper corrective action. This may occur because the cost of corrective action may be higher than the management is willing to pay. The time required to restore or develop effective performance may be too long, or the management may determine that it would be more efficient to change the procedure completely.

4. Placement error: When the wrong person is assigned to a job, it is more likely than not he will fail. However, many assignments are made without real consideration of the qualifications of the participants. This often results from emphasis on such factors as seniority, arbitrary or random selection of people by supervisors for new assignments, etc. It may also occur because in assigning people to a job, managers give major emphasis to technical qualifications and often ignore the very important intangibles, such as intellectual, emotional, motivational or physical factors, which frequently are prime determinants in whether a person will succeed or fail.

5. Overpermissiveness: When a company is lax in enforcing its own policies and procedures, employees tend to take advantage of the situation and work less efficiently.

6. Excessive span of control: If a supervisor has too many people under his immediate command, he will not be able to deal with subordinates as individuals. The organizational struc-

ture should be so designed as to enable the manager to work effectively with each of his people, and to provide performance evaluation, guidance and support for all.

Corrective Procedures

Some of the methods managers can use to correct failures of performance are:

1. Transfers: A transfer involves shifting an employee from one job to another in the same grade level. Normally, it does not involve loss of increments in pay or changes in the level of position held. Workers or subordinate managers who do not have the necessary skills or background for a particular assignment but are basically satisfactory employees should be given the opportunity to transfer to a job in which they would be more adequately suited. This saves the employee for the company and gives him the chance to meet his own needs at a level and in a position where he has a better chance of success.

2. Promotion: There are countless cases of persons who are working in positions below their capabilities and are therefore failures. Persons with high potential and with the motivation to advance and achieve may often be salvaged by promotion to jobs which utilize their full capabilities.

3. Demotion: When a person is put in a position above his level of competence, he may be demoted to a job which he can handle more effectively. Demotion is not often used by companies because it is thought that a person who is demoted will be resentful and therefore uncooperative. However, it sometimes happens that an employee who has been successful in his original job is moved up to a higher job before he is ready for it. If it turns out he cannot cope with it, it is better for both the man and the company to return the worker to his former job or one similar to it. If this demotion is accompanied by proper counseling, it can be a favorable move for all concerned.

4. Punishment: Implied in all employer-employee relations is the threat that failure to perform will result in some form of pun-

ishment. These negative sanctions are often used indiscriminately and as a result lead to poor morale; instead of correcting the situation, they only aggravate it. When it is possible to improve a situation by positive action, that is usually more effective.

Sometimes the fear of punishment—especially when not justified—makes workers less productive rather than more productive. Managers should analyze the reasons for failure to produce. If poor productivity is caused by malingering, discipline by threat of punishment may be effective. However, if the lower productivity has other causes, correction of the cause is a more logical approach than discipline.

The most common method of using threat and punishment is informal. The supervisor speaks to the individuals involved (or to the entire unit, if applicable) and demands improved performance; he couples this demand with a threat of future managerial action if improvement does not occur.

If the individual (or group) does not improve, the manager must take some action. Often threats made are not followed through. Once the employees recognize this pattern, threats of punishment become useless.

5. Formal disciplinary action: In many companies a definite policy on disciplinary action is spelled out in the personnel manual and/or the union contract. This is usually implemented by a grievance procedure (especially when there is a labor union) so that claims of inequity can be adjudicated.

The mildest level of formal disciplinary action is an official warning. This may be used for such offenses as unexcused absenteeism, leaving the job without permission, slowing down production or other first offenses. The warning is prepared in writing and must be acknowledged by the employee.

The next level of discipline is suspension. This may be imposed for such offenses as disorderly conduct on the job and safety violations, and for second offenses where warnings have been given. Most companies do not as a rule suspend a worker for more than one week.

The ultimate punishment, of course, is discharge. This is invoked only in serious cases such as stealing or insubordination or after several official warnings or previous suspensions on other offenses.

How effective is this type of discipline? There is much controversy over whether punishment really corrects the problems it is meant to correct. Studies have shown that people who have been punished by warning or suspension frequently repeat their offense. Persons whose punishments have been reversed by arbitrators often commit the same offense again. But other studies have come up with opposite results. Most students of this subject are vague about results, saying only that punishment works for some types of people and some types of offenses, and not for others.

6. Personnel and psychological counseling: Some companies have instituted programs of psychological counseling to help employees who need help. Severe emotional problems are referred to outside psychotherapists. Company psychologists usually limit themselves to helping employees overcome short-term emotional disturbances. Many firms disagree with the policy of using a staff of psychologists of their own. That is often considered an invasion of the privacy of the employee; therapy is not the business of the company at all.

In recent years many companies have attempted to help employees who have alcohol or drug problems. Many companies will not hire people with problems of this sort, but as such problems are not always uncovered in advance, or may develop after employment, the company must decide whether to terminate or rehabilitate the employee. Some firms believe that a good employee can be salvaged from the alcohol or drug habit, and attempt to do so through organizations such as Alcoholics Anonymous, hospitals, clinics and similar groups.

Workers and subordinate managers can obtain significant assistance in overcoming work problems (as against personal problems) from their own bosses or from the personnel specialists in the company. Heart-to-heart talks between supervisor and subordinate often lead to solution of work problems and to a better relationship between the parties in the future.

Handling Individual Problems

One of the major responsibilities of any manager is handling problems which develop in his department. When faced with a personnel problem, it is important that the manager give it the same type of consideration he would give to any business problem. He should apply the systematic analysis technique to this.

There are three general steps in this process:

1. *Recognize the problem.* Does a problem really exist? If so, what is its nature? How is it manifested? Is morale low? Are there an unusual number of disciplinary actions required? Is production falling below standard? A vague feeling that something is not going right is not enough. Specific identification of the problem is necessary.

2. *Make an estimate of the situation.* Who is involved? What are the circumstances? Where and when does the problem occur?

Determine the cause. Why and how did the problem arise? Investigate the circumstances and ascertain the facts.

Consider all possible solutions. What can be done to correct the situation? Are there several alternatives to choose from? Usually a variety of choices exist.

3. *Evaluate the alternatives.* Compare the advantages and limitations of each.

Select the best possible solution. Then take action to implement your decision.

Let us examine this system with specific reference to an on-the-job situation: Alex Parker has been just barely getting in on time each day. Four out of five days he punches the clock seconds before the starting whistle. On the fifth day he is a few minutes late. The other men have nicknamed him "the minute man."

His supervisor has been annoyed by this pattern of behavior and has warned Parker he had better be on time and ready for work every day. After two weeks of cooperative promptness, Parker has again rushed in five minutes late. His supervisor now bawls him out and suspends him for three days (the appropriate discipline, according to company policy).

Later it is brought out that Parker's wife has been ill for some time, and he has had to get his children ready for school. This has caused his last-minute arrivals. After his warning, Parker had arranged to have a neighbor take the children to school. The day of his recent lateness the neighbor had become ill at the last minute, and he had had to take the children to school himself.

By not handling this problem in a systematic manner, the supervisor had made an inequitable decision causing hardship for Parker and, when the other men in the department heard the whole story, he caused poor morale and resentment in the department as a group.

When a violation of company rules occurs, or an employee requires correction in some aspect of his work or behavior, the manager must take some action. Inaction is the equivalent of condoning the violation or being lax in managing the department.

These guidelines will help a manager in his handling of disciplinary problems:

DO'S

1. Remember that maintenance of good discipline in his department is an integral part of the supervisor's job.

2. Before taking action, figure out logically not only what the problem is, but why it has happened.

3. Be certain the offending person knows what it is that has caused the concern. Give him or her a chance to explain his or her action. If an explanation is given, investigate it and determine if all the facts have been presented.

4. Give the offender a chance to make amends before taking disciplinary action.

5. Take action promptly. Delays in looking into the matter and in making a decision reduce the effectiveness of the action.

6. Make certain the action is sustained by the evidence and that all parties concerned know the reasons for the action.

DON'T'S

1. Don't suppose that disciplinary problems can be solved by ignoring them or by failing to take positive action.

2. Don't act when the supervisor or the offender is under the influence of strong emotions. Wait until the situation calms down.

3. Don't try to reform the incorrigible subordinate. However, if the supervisor feels that there are emotional problems that might be alleviated by counseling, this should be conveyed to the personnel department.

4. Don't take the easy way out by transferring a person who cannot do the job or is a personality problem unless the transfer is for the best interests of both the person and the company.

5. Don't reprimand a subordinate before others. This usually embarrasses the person, causes resentment and rarely corrects the situation. Any reprimand that is necessary should be given in private.

If the supervisor keeps in mind that "people problems" are solved not by emotional outbursts but by logical systematic approaches to the situation, the department will gain by higher morale, lower turnover and greater productivity.

PART V

Coordinating and Controlling

*Executive ability consists in
getting the right men in the
right places and keeping them
willingly at the top notch.*
            Herbert G. Stockwell

16

COORDINATION

In order for an organization to succeed in meeting its goals, it must be well balanced. Even at the department level, unless there is coordination among the various components of the organization, there is little chance of attaining the results desired.

It is management's responsibility to bring into balance the various aspects of the work and to coordinate the efforts of all persons involved in meeting the goals of the department or company to achieve maximum contribution from these efforts.

The manager accomplishes this by making appropriate decisions that take into account the interrelated activities and blending them for effective results. His job is to see that any aspect of the work which is at cross purposes with the goal accomplishment is avoided.

This overall area of management's job is called coordination —the first "co" in the acronym "PLORDI*CO*CO" which we have used to sum up management's function.

Coordination has been defined as the orderly synchronization of the efforts of a group to assure that those efforts are properly timed and are correct as to quantity and quality of work expected. Finally coordination involves directing the execution of these efforts so that they are unified and result in the effective accomplishment of a goal or set of goals.

There are three aspects of coordination that managers must keep in mind:

1. Coordination among the individuals in a group: If all the musicians in an orchestra played their notes correctly, they would be doing their jobs, but the result might be cacophony. When the conductor coordinates their efforts, the result is beautiful music. This is an example of coordination within a group. Each manager from the first-line supervisor to the chief executive officer has the responsibility of coordinating the work of the persons directly responsible to him.

2. Coordination among groups of an organization: Each department of a company must know what other departments are doing and must coordinate its actions with theirs. If the Sales Department plans to push the sale of a specific item, Manufacturing must be prepared to produce it, Purchasing must buy the needed raw materials, Accounting and Finance must make arrangements for funds to be available and set up collection procedures, etc., and Personnel must recruit people to make the goods.

3. Coordination among various organizations: In today's complex economy, businesses become dependent upon one another. Management must know what is going on in the world and how that affects the company's plans. If an energy crisis or a raw materials shortage develops, management in each company affected must coordinate its needs with others using the same materials and in accordance with the government regulations that concern it.

Coordination results from decisions made by managers in the execution of their jobs. When the managerial functions of planning, organizing, directing and controlling are performed properly, and adequate consideration is given to their interrelatedness, the results should be a well-balanced and integrated effort.

Coordination starts with planning. All plans must be interrelated and designed to fit in with the plans of all other aspects of the organization. Short-range and long-range plans should be integrated so that their respective objectives harmonize. It is not uncommon for short-range plans to be made which are in conflict with long-range goals. Companies may make these short-range plans as a matter of expediency in a particular situation, even though a more careful analysis of the concept in light of the long-range goals would have resulted in a different decision. Senior management must always be alert to this tendency on the part of subordinate managers, who are primarily interested in their own departments, and may either not be aware of the overall objective or choose to ignore it.

Coordination in the implementation of plans will be smoother if those persons who are to be responsible for carrying out the plans participate in the early stages of planning. If everybody knows what is planned, and has had a hand in developing the plan, there will be little difficulty in coordinating the activities of the people within the group.

Coordination should also be built into the organization structure. In setting up the departments, chain-of-command and line-and-staff relationships as a base for future coordination must be established. The exact place in the structure where any function or activity is assigned constitutes the very essence of coordination. It also determines the amount and extent of the coordination each unit will receive.

In the "directing" aspect of a manager's job, the importance of coordination is self-evident. In a small company the personalities of the management people play a big part in coordinative efforts. Because of the managers' intimate knowledge of the situation and the short lines of communication, there is an ease of coordination that is difficult to achieve in a larger organization. It is much simpler to achieve a balanced, coordinated effort when all parties know each other and work closely together. When this sort of relationship cannot be attained because of the size or complexity of an organization, the need for more formal means of coordination develops.

Finally, controlling has a direct bearing on coordination in that frequent evaluation of the progress of the work can be used to balance the efforts of each component of the organization.

Coordination exists in each phase of the manager's job and is the lubricant which makes all of the parts work smoothly together.

Kinds of Coordination

Vertical coordination: This term refers to coordinating the various levels within the organizational structure. It is usually achieved through the channels of command. The act of coordinating starts at the top of the pyramid: Manager M1 directly coordinates the work of his subordinate managers, Managers M2 and M3, and thus indirectly the work of their subordinates, and so on down the line.

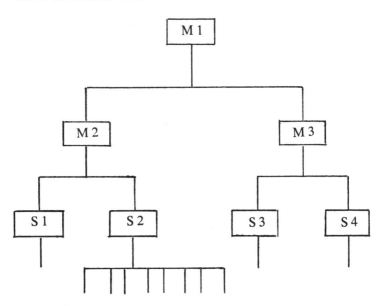

Horizontal coordination: This term concerns the activities within any level of the organization. In the preceding chart it would represent coordination between M2 and M3 and among the supervisors, S1, S2, S3 and S4.

Although in theory coordination among peers should be the function of the superordinate manager, in practice it depends to a great degree on the relationships among the peers. Coordination can be facilitated by good communications and provision for bypassing channels where necessary to achieve close working relationships.

The Use of Staff as Coordinators

Although good organizational structure may build coordination into the company's hierarchy and good planning establish coordinative systems within the standard operating procedure, many companies find it necessary to augment their coordination by other means.

The most frequently used coordinative device is the assignment of staff people to assist in synchronizing the activities of the sections or departments under the jurisdiction of their managers.

As discussed in a previous chapter, staff jobs may be either general or special. The generalist—for example, an administrative assistant or assistant to a senior manager—is often called upon to coordinate various activities.

The staff assistant is particularly helpful in horizontal communication and coordination. As he can deal with each of the subordinate managers as the representative of a higher ranking manager, he is able to convey information, obtain feedback, uncover problems, deal with personality conflicts and do anything needed to assure smooth operation.

The power of the staff assistant to compel action on the part of the subordinate managers depends on how much authority he has. In some cases he acts as an alter ego for his boss and so has considerable clout in dealing with problems. In most cases, however, he must depend on diplomacy and his own persuasiveness to achieve his goals.

At lower levels in an organization, some companies use persons with the title of "expeditor" to help coordinate diverse activities in their departments.

All coordination of this type is really extrinsic to the well-managed operation. With good organization and control, coordination should be so well constructed within the company that department heads and other managers can coordinate effectively without outside assistance.

Committees

Much business activity today is conducted by committees. These groups of executives or other personnel are also important in the coordinative process.

At a committee meeting different views can be unified and integrated. Prescribed courses of action can be outlined, the degree of coordination and cooperation required can be established, and procedures set to assure that all participants will abide by the decisions made.

Committee work also encourages participative management. At committee meetings all persons who will have a part in the implementation of the idea will be present, and this ensures that they will have a say in the decision. That will motivate them to work hard to achieve the goals set. Usually this means working closely with other people on the committee.

To some managers committees are the most effective coordinating tool they use. Other managers find committees more frustrating than helpful.

Committees are only as good as the members and their understanding of the goals that they are trying to meet. Unless all members are competent and work together, the meetings will waste the time of all participants and will probably work against coordination rather than for it.

Maintaining Balanced Operations

Because of the constant changes in circumstances that affect a business organization, managers must be alert to the ways in which outside conditions, internal personnel changes, and the dynamics of the business situation may disturb the balance of the company's operations.

A shift in managers in a department may bring into the picture a hard-hitting department head to replace one who was more pliant. The result might be a shift in the balance of power in that aspect of the company. Management must assure itself that the activities of other departments are not adversely affected by such changes.

The opening of a new plant, the introduction of a new product, the loss of a major contract—any of these may change the company's activities and upset the equilibrium.

Maintaining balance under these circumstances becomes more difficult. To accommodate these changes, management must constantly review its role and the relationships that exist between top management and the middle and lower ranks of management, as well as the horizontal relationships among the middle management personnel.

To keep its coordinative activities up to date and ensure the highest degree of coordination, management must:

1. Continually review the goals of the company and each component of the company. Determine the relative importance of these goals and direct its greatest effort toward realizing its most important goals. Reserve enough effort, however, to make satisfactory progress in attaining all goals, even when the major effort is directed toward the prime objective.

2. Review the sub-goals that are being worked on. Make sure that these are in line with the prime goals and that responsible managers see the relationship between the sub-goals and prime goals.

3. Keep all aspects of the business in balance. A major problem is that often managers play up their own pet projects instead of thinking about the total picture. This may not only defeat the prime goal, but discourage other managers, who feel that the personal whim of the boss has taken priority over what should be a major objective. A similar problem which often occurs is that a general manager who has risen from a specific area—for example, marketing, or an even more narrow specialty, product management of a specific product perhaps—now gives first thought to this narrow field, instead of to the total picture.

4. Keep alert for continuing improvements of methods. If methods become obsolete, if new ideas are not at least studied and considered, the company will fall behind. If the work of one department suffers because of this, it will reduce the effectiveness of the whole organization by throwing it off balance.

5. Set up a system that will enable the company to make regular analyses to ensure that a balanced operation is being maintained. Some of the Management Information Systems now in use in companies with computers can do this.

6. See that balance is maintained not only in the manager's immediate area of operation, but down the line as well. The farther down the structure an imbalance can be discovered, the easier it will be to solve the problem and bring the company back into balance before serious damage is done.

7. Use the control system to see that each job is producing the results expected; if it is not, see that corrective action is taken.

8. Make sure that all personnel are devoting their time to important phases of the work and not dissipating their efforts on unessentials.

All managers should have a clear understanding of their duties and the limits of their authority. One of the big headaches management often has is conflict over duties and authority. These should be written out clearly and provided to all parties concerned. If cooperation is to be attained (and coordination cannot exist without cooperation), intracompany conflict must be eliminated or at the least, minimized. Rivals will not only fail to cooperate, but may sabotage the entire effort.

A climate of cooperation should be established and maintained. This can be done by a sincere effort on management's part to work closely with all subordinate managers. Working closely includes participation in decision-making, opportunity to air ideas and gripes, fair treatment for all subordinates, and the maintaining of a high morale.

One of the most important parts of developing a climate of cooperation is establishing and maintaining an understanding of the mutual interdependence of departments for the achievement of the overall major goals and objectives of the entire organization. Because of the overemphasis in many companies on "the bottom line" for each department, particularly in decentralized operations, there has been an increasing tendency for each department to look out for its own interests even at the cost of sacrificing other units of the company.

All managers should be trained and retrained to think in terms of the entire company, rather than their parochial interests. This must be encouraged by management by giving them recognition, not only for what their own department accomplishes, but for the way department achievement fits in with the whole company's goals. For example, an engineering manager should be given credit for improving a manufacturing process which contributed to the profits of the production department, but caused his own department to go over budget. If this is not done, the department head would be encouraged to watch his own budget first, and the company's long-run interest second.

General management should make clear to all specialized departments what their interrelationships are and how they fit together. Frequent meetings of department heads to discuss overall goals help in this. A clearly written organizational chart with good job descriptions avoids misunderstandings and conflicts over who is responsible for the various aspects of the work.

Most important of all is to have the results expected from each manager clearly understood, and a clear picture drawn to show that these results can be attained only with the help, cooperation and support of all the other facets of the company's organization.

Coordination With External Forces

Many managerial decisions must take into account conditions and activities outside the company itself. In today's society no company can make decisions without considering the changes in the economy, the rules and regulations of government and the pressures of various groups in the community.

Managers must be familiar with these problems. They should know the laws concerning pollution control if they are involved in decisions where this may be a factor; they should be familiar with the equal employment laws if they deal with personnel, etc.

Decisions are affected, not only by these pressures, but by the national economy and the world economy, by improvements in technology and by the actions of suppliers, competitors and customers.

The methods to be used for achieving coordination with forces outside the company depend upon the situation. In dealing with government activities, managers must not only know the laws under which their businesses must operate, but the interpretations and rulings related to these laws. They must be able to anticipate changes and be aware of any actions by government or pressure groups to modify the rules and regulations. Many managers take active part in industry associations which lobby on matters concerning their industry.

The effect of consumer groups on management decisions is best exemplified in the automobile industry. Because of adverse publicity spearheaded by consumerists, the management of automobile manufacturers has had to change their attitudes on design, safety and other aspects of manufacturing and marketing their products. This has also been true in many other industries. Managers have to deal with representatives of various pressure groups and coordinate their plans so that they may achieve by voluntary action what might be forced on them by law in a less desirable manner. Management cannot ignore pressures of this kind and hope they will go away. Active relationships with community groups on matters that pertain to the company will pay off in better relations with the community, with customers and potential customers, and even with government.

Technology is another important external influence on the efforts of management. Survival of the enterprise may depend on keeping up with the latest technologies. This can be achieved in part by coordinating activities of the company with the work of the various technical societies. Many firms encourage their technical managers to take active roles in these associations.

They also keep up with research done by universities and in government-sponsored projects—often assisting in their financing or providing personnel or equipment to aid in research.

In nearly every case, a business depends for its success upon the activities of other enterprises. For that reason, coordination between a company and other organizations is not only common practice, but almost essential for growth or even survival. Production departments must have close relationships with suppliers or materials; shipping departments must be familiar with what is going on in the transportation industry. This necessary coordination is obtained through the application of knowledge of these industries and companies—knowledge obtained from studying directories, reports and catalogues, from attending meetings of trade associations, from personal contacts etc.

Coordination does not come into existence just because people work together. Specific efforts and considerations in making decisions are required to maintain coordination among the diverse groups that make up an enterprise, as well as with the outside forces that affect company activities.

Coordination cannot be forced. When pleas are made for people to cooperate and coordinate activities, all that results is lip service to the concept.

From the top to the bottom levels of the organization, an affirmative program must exist to develop coordination. It starts with the planning and permeates every aspect of the management process.

It will succeed only if there is a free flow of information throughout the organization, a thorough understanding of the goals to be achieved and a group of committed managers and employees who know the results that are desired and are motivated to cooperate with each other to achieve these results.

17

THE CONTROL
PROCESS

The ultimate step in management's responsibility is *control,*
symbolized by the last syllable in the acronym "PLORDI-
CO*CO.*" The primary objective of the control process is to
assure that what has actually occurred conforms as closely as
possible to what had been planned.

A systematic control process must include three steps: 1.
Performance standards 2. Comparison of actual results against
these standards and 3. Corrective action.

Setting Performance Standards

Performance standards must be established so all managers
will know just what is expected of them and how they will be
measured in achieving these standards.

To set performance standards which are meaningful, here is a
ten step approach:

1. Responsibility for the preparation of the standards rests
jointly with the individual who is to carry them out and the
manager who supervises his work.

2. In preparing to set up standards, the best way to start is
for the manager to take a sheet of paper and answer in writing
the question: "What conditions *should exist* at the end of the
period, if the individual for whom I am setting this standard

carries out his duties and performs to my complete satisfaction?" The subordinate should get his thinking started in the same way by asking, "What conditions *should exist* at the end of the period if my responsibilities are carried out to my satisfaction and to the satisfaction of the manager to whom I report?"

3. In their final form, performance standards should first identify the most important areas of matters for which the individual is personally accountable, the areas where attention should be focused. It helps to state the "as is" situation and to indicate the general objectives under each situation.

4. Manager and subordinate should then set out the *end-results* planned, or the conditions which should exist in order to discharge fully and capably each area of accountability and attain each objective in the period ahead. These end-results become the standards of performance to be expected.

5. End-results should not be generalities. They should be specific and tangible plans to be carried through: actions to be started, relationships with others to be established or improved, accomplishments, and progress to be made. These should be expressed in terms of quantity, quality, experience, time, service, etc., so that at the end of the period their attainment or lack of attainment can be readily ascertained.

6. End-results should briefly specify:

What specifically is to be done
How each job is to be accomplished
How the work is to be divided
How well the work is to be done
By whom each job is to be done
When each job is to be started and finished.

7. Since the standards of performance are to be used for analyzing the caliber of each individual's work and for evaluating his contribution, as well as for determining whether what has been planned has actually been done, the standards should be carefully thought out and agreed to by both manager and subordinate.

8. To keep performance standards within manageable limits and to make them as useful as possible, the statement of end-results should be limited to the most important ones to be accomplished during the period under consideration.

9. Include in performance standards not only the tangible factors, such as costs, production, sales, etc., but also such intangibles as development of subordinates, improvement of interpersonal relationships, self-development, etc.

10. Finally, show a comparison between what the "as is" situation looks like at the start of the period and what is expected by the end of the period in each area being measured.

Selecting Control Points

Management cannot wait until the end of a period to determine if things are going according to plan. To make sure that any trouble will be caught while it is forming, strategic control points must be established.

A control point should be set at a time when enough of the work should have been done to obtain a clear picture of the accomplishment to date. It may be set at a time just before a new aspect of the work is to be started, so that management can make sure that the work that has been completed is correct.

An example of setting control points may be taken from the Quality Control field. Before a production process commences, a control is set to determine if the preceding processes have been correctly completed. It is better of course to correct defects in the components before they are assembled than to have to check them out after the product is completed, looking for a defective part.

In a higher level management situation, a control point could be set at the end of a specific time period (for example, a month) to determine the status of each aspect of the work before the next period begins. If there are problems in timing, quality or any other aspect of the work, corrections can be made before it is too late.

The *exception principle* which was discussed in an earlier chapter is especially effective in the control-point approach.

Managers need only look for exceptions from the standards expected at each point and take appropriate action.

Often, in quantifiable matters, control points can be designed by dividing the figures for the year by the number of control points and making seasonal adjustments, if necessary. However in intangible end-results, it is very difficult to establish sub-results at intermediate points.

Evaluating Performance

Once the standards have been established and control points set, the manager has to determine what methods can be used to best evaluate how close performance comes to expectations.

Some of the techniques used are:

1. *Personal observation:* In most organizations the managers frequently visit various areas of the business under their jurisdiction to observe what is being done. They may check the quantity and quality of work, the attitude of employees and the general operations of the department. There is an advantage of seeing with one's own eyes what is going on, and a manager can often take quick action to correct problems right on the spot. Personal observation also gives a manager a better "feel" of the situation than any other control method. The subordinate managers and workers see the manager at the scene of operations, and it is helpful to their morale to know that there is interest in what they are doing; at the same time, it keeps them alert.

Personal observation is especially good for checking intangibles. There is probably no better way to check the morale of a group, to observe how employees are being trained and treated, and to maintain close liaison with subordinates.

On the other hand, personal observation has many disadvantages. It rarely provides accurate quantitative data. Information is acquired only in broad terms and is not precise. Another negative is that it is very time-consuming and takes the manager away from his other duties. An intangible disadvantage is that sometimes, instead of the personal visit's being interpreted by the workers as an interest in them, it may be considered "snooping" and a sign of mistrust. Another limitation is that direct contact at best is limited to seeing only a small sample of the personnel under the manager's jurisdiction and to seeing only random examples of the entire operation.

2. *Use of statistical data:* As it is usually impossible to observe everything personally, managers depend on various statistical data to know what is happening. This method may take the form of sampling, studies of computer printouts and other mathematical analyses.

Sampling is frequently used in such control situations as quality control, production control and other easily quantified areas. For example, the Save-a-Watt Electrical Products Co. keeps accurate records of the number of toggle switches produced in that department each day, and also of the number of switches which are rejected by the inspectors. As it is economically unfeasible to check every switch that is produced, they determine by mathematical means what proportion of the switches are rejected. If they determine that one out of every hundred fails to meet inspection standards, they may decide to take a random sample of one percent of production from each machine each hour for inspection. If the number of rejects in the sample exceeds the expected quota, a more detailed inspection will be made.

Statistical Probabilities may be useful in dealing with large-scale data. Whenever products are produced in large quantities, it is generally advantageous to use statistical probabilities to determine when the number of errors becomes large enough to warrant stopping production. It is usually too expensive to inspect every item, except in situations where the risk of failure of the product to function is very serious, as in the case of an electronic pacemaker, where failure would cause the death of the patient.

Management Information Systems (MIS) provide for a form of statistical observation of what is happening in a variety of situations. Computer information is given to managers rapidly, and a relatively quick check of the figures will tell the manager when any aspect of his operation is deviating from expectations.

Using Symptoms for Control

In cases where it is not possible to observe the specific problem directly, managers look for symptoms which might indicate problems that are developing. For example, employee morale is difficult to measure. Some companies keep statistics on turnover of employees, number of absences and tardinesses, number of grievances and suggestions submitted, and regard those as symptomatic of the morale of the group. When turnover, absences and grievances increase and suggestions decrease, they investigate further to determine why morale has fallen.

Written Reports

In most larger firms, the written report is the chief method of obtaining information on performance. Two types of written reports are used:

Periodic reports: These are the very commonly used daily, weekly, monthly, etc., reports that are required in most businesses. These reports are usually statistical in nature and are prepared on standard forms. The subordinate manager submits them at regular intervals to his boss. As they are standardized, it is easy to note how each aspect of the job is progressing and to compare it with expectations. Most report forms have provision for special comments so that superordinate management can understand the reasons for any deviations. Most periodic reports are quantitative and cover routine matters. Occasionally companies require periodic narrative reports to cover aspects of the work which are not easily quantified.

A major negative aspect of periodic reports is that they often cover so much material that it is impossible for the reader to absorb it all. To overcome this difficulty, summaries should be prepared which point out the major factors—good and bad— about the matters in the report.

Timeliness is important in all reports used for the measurement of performance. Too long a delay in obtaining the information may make it difficult to correct a problem before it becomes too serious.

Often managers have so many reports to complete that they tend to become careless about them. Many reports are not really necessary, or have outlived their usefulness, but are still required. All reports should be examined periodically to see if they are still valuable. Often daily reports are required when a weekly report would be adequate.

Special reports: In addition to the regular periodic reports, many situations can only be controlled by special reports. These usually cover specific situations such as reports on recommendations for changes in methods, purchase of new equipment, introduction of a new personnel policy, etc. Follow-up reports on non-routine matters usually take the form of special studies. In the final chapter of this book, we will take a close look at how a manager might write an effective report.

Comparing Performance with Standards

Most periodic report forms provide for a comparison of the standard (i.e. result expected) with actual performance. Most managers have a definite concept of what tolerance will be acceptable in variations from the standard. This is a matter of executive judgment. Only a person who is familiar with the situation can determine if a five percent fall-off in production is permissible in one instance, while even a one percent deviation may be critical in another. Even these factors may change from time to time depending upon circumstances. The manager should have the authority and flexibility to analyze, evaluate and judge the results as a part of the control process.

Here again written reports can be of great help. If the report requires the writer to point out the deviations, explain the reason, if he knows it, and make suggestions for correction, it will help the senior manager make the necessary decisions and encourage the subordinate manager to think out his problems and present concrete suggestions to his boss.

The controlling step of comparing performance with standards should be taken as close to the point of performance as possible. As much of the correction procedure as can be should be carried out (or at least recommended) by the line-supervisor in direct charge of the department. Where higher authority is required, the information should be forwarded promptly up the line and the decision returned to the operating manager as soon as possible.

Corrective Action

Using the exception principle, managers will focus on deviations rather than on the entire problem. As soon as possible, the manager should investigate the reasons for a deviation and decide how to overcome it.

This may involve a re-study of the original plan to determine whether the fault lay in the plan or in the execution of it. A well-known men's toiletries manufacturer introduced a new after-shave lotion and planned for production in time for the Christmas season. The first feedback reports showed a much lower sales volume than the original plan anticipated. Was the fault in the sales effort? distribution? merchandising? Investigation showed that the original plan was based on an overly optimistic sales forecast. A quick correction in this enabled the firm to cut back production before they were overstocked with inventory.

Perhaps the reason for a particular deviation lies in the implementation of the plan. There may be a problem in obtaining raw materials, labor or equipment, or the deviation may be due to inefficiency of management or low morale among the workers. A careful evaluation must be made. Guesses should be substantiated by studying the facts. Many deviations are easily corrected; others require a complete overhauling of an operation.

In determining what the deviation really means, one must distinguish between obvious and more subtle problems. An easily understood deviation from expectations might be a sudden increase in cost of raw materials which reduces significantly the profits anticipated for an item. Corrective action might include substituting a cheaper raw material, raising the price to the consumer, or absorbing the added costs for this item and making it up by adjustments in other items sold.

A less obvious deviation might be a reduction in sales of a certain item. The cause of the reduction may appear to be poor economic conditions, but a study of the facts may show that a competitor's sales have not decreased. Further analysis might disclose a variety of reasons for the fall in sales, such as increase of the competitor's advertising, overemphasis of other product lines by the company's own salesmen, poor quality of product or other internal reasons which could be corrected.

Too often decisions are made on the basis of the manager's hunch about a situation. Unless this is verified by careful analysis, it can be very costly to the company. Hunches sometimes are right, but good management cannot fly by the seat of its pants. A real analysis must be made.

The cause of a deviation is called the "critical factor"—that means it is the one thing that must be changed or corrected before the problem can be eliminated. This critical factor is often elusive. One must use careful and deep analysis to locate and identify it.

Managers must probe by asking themselves such questions as:

"How did this situation come to be?"

"Is this the complete situation or is it part of a larger problem?"

"Is the deviation a symptom of deeper trouble?"

"Where are the roots from which this problem developed?"

"If the obvious deviation is corrected, will the problem be solved?"

To find the answers to these questions, managers should use the techniques of problem analysis discussed earlier in this book. (Chapter 5). Managers should not hesitate to call on experts in the technical areas involved if they are available in the company, and should if necessary obtain outside advice. Just as a medical doctor will call on specialists to help diagnose or confirm a diagnosis, a good manager will not depend entirely on his own judgment in complex cases. If the problem concerns manu-facturing productivity, an industrial engineer may be helpful in analysing technical causes, if any; a personnel specialist might determine if there is a problem of motivation or of some aspect of human relations.

Taking the Corrective Action

Corrective action should be put into effect by the manager who has direct authority over the actual performance. He should be given the support he needs by top management. Unless this backing exists, subordinate management will not be able to make the changes that are needed to effect the action.

It is best to assign individual responsibility for correcting problems. Holding a particular manager accountable for the expected results is one of the best means of achieving them. This should be made a positive rather than a negative factor. To obtain good results it is better to accentuate the potential reward and recognition for doing a good job than to emphasize the penalty for failure. Too often accountability is equated with blame rather than with credit.

The focus of corrective action should be the results expected. The measure of success will rest on the attainment of these results.

The final step in correcting the deviation is to test the solu-tions suggested to make sure they do indeed correct the prob-lem itself, rather than just alleviate the symptoms. Feedback should be obtained as soon after the corrections are implemented as possible, to measure the new figures against expected results. Do not wait until the next reporting period. Keep checking regularly. If the desired results are not being reached, the good manager must step in once again and start the process from the beginning, going on until a satisfactory solution is found.

Budgetary Controls

One of the common techniques used by management for con-trolling is the budget. In the discussion of the budget in Chapter

6, methods of setting budgets were analyzed. One of the uses of the budget is planning—that is, expressing goals as targets segregated by specific activity and covering a definite period of time. The use of these budget targets for controlling is a natural follow-up.

Budgetary control is the process of finding out what has been done and comparing these results with the corresponding budget data. In this sense the budget becomes the "should be" phase of the control system.

Actual performance is reviewed against the budget at regular intervals, and variances are analyzed. It is the responsibility of the budget director or other designated manager to review these figures with the department heads and use the information to assist in pointing out problem areas.

This is usually done by means of the same type of reports discussed earlier in this chapter, but instead of goals listed in different forms, goals are now expressed in budgetary terms.

Good budgetary controls utilize a systematic reporting system so that responsible managers can be kept informed. Reports are issued regularly and as often as the situation warrants. Information is kept timely, as long delay lessens the viability of the information. It is particularly effective if the report includes comparisons with previous (comparable) periods as well as with the specific goals for the current period.

Budgets may be created separately for each specific department, or they can be developed for the entire organization. They may cover a single field, such as sales or production, or they may cover income and expenses for the entire company.

Budgetary control helps to provide the management with an overall view, an all-inclusive look at the organization. It helps put all activities in proper perspective so the manager can see how any one aspect of the operation meshes with what is being done in all other areas.

Some of the other advantages of using budgets for control are that they help focus on the expenditures and let management know if too much or too little is being spent on any phase of the work. A budget solidifies the goals by quantifying them and enabling the manager to have a better understanding of the results expected. It shows up weaknesses in the organization, including structural defects, inefficiency of managers and faults in the planning.

On the negative side, budgets can be dangerous as a control device because they often emphasize the factors that are easiest to observe—the tangibles—and do not bring out intangible problems. For example, the cost of customer service may be shown in the budget, but not the quality of the service given.

Another danger is that the budget may spotlight symptoms which may be mistaken for the basic problem. We become so absorbed in the numbers that we fail to probe what lies behind them. If the advertising costs are higher than expected in relation to sales, we may cut down on cost of advertising rather than examine our ads to see if the answer is the content or placement of the ad rather than its cost.

Another danger is that a company may go through the form of budgetary control without real meaning. The budgets are prepared routinely and mechanically. No real thought is given to how to improve the operation. The budget in that case is no more than a piece of paper which may be so worthless as to be more of a handicap than a help in control.

No matter how small a company may be, the use of a budget as a planning and control device can be useful. Reviewing what is expected on a regular basis and comparing that with what has actually happened should be required of all managers at all levels. If the budget is a live, dynamic tool instead of a series of meaningless figures on a chart nobody looks at, it can become a significant means by which the manager of a company or a part of a company can run a well-balanced and profitable operation.

18

THE HUMAN ASPECTS
OF CONTROL

In managing through people we must always keep in mind the probable reactions of the people concerned to managerial actions. As control is a highly sensitive area, there is a strong likelihood that there may be some resistance to it on the part of the people being controlled.

In order for controls to be effective, the behavior of the people involved has to change. The only purpose of control is to ensure that if goals are not being met, changes will be made, and that the behavior of the persons—managers or workers—who are not meeting the goals will be adjusted so that the job will be accomplished.

Many factors influence the reaction of persons to controls. Among them are the way they feel toward the company and specifically toward the immediate supervisor, whether or not they like their work, the opportunities in the organization for expressing one's feelings and their degree of participation in setting the goals and implementing the operation.

Most controls are disliked. People generally feel ill at ease with any action which circumscribes their activities, and particularly so if such actions can lead to discipline, affect their future with the organization or force them to change their ways of doing things.

The word "control" itself has negative connotations in the minds of most people. People being "controlled" look at control as a downward police action carried on by supervisors rather than as an effort on the part of management to assist them. The records that are used for control purposes frequently appear to be signs of a lack of accomplishment rather than a means of indicating trends.

A frequent complaint about control systems is that they seem machinelike to those being controlled. They view the control system as a mechanical monster that monitors performance and imagine all mistakes are reported and the reports sent on to the boss, who is anxiously looking for negative evidence or deviations from established norms.

Performance standards are often looked upon as unclear and unfair, as being imposed upon the worker by the management, which does not really understand the problems the worker faces. People do not understand the control system. They look upon it as a villain—they do not accept it as a means to help them grow and be successful.

Let us examine these and some other reasons why people object to controls.

Failure to Accept Objectives

A common problem in management is finding that the people engaged in a job have no interest in accomplishing the objective set for them. They may see no real value in it for themselves, or they may feel it is not important enough to take trouble over.

Barbara Collins is the Atlanta sales representative for Sweet Sixteen Cosmetics. Recently she received a memo from her boss in New York changing her sales goals from emphasis on department store sales to variety stores. Collins has worked hard building contacts in the department stores and now feels she has to start all over. She disagrees with the judgment that the variety stores are a better outlet for the product line she carries, and considers the decision to be arbitrary, unreasonable and basically unfair to her.

Can the company depend on her full cooperation? She does not accept the objectives, so the results will be less than expected; the controls will show considerable deviation, and Collins's boss will be irritated with her.

This situation could have been avoided if Collins had been asked to participate in the change of objectives, if the company had explained the reasons for suggesting the change, and perhaps modified the objective on the basis of suggestions made by Collins.

All this might have been done in the first place if management had been more sensitive to the ideas, feelings and needs of the operating people. Collins believed she was unfairly treated not only because she had not been consulted, but also because much of the work she had accomplished in building contacts with department-store buyers was now being ignored, and the time and energy she had spent had been wasted. She was emotionally involved in this project because her own ego had been bolstered by selling a "prestige" line to department stores, and now this assignment was being downgraded. Management should have considered her feelings and helped her overcome the sense of deflation by appealing to other ego needs she had, such as her desire to earn more money, to be associated with a product with wider distribution, and perhaps thinking of her line as "the top line in the variety store" instead of the lowest priced cosmetic in the department store.

In setting objectives and controls, the manager should never overlook the personal needs and social pressures of the subordinate. In fact, in any situation involving people, feelings and attitudes must always be considered.

As frequently stated in other parts of this book, if the subordinates participate in the setting of objectives, there is more likelihood that these objectives will be understood, accepted and worked at.

Feelings That the Performance Standards Are Unreasonable

Often a person may agree with the objective but be unhappy about the control because he feels the performance standard is too high. This is often the case in situations where there are frequent changes in standards. Joe Pitt has had his job reevaluated three times during the past year. Each time management has increased his quota. Joe accepted the first change because he realized he could readily perform at the increased rate, but he felt the other two changes were unreasonable—a "speed-up" technique which he resented.

Managers slough off such objections on the ground that workers always feel they are being pushed too hard; they feel most workers do not work up to capacity. Whether or not this is true, the worker whose quota is raised feels he is being treated unfairly. The setting of unreasonable standards, whether at the factory level, in sales quotas, or in profit goals for the manager of a unit, can only lead to dissatisfaction, failure to try to meet the goals and ultimate loss of productivity. The manager should work closely with his people in setting performance andards Where objective criteria have been used in establishing the standards, all parties should be shown how the criteria were established and be given the chance to express their ideas and feelings about them.

The Effect of Social Pressures

Group pressures operate both for and against management. A member of a group is usually more anxious to be accepted and approved by his group than by management. Successful managers are able to integrate the need for group approval with the goals of management. This takes great skill and understanding, but it can be the key to success.

The conflict between group pressure and management is more pronounced at the lower levels. Factory workers tend to follow the informal leader in preference to the foreman; clerks and office workers may gang up against the office manager. However, the social pressures of professional and management personnel are more likely to be supportive of management. If these persons believe that the control system is equitable, they will put the pressure of their group behind management in trying to achieve the goals.

Other groups within the organization may be neutral or unpredictable in their approach toward controls. Management must keep alert to group thinking and attitudes so that it can take the necessary steps to gain group support when that is possible, or overcome resistance where that is necessary.

Gaining Acceptance of Controls

As the real purpose of control includes the assistance of all persons concerned with the operation in meeting the goals, the persons involved must be constantly made aware of how they will benefit by adhering to management objectives. Among the points management should consider in this matter are:

1. Be aware of personnel needs and social pressures. The best controls have a motivating effect. They stimulate in the employee a desire to meet the performance standards. Management should recognize this and work with their people to help them meet their own needs through the goals set forth. If the persons concerned believed control standards are fair and necessary, they will give the support needed to meet those standards. Support of the employees as individuals and in the groups within which they function is essential to the effectiveness of the program.

2. Develop mutual interest in achieving the objectives. Control efforts are facilitated when each member of the organization knows the major objectives and is thoroughly familiar with the intermediate objectives of his own section or unit. When every employee knows what is expected of him, knows the reasons for these expectations and what benefits he will derive from reaching these objectives, he will be more likely to give the goals his full support and accept the controls established by management.

3. Explain control measurements used. Both rank-and-file and management personnel should understand how the performance standards have been set and what measurements are used to determine whether they are being met. Standards are best set cooperatively, and changes in the performance standards should not be undertaken without giving the concerned personnel a chance to participate in the decision.

4. Take into account special factors: If local conditions or special problems relating to a special situation develop, some flexibility should be allowed in the controls. However, if the control system is to be meaningful, standards should not be too easy to change. One good system which is equitable to all is to build in automatic changes of standards when certain specific changes in conditions occur. For example, sales quotas could be automatically lowered or raised on a seasonal basis; production standards could vary with the availability of raw materials, etc. This alleviates the need for participants to ask for changes in standards every time a problem arises. Such a practice is fairer than having to fight for a change each time. In addition, all standards should be reviewed periodically with the participants to determine if any changes should be made in them for the benefit of either the worker or the company—or, hopefully, for the mutual advantage of both.

To summarize, here are eleven ways to make a control system more positive:

1. If possible, the persons being controlled should be involved in the design of the control system.

2. The desired results should be clear to everyone. They should be reasonable and attainable. Those being controlled should want to achieve the desired results.

3. Performance standards should be derived from these desired results, and the persons being controlled should feel these standards are fair.

4. The indicators used should provide current information.

5. Persons being controlled should feel free to seek information from the control system which will help them meet their objectives.

6. Persons being controlled should be aware of their limits—for example, as to decisions, finance, size of errors, number of errors, operation, time, etc.

7. Accountability should be built into the control system.

8. Control systems should give purpose to jobs.

9. Management by the exception principle should be the rule. This will eliminate the need of supervisors to "oversupervise."

10. The control system should be established in such a way that it can be viewed through the eyes of the persons being controlled rather than only through the eyes of management.

11. The ultimate objective of the control system should be self-control.

Resistance to Change

In order to correct problems that are uncovered in the control procedure, changes must be made in either the technical aspect of the operation or in the way the persons involved are performing. It is easy to make mechanical adjustments, but when it comes to changing a human being's manner of working, thinking or performing a specific task, management must be prepared to meet serious obstacles.

People tend to identify with the way they act, and any attempt to change that often results in resentment and resistance. Such an attempt is considered a personal rebuke rather than a means of helping the individual reach the goal.

Even in making changes in the technological aspects of a job, resistance often occurs. This may be caused by concern that the change will make the worker work faster or harder, or that it may require the acquisition of new skills, which may be difficult for some of the workers to learn, or that it may in some way depreciate the value of their current skills.

Other forms of change are also resisted. Some of these are changes in the organizational structure, in methods of compensation, in working conditions, etc.

Resistance to change may manifest itself in many ways. Most frequent are increases in absenteeism, resignations, requests for transfers, and complaints and gripes about minor aspects of the job. These are, of course, symptoms of deeper problems—usually of fear of what the changes may really mean to the worker.

Causes of resistance to change: The most obvious cause of resistance is economic. Workers are afraid that change may result in loss of jobs, reduction of the value of their skills, or in reduction in overtime or incentive pay. This is most common in resistance to automation or other technological improvement.

Change also adds a degree of uncertainty to what has hitherto appeared to be a stable situation. The company introduces a new system in its clerical operations. The clerks who had thought they knew what the company expected of them and what their future advancement opportunities were, now find that the new system makes all of this uncertain. Their tendency is to resist the change, and they are reluctant to give the new system their full support.

A major problem is the psychological impact of change on the affected parties. How does the change affect their status? their interpersonal relationships? A management consultant suggested that a firm centralize its purchasing activities to take advantage of quantity discounts, better bargaining strength in dealing with vendors and more effective control. Previously all purchasing had been done by the various plant managers. The plant managers and their staffs resented the change because, even though they agreed it was more efficient, it lowered their status in the eyes of their subordinates, who interpreted the change as a lack of confidence on top management's part in the plant executives.

Whenever management institutes changes, the number of orders given to those subordinates who must carry out the change is usually increased. As some people resent taking orders, or have become accustomed to a certain degree of autonomy, they may resist the new controls. It reduces their feelings of independence and is a blow to their egos to now have to accept direction in areas where they had previously made their own decisions.

Reducing Resistance to Change: Although it is not always possible to overcome resistance to change—it is too deeply ingrained in the human psyche—there are steps management can take to reduce this resistance and thereby increase the chances of success in effecting the changes.

1. Using economic incentives: As much of the resistance has an economic motivation—fear of loss of job or money—an easy solution (but an expensive one) might be to guarantee that there

will be no loss of income during the changeover. Some companies do this when introducing a new machine. The workers will produce less while learning the operation of the new equipment, but they are paid the same amount of money during the transition as they earned before, even though they do not produce as much.

2. Better communications: Much resistance to change is caused by fear of the unknown. This can be alleviated by providing appropriate information. It is best to explain not only what changes are to be made but why. For communication to be really effective it must provide feedback, so that management knows not only whether the information has been understood but also whether it is accepted. When a major change is contemplated, management should be sure to set up two-way communication facilities so that the supervisors and subordinates can discuss the proposed plan in a way that will bring any potential problems into the open and prevent resistance before it occurs.

3. Participative decision-making: Using a pattern of leadership that encourages all members of the group to participate in making decisions that affect them will facilitate the process of introducing change and enhance their sense of control over their own activities. (See Chapter 12)

People often resist change because they have certain fixed attitudes to which they adhere in spite of all evidence to the contrary. If they participate in making the decisions to change what has been done, their participation helps unfreeze these attitudes so that they can be reexamined. This participation also commits each member of the group to work hard to carry out the decisions that have been reached and serves as an incentive to achieve success.

4. Bargaining: When group decision-making is not practiced, bargaining with the group to achieve approval of the management's concepts is often used. Though management does not agree in advance to accept any decisions made by the group, it usually listens to group proposals, weighs them, accepts changes in the original plan that are workable, and sometimes trades off

some of the original proposals to gain acceptance by the group of the balance.

5. Making changes tentative: It is often useful to test proposed changes before making them final. This enables the employees to test their own reactions to the new situation and provides them with more facts so they can understand the reasons for the proposals. When people have the chance to work with a situation, they obtain a better view of what should be done; often it reduces their own emotional objections to see that the change will not affect them adversely. Of course, it can work against acceptance if the trial period shows many negative factors. Management should be careful to prepare the participants properly by telling them what to expect—both good and bad—from the new situation. If they know that some negative factors will occur, but can see how the positive aspects will more than compensate for them, there is greater chance of acceptance and success.

6. Bringing in a new manager: One of the major problems in change is the changing of department heads. A new manager of a section or unit is an unknown quantity to the subordinates. There is usually considerable worry and uncertainty. Will the new boss make changes which will adversely affect them? Will he or she be easy to work for, or much more difficult than the predecessor? How will the change affect the future of each of the subordinates? To overcome this anxiety, the company must carefully prepare both the new manager and the staff for the transfer of authority from the old to the new supervisor. The new manager should be given a careful review of the situation in the department: the status of work being done, the objectives, the failures and successes of the predecessor, etc. Most important, he should be given a thorough briefing on all of the people in the department. He should know the assets and liabilities, personality problems and ambitions, and special interests of each subordinate. In a large department, this may not always be possible, but he should be given this information at least on key subordinates, including the informal leaders of the group.

The new manager should be cautioned not to make any major

changes until he has had sufficient experience in the new job to understand the situation and to have won the confidence of his people. He should use the techniques of instituting change discussed in the preceding paragraphs.

The staff should be prepared for the new manager by being given some background about him to give them confidence in his capability. Some firms introduce the new manager in a formal ceremony to show the concerned subordinates that he has the full confidence of management.

Proper preparation can overcome much of the innate resistance to a new boss. If the new manager makes a strong effort to gain cooperation—even at the expense of immediate improvement in operations—it will pay off in the long run by achieving more cooperation with less chance of resistance or even sabotage of his efforts and a smooth running team which will accept changes when presented.

Effecting Change in an Individual

In many cases the problem of making a correction in the way a job is done or in other business problems comes down to changing the attitude or approach of a specific individual. All of the techniques mentioned earlier in this chapter can be applied to specific persons: participation, two-way communication, trial runs on new ideas, etc. However, often a personalized one-to-one discussion with the problem-person is more effective.

The manager must keep in mind his overall objective: to correct a situation without incurring resentment. Most often the supervisor will "bawl out" a subordinate who is not performing according to standard, instead of really correcting the situation. Let's examine a specific instance.

Jim Burke, the company's sales manager, checks the weekly sales report of Bill Williams, a good salesman but a poor report-writer. He calls him into his office and says, "Williams, how the heck did you get through college? Can't you even write up a simple sales report?"

Let's examine this situation. What should its objective be? To correct Williams so he can submit proper reports in the future.

Does this bawling-out accomplish the objective? Not only has it failed to show Williams how to do a better job, or even how to find out where he could learn the proper method, but it has made him feel small and inadequate.

Let's now try to look into the mind of Williams. Is he thinking: "I'd better find out where I went wrong and learn how to do it right"? Probably not. He is more likely thinking: "That Jim Burke is a ———." Resentment, not correction, is the result.

How should Jim Burke have handled this matter? Let's review his objectives:

1. To teach Williams the proper way to complete a sales report.

2. To make sure that Williams will hand in correct reports in the future.

3. To do all this without developing resentment toward himself and the company.

A better way to accomplish these purposes would have been to ask Williams to meet with him when they both had some time, so that he could show him where he erred, and what corrections should be made. Jim Burke should have avoided sarcasm. The discussion should have been constructive. Instead of saying or implying that Williams was stupid, it would have been more effective to ask, "Williams, are you familiar with the SOP concerning sales reports?" In this way the emphasis is put on the correct procedure, not the *man*, on his *error*. He then would suggest that they go over the SOP again, point out the specific errors made, and get feedback to make sure that Williams understood the procedure and would complete the report satisfactorily next time.

To summarize, in dealing with correcting a problem with a subordinate:

1. Discuss the problem with the subordinate as soon after the error is discovered as possible.

2. Do this on a person-to-person basis in private.

3. Begin the discussion with a question. Do not, however, let the question take the form of an accusation.

4. Listen to the subordinate's response. Be attentive, patient, open-minded. Let him tell his whole story. This is particularly important if the behavior that is under discussion is a matter of personality rather than a technical aspect of the work.

5. Always emphasize the *what* rather than the *who*. Base the discussion on criticism of the action that was wrong, rather than on criticism of the person whose action is involved.

6. Conclude the discussion with a definite plan of action. Be constructive and specific about what should be done. Make sure that the subordinate understands, accepts and will follow your corrections.

PART VI

Conclusion

Thinking is easy, acting is difficult, and to put one's thoughts into action is the most difficult thing in the world.

Goethe

19

GETTING IT
ALL TOGETHER

Most people in management are middle-managers. They report to a higher level of management in the corporate hierarchy. In most instances they have a degree of autonomy in operating their own departments and some influence in the development of policy for the company. Even the top management executives have to account to a board of directors or to the stockholders.

Because being a manager does not necessarily make one a policy-maker, many of the concepts and ideas presented in this book may be received half-heartedly. One might say "It sounds great, but I could never get my boss to do it."

Progress is never made without a struggle. The readers of this book are in a position to persuade their own bosses to accept some of their thinking. All but the most obstinate individualists in management look to their subordinates for ideas. The middle-manager who can sell his boss on improving management techniques is more likely to move up the corporate ladder than one who just follows orders and makes no suggestions to improve managerial methods.

In the preceding chapters we have discussed ways to sell your ideas to subordinates, ways to effect changes in people's attitudes, etc. The same type of approach must be used in selling ideas and effecting changes in the boss's views about the job.

Most management concepts are conveyed either informally—

in day-to-day dealings with the superior manager, or formally—
by oral or written presentations.

Informal Approach

How a senior manager will react to suggestions from his jun-
iors obviously depends on the personalities of both parties. When
one deals with an open-minded executive, it is relatively easy to
make suggestions, recommendations or actual changes. However,
in most cases the subordinate manager has to be able to justify
his suggestion and often actually persuade the senior to accept it.

The best approach is to be specific rather than to make general
suggestions. Instead of saying to the boss "Why don't we use
brainstorming sessions to develop some new alternatives on some
of our problems?" it is more effective to pick a specific situation
and tie the suggestion in with that. For example, a middle-manager might say, "We can't seem to get that new product off the
ground. Perhaps if we called some of the fellows working on the
program together and brainstormed it, we might come up with
alternatives that we haven't thought of."

Be prepared to back up suggestions with good reasons. Bob R.
wanted to promote Sandra D. to a newly created sales position
in his department. His boss had reservations about assigning a
woman to a sales spot. Bob gave him several instances of
Sandra's skill in the handling of customer problems in her present job and so was able to persuade him to give Sandra a pro-
bationary assignment to the job for six months. By the end of the
period, Sandra had proved to be so effective that the boss not
only made the assignment permanent, but is now actively seeking women for similar jobs.

The key factors in selling your ideas to your boss are:

1. Know your boss. Unless you understand what it is he seeks
in his job, what his objectives are for the department or company,
what his previous reactions have been to similar ideas, it will be
difficult to know how to approach him.

2. Be convinced that your idea will work. Do your homework.

Think through your suggestions. If possible, talk them over with other middle-managers and with the people who will have to work with the new method. If the idea can be tested, do so. Then, you can present your boss with data to support the concept— not with just an untried idea.

3. Approach the boss at an appropriate time. Everybody knows that if someone is preoccupied with a problem, it is not a good time to talk to him about another problem. Wait until the "right" moment. Is he in a receptive mood? Is the situation your idea concerns pertinent at this time?

4. Be prepared to show the boss how the idea will benefit the department, the company and his objectives. People want to know what's in it for them, or their department, not how it might help you.

5. Watch the reactions carefully. If he turns you off completely, it may be smarter to retreat and bring your idea up at another, more appropriate time. If he shows a flicker of interest, be prepared to follow it through and present the whole story.

6. Be brief and succinct. Unless the idea is highly complex, give as complete an account of the suggestion as you can in the shortest time. The longer it takes to tell your story, the more likely you are to lose his interest. Proper preparation of what you intend to say will enable you to achieve your purpose.

7. Be ready to answer questions. Have facts and figures. Most managers want to know what any new method or system will cost.

8. Make the sale. If interest is developed, don't let the conversation end without some commitment from the boss. Even if it is "I'll think about it," obtain a time when you can expect an answer.

9. Follow up your plan. Don't let an idea die. If you keep being put off, try to discover the reason. Present new data to support your ideas if appropriate. On the other hand, know when to withdraw. It will do you no good to antagonize the boss by over-persistence.

10. Be flexible. It is better to have part of your suggestion accepted than none. Compromises and trade-offs sometimes are necessary.

Formal Approach

When complex or important matters have to be conveyed to management, it is usually done by submitting a written report. Many managers who are quite capable of expressing themselves in direct conversation with their bosses find it difficult to put their ideas together in written form. Inasmuch as written reports are essential to communication in most organizations, a manager must master the art of writing good reports if he wants to make an impact on his organization.

A good report contains far more than just basic ideas. It must enable the reader to understand the subject as clearly as the person who has written the report.

Careful planning must go into a report. Whether the report is initiated by the boss who asks his subordinate to make a study or develop an idea he has, or whether it is initiated by the subordinate manager, it should be well thought out before being committed to paper.

Heather N., the office manager of Goody Gumdrops Co., saw a new piece of filing equipment at the Business Equipment Show and told her boss about it. He asked her to get more information about it and to write a report that he could present to the Controller.

Heather wrote for some literature, abstracted a few key facts and sent the report to the boss. She got the report back with a page full of questions.

Had Heather planned this report properly, she would have had the answers to most of the questions in the original report. It would have taken no more time to prepare the report properly than to answer the questions asked after the original report was submitted and returned.

The boss would then have complimented her instead of worrying about her ability to handle other than routine assignments. She would have established a reputation as a self-starter, a thoroughly dependable manager.

How should Heather have handled this situation?

1. *Define the problem:* What was it the boss was seeking? Much time and effort have been wasted by not knowing what is wanted. Find out from the person requesting the report what his objectives are. Determine how he plans to use the report. Without knowing this, one might spend three weeks on a report in which there is no more than casual interest and only a few days on one the boss considers very important. This will also enable one to plan one's own work on the project. If one doesn't know enough about the objective of the report, one might end up working hardest on the least important phases of the matter. Don't be afraid to ask questions. The writer of the report and the boss should both understand the objectives that are sought.

2. *Get the facts:* Once the objectives are clear, try to get all the information needed. In the case of the report on the new filing equipment, Heather should have obtained *all* available information. Of course, the manufacturer's literature should have been studied. That was only a start. Perhaps there is other equipment of a similar type on the market. Material about these other brands should be studied and compared with the equipment being considered.

Persons in the departments that will use the new equipment should be consulted to see what their needs are and what the new equipment will do (or not do) that the presently-used equipment does or fails to do.

If possible, the office manager should interview the salesmen of the vendor and see a demonstration of the equipment in operation. If it is a complex system, it would be wise to discuss it with other firms that are using it now. All this takes work and time, but if a full story is needed to enable the company to make a decision to invest in this equipment, it will be well worth the time.

3. *Analyze the facts:* Once the data are accumulated, Heather will have to assemble, correlate and analyze them. She will have to fit the facts together, comparing what this equipment can do and what the currently-used equipment is doing. It is sometimes advantageous to present more than one alternative, to indicate the advantages and limitations of each, and then to make one's own recommendations.

In assembling and analyzing the facts, the report writer should use some system to keep the information together and in order.

Probably the most effective system used by researchers and professional writers is the category breakdown. A separate folder or envelope is made up for each major category of the study. Information on each aspect of the study (reports of interviews, sales literature, cost figures, etc.) are put in the proper folders. This can save many hours of sorting and assembling facts if it is done at the beginning instead of throwing all the materials together and sorting them out later on.

Writing the Report

A good report must be read easily. Its language and form should be familiar to the person or persons who will be reading it. A technician writing a report for a non-technical group should try to couch his report in as non-technical language as the subject permits. His readers are not trained as technicians, so he must translate his thoughts into words that they understand.

The report writer has an advantage when he knows what his superior expects in terms of language, details of content, graphic material, and so on. Some managers prefer terse reports; others prefer great detail. Some want graphs and charts; others would rather have statistical tables giving exact figures.

Know the reader. Gear the report to his interests and desires. The report is written for him, so it should be tailored to his needs.

Although there is no ideal report style, the following format will usually be effective:

1. A brief statement of the problem: State what has been requested, or, if the report has been initiated by the writer, what the purpose is. For example:

"Because our present filing equipment is slow and often inaccurate, I have examined a newly designed electronic filing and retrieving system which should overcome these shortcomings." It is good diplomacy to give credit in the introduction to others who helped provide the necessary information.

2. Summary and recommendations: In a narrative the results are not fully understood until everything that leads up to them is read. A report is different. In a report the summary and recommendation should be presented *at the beginning*. This will enable managers who read it to get the key information at once. They do not have to wade through reams of detail to find out what is recommended. When time allows, they can read the full report.

3. Detailed back-up: This is the meat of the report. In it all the details are presented to support the summary and recommendations. How much information should be included naturally depends upon how the subject, but specific data should be given.

Charts, graphs or statistical tables may make a report more easily understood. Photographs can be helpful if the subject lends itself to that type of presentation.

Watch the language. Keep it clear and to the point. There is no need to use an elaborate, pedantic style. Relate the language to the interests and background of the people for whom it is written. The choice of language is extremely important. Words must be selected carefully and arranged interestingly and grammatically. The good writer writes ideas—not words. A good suggestion is to keep one idea to a paragraph. Start each paragraph with a topic sentence which summarizes the idea.

How long should a report be? Long enough to tell the whole story and not one word longer. Avoid repetition. A common fault in report writing is stating the same idea over and over again in different words.

Dewey Olson of IBM listed in an article in "The Office" the following steps around which a report should be organized:

1. *Gain attention* with a succinct informative lead sentence. Try a straightforward approach. For example, you might begin with "XYZ is wasting $2 million annually on rejected parts." Try to determine what facet of your communication would be of greatest interest to your specific reader and use that for an opening to gain attention.

2. *Arouse interest* by telling your reader how he can benefit from reading your communication. Tell him what he will gain from your communication. Tell him early. The information must be timely, or it is likely to be filed without being read.

3. *Produce conviction* by appealing to the reader's mind, not his emotions. He wants facts. Why is your solution better? Why is it a solution? Don't just dump the facts on him. Analyze them and show him how you reached your conclusion. Start with the familiar to gain his confidence, then gradually lead him to the new approach by defining your terms and substantiating your claims.

4. *Create desire* by motivating your reader. Spell it out for him. Tell him why your idea will work. Creating the need isn't enough, you must create a desire to satisfy this need.

5. *Get action* by spelling out what action is required and out-lining the steps necessary to produce the desired results. Many memos and reports fail to produce action because the action required is not clearly spelled out. Try not to present "obvious" conclusions that are not obvious to your reader, but don't assume he has extrasensory perception.*

Even when the final report has been submitted, the writer is still not relieved of his duty in the matter. He may have to discuss the report orally with his superior, with other executives or sometimes with the chief executive officer of the company. He must be prepared to answer questions on all phases of the report. Inasmuch as not all the material used in preparing the report will be used in the report, he should keep his original material for future reference when defending his ideas.

Oral Presentations

Although written reports are more usual in business, oral reports are occasionally required, and written reports often are supplemented by oral presentations before committees or boards of executives.

The oral report should be prepared in much the same way as the written report. However, the speaker must be prepared to

* Dewey Olson, "Six Steps to Better Written Communications," in *The Office*, April 1966, p. 69.

speak clearly and interestingly to his audience. For most people it is much easier to write a report than to present it orally. In an oral report the speaker has only one chance to tell his story. If the listeners do not accept it then, they will rarely give him another chance. In written reports, the paper can be reread and studied at leisure.

Many middle-managers have improved their speaking ability and self-confidence in presenting their ideas to their peers and superiors by studying the techniques of good public speaking through such programs as the Dale Carnegie Course in *Effective Speaking and Human Relations.*

Presenting one's ideas to others in the organization is a key management responsibility. It is necessary not only to get one's job done effectively, but to communicate to the organization those exciting, vital new thoughts that most people have. Effective communication is essential not only to the survival of the company, but also to ensure the growth of the company, and with it, the development and advancement of the managers that help it grow.

Managing Through People

No matter how good one's ideas are, or how successful one is in selling them to senior management, they cannot be implemented except through the people up and down the line who will work with them.

It has been the total concept of this book to point up the significance of the individual human being to the success of the organization. To ensure that this significance is realized, each manager must give his subordinate managers the opportunity to meet their personal goals through their jobs wherever possible.

The process starts with the proper selection of personnel for each job, and the maintenance of each person in a job that is being performed satisfactorily. If the right person is picked for a job, that person will usually find that the job is meaningful to him. Good managers usually enjoy their work and gain personal satisfaction from it.

However, the time often comes when the job is no longer a challenge, when the individual works routinely with little or no imagination or enthusiasm. Good management can give a person in this position a lift by recognizing the situation and alleviating it either by transferring him to a more challenging job, or by giving him an opportunity to participate in more decisions concerning his department.

Managers should be allowed to move horizontally—to a job on the same level—as well as vertically—up or down in the ranks. Many companies consider horizontal transfers to be bad. They are afraid the manager will consider such a transfer a loss of face, as it is a transfer to a lateral position—not a promotion.

Many modern management thinkers believe that lateral moves are good not only for the man, but for the company. It is stimulating to the individual because it gives him new problems to work with, new people to relate to and an opportunity to learn new aspects of the operation. It is good for the company because it trains personnel to handle a variety of jobs and opens the road to promotion to them in several areas, not in just a limited range. It also allows for persons who are not producing satisfactorily in one type of work to be moved to another without loss of face. It creates a pool of professional managers who can perform a variety of functions throughout the organization.

In making choices for promotion as well as transfer, the interests, capabilities and desires of the individual should be considered, not just the needs of the company. Too many people are promoted to positions above their capability because it is assumed they are ready for the promotion. Many promotions are made on the basis of seniority or competence in a technical or professional sphere, without considering capacity for leadership or managerial responsibility. Such promotions are not only bad for the company, but often deal a serious blow to the ego of the manager who finds himself above his level of competence. The company will have to remove him from the job if it is to succeed, and in doing so, it may lose a valuable employee.

To avoid this outcome, management must be sure to make promotions only after careful analysis of the individuals being considered, and after discussing the new job with them. They should not make subordinate managers feel that failure to be promoted is due to incompetence in their current jobs, but rather that they are not as yet ready for the higher job. Often, the subordinate may not even desire the new job. His own wishes should be considered as well as the company's.

On the other hand, persons ready for promotion should not be kept back because of seniority, favoritism or the need of the company for their continued service in their present spot. Such persons will not long remain in positions below the level of their capability. If the company with which they are employed holds them back, they will sooner or later leave for greener pastures.

Good managers know the interests and motivations of their people. They work with them to channel these toward objectives that meet the needs of both the company and the individual. By recognizing the talents and aims of each person under their jurisdiction, they are likely to obtain their best efforts and loyalty.

Encouraging Participative Management

Another basic premise of this book is that all people should be encouraged to use their full potential. There is a tremendous reserve of capability in most people that is not being utilized. In authoritarian management approaches, this capability is never tapped.

One way to reach this gold mine is to give subordinates (after thorough training, of course) freedom to make decisions on their own, to help develop both short- and long-range objectives—not only for their own activities, but for the entire organization.

It is understood that all men are *not* created equal in terms of intelligence, energy level, physical health, or motivation to achieve. However, each person should be encouraged to contribute to the limits of his capability. The effort will pay off in creative ideas, new approaches and constructive evaluations that will result in a more effective organization.

It will also stimulate the individual to participate. The greater a man's participation in decision-making, the greater importance he attributes to his job, the higher is his commitment to fulfill the requirements of the job.

Conclusion

No matter what approach management takes to operating a business, the final test is the results attained. A company to be successful must not only be profitable now, but must set the stage for long-term profitability.

There are many methods of running a business. Modern management techniques include the use of highly sophisticated computers, application of mathematical formulas and installation of complex management systems. All or any of these may be applicable to specific situations.

No matter what the type of business or organization, we find one factor common to all—the factor of the human resources that in the final analysis determine the success or failure of the enterprise.

By careful nurturing of these human resources, management can bring out the hidden creative powers people have and channel them to work for the best interests of the organization. At the same time, this will give each person involved a greater degree of job satisfaction and make him more successful as an individual.

Managing through people is not a panacea for all management ills. It is not even an answer to specific management problems. It is an overall philosophy for dealing with one's total organizational activities. It makes all management

*HUMAN*agement.

Dale Carnegie, in his preface to *How to Win Friends and Influence People,* quotes William James: "Compared to what we ought to be, we are only half awake. We are making use of only a small part of our physical and mental resources."

It is to the advantage of managers at all levels to bring forth these resources in the people they manage. By applying the principles discussed in this book, managers should fully awaken the talents of their people, and that will pay off in reduced costs, higher profits and a happier, more productive work force and management team.

Afterword

The Dale Carnegie Management Seminar has a documented history confirming its important contributions to the art of management. The curriculum is designed to apply to either individual executives or managers or company groups and has proved highly efficient in training at minimal time and expense.

The Seminar is especially valuable to managers responsible for deciding and implementing both corporate overall objectives and specific departmental goals. Its flexibility and practicality are being demonstrated every day by both large and small organizations.

The Seminar's principles of goal-directed management are designed to clarify, appraise and guide planning for results. Most people react favorably to responsibility and are fully able to assimilate broader training in ways that increase both performance and results.

Dale Carnegie Management Seminars are held throughout the United States and Canada and in many other countries of the world.

Index